Dissecting the Superego

Dissecting the Superego: Moralities Under the Psychoanalytic Microscope offers a comprehensive overview of how the superego, the workings of our moral faculties, may be understood and clinically utilised in contemporary practice.

Drawing on the latest psychoanalytic thinking – as well as neurobiological, psychological and ethical perspectives – this book reinstates the superego as a central concept, and gives a clear guide to its importance in the modern world. In addition to the theoretical background of this construct, the contributors provide a clear guide to the importance of the superego in a range of pathological and everyday scenarios, and particularly in clinical settings.

With an emphasis on the wider social and cultural context, *Dissecting the Superego* will be of interest to trainee and qualified psychotherapists, social workers, youth offender and probation workers and ethicists.

Celia Harding has worked as a Psychoanalytic Psychotherapist in private practice in East London for over thirty years and is a Founder member of the Association for Psychotherapy in East London.

Dissecting the super-ego

Dissecting the Superego

Moralities Under the Psychoanalytic Microscope

Edited by
Celia Harding

LONDON AND NEW YORK

First published 2019
by Routledge
2 Park Square, Milton Park, Abingdon, Oxon OX14 4RN

and by Routledge
711 Third Avenue, New York, NY 10017

Routledge is an imprint of the Taylor & Francis Group, an informa business

© 2019 Celia Harding

The right of Celia Harding to be identified as author of this work has been asserted by her in accordance with sections 77 and 78 of the Copyright, Designs and Patents Act 1988.

All rights reserved. No part of this book may be reprinted or reproduced or utilised in any form or by any electronic, mechanical, or other means, now known or hereafter invented, including photocopying and recording, or in any information storage or retrieval system, without permission in writing from the publishers.

Trademark notice: Product or corporate names may be trademarks or registered trademarks, and are used only for identification and explanation without intent to infringe.

British Library Cataloguing-in-Publication Data
A catalogue record for this book is available from the British Library

Library of Congress Cataloging-in-Publication Data
A catalog record for this book has been requested

ISBN: 978-0-8153-4839-9 (hbk)
ISBN: 978-0-8153-6107-7 (pbk)
ISBN: 978-1-351-11710-4 (ebk)

Typeset in Times New Roman
by Apex CoVantage, LLC

Printed and bound in Great Britain by
TJ International Ltd, Padstow, Cornwall

Contents

List of figures	vii
List of contributors	viii
Preface	xi
Acknowledgements	xiii
Epigraphs	xv

Introduction: the superego in 21st-century psychoanalysis 1
CELIA HARDING

PART I
Theoretical and developmental considerations 19

1 **The good, the bad and the superego: from punishment to reparation** 21
R. D. HINSHELWOOD

2 **A new theory of conscience: the petrified ego** 32
ELIZABETH REDDISH

3 **Reflections on the ego ideal in childhood** 46
ANN HORNE

4 **The neurobiological bases of human moralities: industrial civilization's misguided moral development** 60
DARCIA NARVAEZ

PART II
The role of the superego in different states of mind 77

5 **'Sorry doesn't make a dead man alive': the superego behind depressive states of mind** 79
CELIA HARDING

6	**Superegos in patients with problems of perversion** HEATHER WOOD	95
7	**About the analyst and patient: the superego in borderline states of mind** JACK NATHAN	110
8	**The role of the superego in psychopathic states of mind and personality** CELIA TAYLOR	126
9	**Fundamentalism and the superego** LESLEY MURDIN	142

PART III
The superego in clinical contexts — 155

10	**The superego as a significant factor in clinical training** CHRISTINE DRIVER	157
11	**The analytic superego** WARREN COLMAN	172
12	**The superego's role in ethical practice: hindrance and help** CELIA HARDING	187

Index — 205

Figures

8.1 Hare Psychopathy Checklist (PCL-R) factors 1 and 2 (Hare, 2003: p. 79)   128
8.2 Common countertransference reactions to the psychopathic patient (Meloy & Reavis, 2007: p. 186)   129
12.1 Triangulating modal orienting ethical thinking   191

Contributors

Warren Colman is qualified in couples psychotherapy and a founder member of the British Society of Couples Psychotherapy and Counselling. He was a senior lecturer and couples psychotherapist at what became the Tavistock Marital Studies Institute. He qualified as a Jungian analyst, a training analyst and supervising analyst. He has been in full time private practice as an analyst, psychotherapist and couples psychotherapist since 1997. He teaches, lectures and supervises widely in the UK and abroad. He was the editor-in-chief of the *Journal of Analytical Psychology* from 2007 to 2013 and is currently the consultant editor. He was Chair of the Society of Analytical Psychology. Since 1988, he has published over forty papers on a wide range of topics, including couples, sexuality and gender, the self, the therapeutic process, synchronicity and symbolic imagination. His latest book is entitled *Act and Image: The Emergence of Symbolic Imagination*. New Orleans, Louisiana, Spring Journal Books, 2016.

Christine Driver, D.An.Psych. is a Jungian analyst and psychoanalytic psychotherapist. She was Director of Training and Clinical Services at WPF Therapy, and also teaches, supervises and works in private practice. She has written and co-edited *Being and Relating in Psychotherapy* (2013, Palgrave), *Supervision and the Analytic Attitude* (2005, Whurr) and *Supervising Psychotherapy* (2002, Sage) and also published a number of papers in the *British Journal of Psychotherapy* and the *Journal of Analytical Psychology*. She has also undertaken research into religion and psychology.

Celia Harding B.Ed, M.Sc. Member of the fpc (wpf). She has worked as a Psychoanalytic Psychotherapist in private practice in East London for over thirty years and is a founder member of the Association for Psychotherapy in East London. She Supervises, Consults and Teaches. She edited *Sexuality: Psychoanalytic Perspectives* (2001) and *Aggression and Destructiveness* (2006). She served on the fpc (wpf) Ethics Committee for thirteen years and currently serves as a BPC Ethics Panelist. She teaches ethics to trainee therapists.

R. D. Hinshelwood is Emeritus Professor in the Centre for Psychoanalytic Studies, University of Essex, and previously Clinical Director, The Cassel Hospital,

London. He is a fellow of the British Psychoanalytical Society, and a fellow of the Royal College of Psychiatrists. He has authored *A Dictionary of Kleinian Thought* (1989) and other books and articles on Kleinian psychoanalysis. Most recently he edited (2013, with Nuno Torres) *Bion's Sources: The Shaping of His Paradigms*. His interest in the History of Psychoanalysis led to founding the journal *Psychoanalysis and History* in 1996.

Ann Horne is a fellow of the BPF and an honorary member of ČSPAP, the Czech Society for Psychoanalytic Psychotherapy. Following careers as a teacher of English, college lecturer in Social Policy and Psychiatric Social Worker, she finally trained as a child and adolescent psychotherapist at the BAP (now IPCAPA, a college of the BPF) where she was head of training and later of post-graduate development. Previously a joint editor of the *Journal of Child Psychotherapy*, she co-edited with Monica Lanyado *The Handbook of Child and Adolescent Psychotherapy: Psychoanalytic Approaches* (1st edition 1999; 2nd edition 2009) and the Independent Psychoanalytic Approaches with Children and Adolescents series for Routledge: *A Question of Technique, Through Assessment to Consultation, Winnicott's Children* and *An Independent Mind – Collected Papers of Juliet Hopkins*. Retired from NHS work, latterly at the Portman Clinic in London, she has a particular interest in children who use the body and activity rather than be able to access thought and reflection.

Lesley Murdin is a psychoanalytic psychotherapist trained at wpf in London after a first degree in English Literature and years of teaching in Australia and the United States as well as for the Open University in the UK. She has published several books and papers and chaired the UKCP Ethics committee as well as the Analytic Section. Currently she works for BPC, chairing complaints hearings and sits on the Council. She was head of Training at WPF and then National Director. Currently she has a private practice in Cambridge.

Darcia Narvaez is Professor of Psychology at the University of Notre Dame who focuses on moral development and flourishing from an interdisciplinary perspective. Dr Narvaez's current research explores how early life experience influences societal culture and moral character. One of her recent books, Neurobiology and the Development of Human Morality: Evolution, Culture and Wisdom won the 2015 William James Book Award from the American Psychological Association and the 2017 Expanded Reason Award.

Jack Nathan B.Sc. (Hons), M.Sc., C.Q.S.W., M.B.P.F. (Formerly L.C.P., 1991) & M.B.P.C., a psychoanalytic psychotherapist working in private practice and in the NHS as a Consultant Psychotherapist at the Self-Harm Out-Patients Service (SHOPS) at the Maudsley Hospital, in the Lambeth Psychotherapy Service and Trust Advisor for Psychotherapy for the South London & Maudsley NHS Foundation Trust. Formerly a social work manager at the Maudsley Hospital, and a lecturer in social work at the Institute of Psychiatry, he trained at the London Centre for Psychotherapy (now amalgamated in the British Psychotherapy

Foundation). He is also a qualified therapist, supervisor and trainer in Kernberg's Transference Focused Psychotherapy, a treatment specifically geared to working with borderline patients. He is particularly interested in how to work with the borderline patient group, the meaning(s) attached to their self-destructive behaviours and the countertransference difficulties they arouse. He has written about, lectured and run workshops in this country and abroad on the use of benign authority in work with borderline patients. His most recently published work in the British Journal of Psychotherapy is on *The Use of Benign Authority with Severe Borderline Patients: A Psychoanalytic Paradigm*.

Elizabeth Reddish D. Psych. has worked as a psychoanalytic psychotherapist in London since 1996 and is registered with the British Psychoanalytic Council on the Board of which she served for six years as a director. She worked for fifteen years in the film industry prior to training in psychoanalysis. '*The Petrified Ego*' (Karnac, 2014) is adapted from her professional doctorate 'The Structuring Function of the Superego' (2010). She also consults on career development; her clinical experience of the debilitating impact of a harsh over critical conscience forms the basis of a psychoanalytic model that she has designed to help individuals fulfil their potential at work.

Celia Taylor BSc, MB.BS, FRC Psych, Diploma Forensic Psychiatry is a consultant forensic psychiatrist and lead clinician of Millfields inpatient medium secure unit and Changing Lanes community team in East London. Both services are for high-risk offenders with a severe personality disorder and part of the London Pathways Partnership (LPP) a consortium of four mental health trusts that supports probation officers in supervising these clients, as well as operating specialist services in HMP Belmarsh, YOI Aylesbury and HMP Swaleside. She also runs a module in an M.SC. in Forensic Mental Health at Queen Mary University of London. She has published a number of papers in the field in journals with a focus on 'what works?' with this group and how best to support staff in their roles.

Heather Wood, DPhil. was formerly a consultant clinical psychologist and adult psychotherapist at the Portman Clinic, Tavistock and Portman NHSFT. Having trained as a psychoanalytic psychotherapist with the BAP, she is a member of the BPF and BPC. She has published a number of book chapters and articles with a particular focus on problematic use of internet pornography and the related subject of paedophilia, and clinical aspects of working with perversions. She was joint editor and contributor to Hiller, Bolton & Wood (2006) *Sex, Mind and Emotion* (Karnac), and Bower, Hale & Wood (2013) *Addictive States of Mind*, and co-author of Blumenthal, Wood & Williams (2018) Assessing Risk - A Relational Approach. She now works in private practice.

Preface

The idea for this book was conceived in the latter stages of my editing *Aggression and Destructiveness: Psychoanalytic Perspectives* (2006). I realised – too late in the day – that the source of aggression and destructiveness with which we are all most personally and professionally familiar had not received sufficient attention: the criticism, condemnation and punishment, we direct and target at ourselves and others, disguised as moral righteousness, i.e. superego activities. Despite making various forays into planning such a book and reading around the subject, there were always other things which took precedence over writing.

Aware of my interest in the superego, my friend and colleague, Marie-Jose Loncelle directed me to Elizabeth Reddish's *New Theory of Conscience* (2014). In this innovative and valuable work I found theorized some of the work I had been developing with my patients and in my self-analysis: namely the importance of ego strengthening work to enable a more independent and collaborative relationship with the superego. About the same time another friend and colleague, Sybil del Strother, gave me a copy of Adam Phillips' brilliant and accessible article on the superego 'Against Self-Criticism' (2015). Together I took these publications to herald a renewed interest in the superego within the profession which kick-started me into getting this project moving. Clearly I was not going to write the book myself but an edited volume was perhaps a more viable and even preferable option. When I approached colleagues to gauge interest in the subject I was thrilled to find sufficient enthusiasm for the project to get off the ground. The whole project has turned out to be an incredibly rewarding experience: the professional, dedicated and enthusiastic work of its contributors have made this book a joy to edit and the process has been a source of boundless interest at every level not withstanding the inevitable moments of despondency.

I have been awed by several unexpected personal and professional rewards to editing this book, coinciding as it has with the run-up to my retirement. Although the superego has always been a salient concept in my studies, work with my patients and in my personal analyses, my research for the book revealed depths of understanding which had previously eluded me and which have enriched my clinical work with my patients. In addition, I began to realise that my own contributions to the book have offered me an opportunity to bring together work I've been developing over my career in the consulting room and through my professional interest and involvement in psychoanalytic ethics. When the book was well in progress I visited David Hockney's exhibition of his art, spanning his career, at the Tate. I found myself very moved as I reached its conclusion and realised that my feelings about this 'gathering together of a lifetime's work' reflected something of what I felt myself to be accomplishing through my contributions to this book. Our superego tendencies are a tough and challenging part of our minds to explore, get to know and come to constructive terms with, so it may not be surprising that it has taken so long to tackle it!

References

Harding, C. (2006) *Aggression and Destructiveness: Psychoanalytic Perspectives*. East Sussex, Routledge.
Phillips, A. (2015) Against self-criticism. *The London Review of Books*. 5 March, 13–16.
Reddish, E. (2014) *The Petrified Ego: A New Theory of Conscience*. London, Karnac Books.

Acknowledgements

My thanks to the contributors whose enthusiastic and dedicated efforts demonstrate the continued relevance of the superego in the psychoanalytic endeavour. Special thanks also to Stan Ruszczynski for his help in directing me to excellent authors for two of the essential chapters in this book. Also to Ian McGilchrist who recommended Darcia Narvaez to write the crucial chapter on the neurobiological understanding of our moral sense.

I am indebted to my patients for the privilege they have accorded me by allowing me into their inner selves and for all they have taught me in the process. Also to my supervisors over the years for all the help they have given me to understand my patients better and to work with them more effectively. Also to my analysts for the understandings they have given me of myself, especially of my superego tendencies. I am particularly grateful to Astra Temko for her help with my sensitised superego over the duration of this project.

I am grateful to members of the Foundation for Psychotherapy and Counselling for the opportunities they have provided over the years to develop, with colleagues, my interest in psychoanalytic ethics and for offering me forums to present and further develop my clinical and theoretical thinking. Too many colleagues have shown interest and support for this project to mention by name but I have found their enthusiasm greatly encouraging and thank them for it. In particular, my immense gratitude to Gill Bannister, Sybil del Strother and Marie-Jose Loncelle for the editorial and moral support that they have generously given me over and beyond the calls of colleagueship and friendship. Thanks are also due to Ian Lyon, Chorister from ASTMS, for his efforts to source the antiphon which serves as an epigraph to the book.

I am profoundly indebted to Marianne Parsons for her unstinting generous help with my contributions to this book. Also to Elizabeth Reddish, for her generous interest and help with this project in general, my introduction in particular and with forging a title for this book.

Finally, my heartfelt thanks, appreciation and love to Michael Lamprell for his steadfast support and encouragement through the coming together of this book, without which this project would not have been possible.

Reprinted by kind permission:

Epigraph 1 Communion Antiphon, 20th Sunday in Ordinary Time. Si iniquitates observaveris: Psalm 130:3; Apud Dominum misericordia: Psalm 130:7. Weber, S.M. (2015) *The Proper of the Mass for Sundays and Solemnities. Chants for the Roman Missal in English*. San Francisco, Ignatius Press, pp. 600–601.

Epigraph 2. Used with permission from the British Broadcasting Corporation Dr Who, series 9, episode 2 The Witches Familiar. [accessed 15.3.2018] *www.springfieldspringfield.co.uk/episode_scripts.php?tv . . . doctor . . . season=9*

Epigraph to Chapter 2, an excerpt *From Letters to a Young Poet* by Rainer Maria Rilke, translated by M. D. Herter Norton. Copyright 1934, 1954 by W. W. Norton & Company, Inc., renewed (c) 1962, 1982 by M. D. Herter Norton. Used by permission of W. W. Norton & Company, Inc. permission granted to Elizabeth Reddish.

Examples from The Sopranos, Series 1, Episode 1 and Series 3, Episode 7. Permission granted to Celia Harding for use in Chapter 12. © Home Box Office, Inc., All Rights Reserved.

An extended version of Chapter 11, 'The Analytic Super-ego', was first published in the *Journal of the British Association of Psychotherapists*. Volume 44, 2, 1–16, 2006. Re-published in this publication by kind permission of John Wiley & Sons Limited.

Epigraphs

If you, O Lord, should mark iniquities, Lord who shall stand it?
With the Lord there is mercy; in him is plentiful redemption.
(Psalm 130: 3, 7)

Young Davros to Dr Who: Which side are you on? Are you the enemy?
Dr Who: I'm not sure if any of that matters. Friends, enemies. So long as there's mercy. Always mercy.
(Dr Who: 9, 2)

Introduction
The superego in 21st-century psychoanalysis

Celia Harding

From birth, some might argue, from the moment of conception, we are shaped by and shape our relationships, formatively influenced by the 'moral function' (Rickman, 1951) of those involved in this 'becoming'. The contributors to this book offer detailed understandings of the workings of our moral faculties and sensibilities, known in psychoanalysis as the superego. In this introduction I look at some external and internal contextual moorings which may shape the types of superego functioning emerging in clinical work.

Human beings are complex creatures. This statement of the obvious underlines the importance of looking at human phenomena from different viewpoints: no single perspective, however informative or enlightening, as psychoanalysis surely is, can do justice to complicated human behaviours such as a person's moral function. As Mary Midgley (1994) argues in the philosophical case she makes for benign pluralism: 'overlapping pictures taken from different angles provide the right way to get a reasonably unified notion of an object' (p. 56).

To provide a fuller picture of the contexts of superego functioning, I draw on interdisciplinary viewpoints from psychological and developmental research, neuroscience and philosophical exploration to deepen and amplify our psychoanalytic understandings (Wurmser, 2004: p. 187). This background helps us appreciate the power that received moral imperatives can exert over a person's psychic economy and homoeostasis (Glasser, 1996). Also, the magnitude of the psychoanalytic task, as documented in the following chapters, of helping patients to develop their own moral compass informed, rather than driven, by the social values and principles internalised in their superego.

The social nature of human beingness

Freud (1923) arrived at his concept of the superego with his topographical model of the mind. Way-stations included 'conscience' (Freud, 1913: p. 67); a specialist ego compartment standing over the ego as its judge (Freud, 1917: p. 247); and an 'ego ideal' against which the ego measures its worth (Freud, 1914: p. 93ff, see Horne, Chapter 3).[1] Freud primarily focused on the development of individuals as instinctual beings obliged to import from their social and cultural worlds the ways and means of civilising their anti-social impulses to equip them for social life (Freud, 1930). Children begin to develop a superego, building on the neurological, emotional and physical foundations established in the earliest mother–baby relationship (see Hinshelwood, Chapter 1; Narvaez, Chapter 4), as (m)others induct them into the social rules of getting on with others. The superego thereby becomes the guardian of personal social probity and belonging, pressurising the ego to moderate and modify instinctual impulses and holding the ego to its ideals of the person they aspire to be. At this point, the superego appeared as the 'representative-of-society-in-mind' as a necessary 'add-on' in order that people may become socially acceptable.

Before long, psychoanalytic focus extended – beyond the child's instinctual development and interest in objects as satisfiers (or frustraters) of their instinctual desires (Freud, 1905) – to the child's relational environment. For example, Fairbairn (1952) proposed that 'libido is not primarily pleasure-seeking, but object seeking' (p. 137). Infants were now understood as orientating themselves to (m)others as incipient social beings, seeking intrinsically valuable connexions with her. Individual development came to be seen as evolving in the context and matrix of relationships:

> the development of the infant has come to be seen increasingly as something happening within, and shaped by a human context, not, as Freud might have at times liked to think, a spontaneous unfolding of preprogrammed instincts.
> (Wright, 1991: p. 3)

Once children are recognised as having an innate pre-disposition to sociality they can be seen as internalising constraints over their self-expressions because securing (m)other's love matters to them. Such incipient moral regulation of a child's behaviours with others develops into a need to take other peoples' feelings into account and nurture the positive regard of others, even at the expense of free self-expressions of individuality. In short, developing a morally regulating part of the mind appears from the relational viewpoint as fundamental to the development of social human beings, not an 'add-on'. However a child's sociality is not a given: it has to be 'grown'.

Neuroscientific findings also locate the foundations of an infant's social capacities within the fabric of their primary relationships (Schore, 1994 [2016], 2012; McGilchrist, 2009; Narvaez, 2014). Equally, evolutionary, psychological, developmental and attachment perspectives support the contention that children are naturally and essentially 'other-interested' and 'other-sensitized' from an early age (Music, 2014).[2] Schore (1994 [2016]) integrates neurobiological, developmental and psychoanalytic evidence to propose that human social capacities originate within mother–infant relating. We are born with billions of neuronal possibilities which, when activated in the infant's experiences of mother, during critical stages of brain development, establish the neural pathways necessary to engage socially with others (Schore, 1994 [2016]; Eagleman, 2016; Narvaez,

2014; Narvaez, Chapter 4). During the early months, mother regulates her infant's sense of well-being, excitements and distresses to restore comfortable states of mental, emotional and physical equilibrium. Mother's capacity to regulate her infant's inner states is conducted through her finely attuned responsiveness to her baby. Much of this mutual and reciprocal communication is conducted through gaze (Schore, 1994 [2016]; Wright, 1991; Horne, Chapter 3). Such ordinary processes of a mother's loving devotion to her baby lay the neurological foundations for empathic relating to others, particularly in the right hemisphere of the infant's brain. These set unconscious expectations of how relationships work registered in acute, instantaneous, emotional perceptiveness of the other's mental state in relation to self. As growing children find their feet and begin to explore their extending worlds within expanding circles of others, they gradually learn to regulate and adjust their own self-expressions guided by the encouraging smiles and discouraging frowns of (m)other. In later childhood, their developing empathic capacities equip the child to see the world through the eyes of (m)others (Wright, 1991) enabling them to make sense of other people's behaviours and mental states, that is, to develop theories of minds (Fonagy & Target, 1996). Social skills and capacities continue to develop during phase-specific neurological growth periods in childhood, adolescence, early adulthood and throughout life (Schore, 1994 [2016]; Eagleman, 2016; Narvaez, 2014; Narvaez, Chapter 4). Such psychological, neurological and physical developments establish sociality as integral to the individual's personal ontogenic development.

Human sociality is also integral to our phylogeny: psychological research into human morality locates the roots of social values deep in our evolutionary biological inheritance (Haidt, 2012). Haidt identified six fundamental value systems evolved by human beings to uphold effective social organisation: the social imperative to care and protect dependent and vulnerable others; a premium on fairness and justice to promote cooperation between people and discourage cheating and exploitation; loyalty to others underpinning commitment to common tasks and deterring unreliability and betrayal; respect for authorities and hierarchies secures the social advantages of leaderships and co-ordination of social roles for the common good; agreements about what is treated as sacred or taboo protects members from contamination by harmful substances and practices and promotes social bonding through sharing common values; respect for the liberties and rights of others checks inclinations of a powerful few to dominate and exploit the many. In transgression these values accrue the force of taboos, triggering outrage and recoil, much as Freud explores in his mythological account of the phylogenic origin of morality in Totem and Taboo (1913) (see Murdin, Chapter 9). Freud (1913, 1923) proposes that prohibitions of murderous and sexual impulses lie at the foundation of human morality, both in the individual's phylogenic inheritance and their ontogenic resolution of the Oedipus Complex, subsequently internalised as the superego.

If sociality is integral to human nature, and the morality that regulates it is rooted in the individual's phylogenic (Freud, 1913; Midgley, 1994) and ontogenic social development (Schore, 1991, 1994 [2016]), why may people feel torn between their needs to be free, autonomous individuals and their needs for, and responsibilities to, others?

Narvaez (Chapter 4) suggests that infants are born evolutionarily primed with neurological equipment to develop into social beings but this development depends on a mother's capacities to adaptively attune and respond to her infant's needs as an incipient unique individual. In this event, the child's sense of safety with mother extends to become an openness to engagements with others. However, without this maternal provision, the neural pathways and limbic circuits needed for social relating cannot develop: such infants are liable to grow up regarding relationships as threats to their survival, disposed to develop 'safety' ethics based on self-preservation. Narvaez proposes that our neurological social pre-dispositions developed within hunter-gatherer, small scale, socially intimate societies. In contrast our contemporary societies are complex, large-scale, industrialised and globalised, organised around divisions of roles and tasks. Social, familial and individual pressures generate conflicting priorities on parents which may translate, for example, into returning to work from maternity leave rather than providing the baby with the 'companionship care' necessary for the neurological and psychological integration of their individuality and sociality (Narvaez, 2014; Schore, 1994 [2016], 2012). Narvaez argues that the adaptive solution to such conflicts in modern civilisations becomes the development of a superego to manage the conflicts between our individual and social natures, rather than developing a sociality arising naturally from our individuality, and vice versa.

Freud maintained that human aggressivity posed a threat to civilisation necessitating the internalisation of a superego-in-mind:

> What means does civilisation employ in order to inhibit the aggressiveness which opposes it, to make it harmless, to get rid of it, perhaps? . . . to render . . . desire for aggression innocuous? . . .
>
> His aggressiveness is introjected. . . . sent back to where it came from – that is directed towards his own ego. There it is taken over by a portion of the ego, which sets itself over against the rest of the ego as super-ego, and which now in the form of 'conscience', is ready to put into action against the ego the same harsh aggressiveness that the ego would have liked to satisfy upon other, extraneous individuals.
>
> (Freud, 1930: p. 123)

Narvaez views the necessity for a superego as the failure of civilisation to provide the conditions necessary to develop our neurological disposition to become integrated social and individual beings. This view resonates with Fonagy (2003) when he writes that:

> Violence ultimately signals the failure of normal developmental processes to deal with something that occurs naturally. . . . Biological predisposition

and social influence do not create destructiveness, but rather compromise the social processes that normally regulate and tame them.

(2003: p. 190)

Here Fonagy and Narvaez, from different perspectives, converge in their understanding that psychical conflicts are generated by 'the failure of normal developmental processes' to integrate love and aggression, autonomy and sociality, in harmonious, balanced brains and minds.

I have suggested that individuality and sociality are closely interwoven, each forged from and within the other, both rooted in human neurobiology, psychology and physiology. Conflicts arising between and within these aspects of our minds are regulated and mediated by the superego. We now turn to consider the superego in action.

What is the 'superego' and how does it work?

In common parlance, the superego is our conscience, telling us 'right from wrong', holding us to 'the straight and narrow', 'making us guilty' for straying and prompting us to make amends. However the psychoanalytic concept of superego is more complex, comprising constituents from ego, ego ideal and external reality, deeply rooted in the unconscious id.

Freud presented the superego as a specialist ego facility, set apart to judge critically the remaining ego (1917: p. 247). The superego utilises certain ego functions for moral duties: setting limits on expressions of impulses and narcissistic wishes; observing reality from a morally augmented viewpoint; monitoring and judging the ego's efforts to reach its ideal standards of behaviour and self-worth. It follows that the nature of the superego varies according to the baseline ego's development and the quality of the maturational environment in which it evolved (Hartmann & Loewenstein, 1962; Harding, Chapter 5): an immature ego's perception of reality, self and other which has been distorted by primitive defences, is liable to generate a more suspicious, harshly judgemental, condemning and punitive moral estimation of the ego. Observance of values is more likely to be based on fear of punishment than love and concern.[3]

The superego is also rooted in the unconscious mind (Freud, 1923, 1930). The aggression accruing from frustrated impulses is diverted from loved objects and relegated to the unconscious id to be harnessed by the superego to keep the ego to the task of managing anti-social impulses. This 'proscriptive' superego (Glasser, 1996) defines what a person 'shalt not' do: transgressions are punished with redeployed unconscious aggression. Superego rectitude and judgements of self and other are powered by recycled aggression disguised as morally justified censure and punishment. The harshness of the superego is directly proportionate to the aggression the ego swallows in order to safeguard his relationships (Freud, 1923: p. 54; Harding, Chapter 5).

A third aspect of the superego is imported through identifications with, and internalisations of, parental social and cultural values instilled during socialisation of the child's behaviours with other people. In particular, as 'heir to the Oedipus Complex' internalised parental constraints on sexual and aggressive impulses form the baseline of morality. The superego monitors the ego's attempts to restrain incestuous and aggressive impulses punishing failures with guilt (see Murdin Chapter 9). Klein proposed an earlier developmental origin of the superego (see Hinshelwood, Chapter 1).

A fourth contribution to the superego is the ego ideal which 'prescribes' the person the ego wishes and strives to be (Glasser, 1996), and Horne adds, is seen to be by others (Chapter 3). The ego ideal was envisioned by Freud as successor to infantile narcissism, that illusory state of blissful at-oneness with mother, unconditionally loved and lovable, as and for, themselves. As young children 'find their feet' they revel in a grandiose sense of omnipotent powerfulness. But as mothers' pleasure and pride in their achievements fails to mirror their own (Schore, 1991), the reality of their littleness, helplessness and dependence on mother as-a-separate-being begins to dawn; shame accompanies the realised discrepancy between their inflated self-estimation and the reality of their limitations. Children who were helped to adapt to their limitations and discover their abilities, become better equipped to expand their efficacies and modify their ego ideal accordingly. Children left to cope with their shame alone when faced with their actual dependence and helplessness, are liable to fill the gap between how they are, and how they want to be, with illusory omnipotence and grandeur (Novick & Novick, 1991). The ego measures its worth against its success or failure to reach its ideals. The superego enforces ego ideal standards and diminishes the ego with shame for falling short and expands it with pride and self-esteem when standards are reached.

The ego ideal is sometimes identified with a protective aspect of the superego (Freud, 1923; Rickman, 1951; Sandler, 1963). This offers the ego benign protection from overstepping the line between socially acceptable and unacceptable behaviours, between disregard for, and consideration of, others. When lines are crossed a benign superego helps the ego to repair damage done, (Klein, 1937) and learn from experience rather than simply suffer punishment for transgressions. A key developmental variable predisposing the harsh or benign character of a person's superego, is their experience of parental superego reactions and responses to their behaviours and sensitive feelings (Freud, 1933: p. 67; Schafer, 1960: p. 183).

Such understandings coincide with subjective experiences of a superego as authority figure, a judge (Wurmser, 2004), monitoring how we relate to others, accusing and condemning 'wrong doing', reinforcing and rewarding 'right doing'. However, the idea of 'the superego' as if a reified entity (Schafer, 1983) imported and installed in the mind is 'linguistically misleading' (Money-Kyle, 1952) and generates conceptual, developmental and clinical disadvantages.

The superego is more accurately conceptualised as an overarching concept encompassing a complex network and inter-relation of functions and processes, working in concert to enable us to exercise our moral sensibilities, rather like a group of musicians: each musician and instrument contributes to the music made. Analogously, four aspects of the mind come together in superego functioning:

morally augmented ego functions are interwoven with recycled aggression from the id, ego ideals which measure the ego's performance, and social rules and expectations which order and regulate the individual's conduct with others. The superego music thus produced impacts on its listener, the experiencing ego, who responds in different ways. When superego music is harmonious and mellifluous to the mind's ear, the experiencing ego can listen with relative equanimity, absorb and evaluate it freely and use it to guide decisions and behaviours. When superego music is discordant and disturbing, painful to hear, the listening ego is liable to reach for metaphoric ear-plugs to muffle its loud and insistent riffs; or more drastically, switch-off and replace the superego's harsh tones with more amenable tunes. Such experiences prompt the ego to develop defences to survive and manage the moral racket to which it feels subjected. But when the superego music activates terrors of a tsunami of shame (Bromberg, 2011; Schore, 1994 [2016]) the experiencing ego may become frozen and petrified, or fragment, surviving by dissociating this experience as 'not me', in order to forestall re-traumatization.

This conceptual representation of the superego more closely reflects the neurobiological substrata of our moral functions and sensibilities. Our moral sense is not located in a specific part of the brain: 'all activity in the brain is driven by other activity in the brain, in a vastly complex interrelated network' (Eagleman, 2016: p. 166). This suggests that our moral function comprises an interaction of complex networks of neural pathways and circuits contributing to moral engagements with self and others. This said, the pre-frontal cortex is the neural hub of control and regulation of actions (Eagleman, 2016); neuronal pathways centred in and emanating from the orbital frontal cortex process affect related meaning, mediate empathy, emotional expression and regulation (Narvaez, 2014: p. 114f).[4] The network of skills involved in ethical expertise include: 'ethical sensitivity (perception, imagination, feeling), ethical judgement (reasoning and reflection), ethical focus (attention, motivation, moral identity) and ethical action (effectivities, steadfastness)', (Narvaez, 2014: p. 293) engaging cognitive and emotional networks and circuits deeply rooted, in our physiological, neurological and psychological being (Schore, 1994 [2016]; Narvaez, 2014).

Treating the superego as a reified entity in mind may also have misleading implications for our understanding of the ego developments necessary for patients to forge their own moral function. When superego music traumatises our experiencing ego, we turn deaf ears to it and/or develop defences (such as those described in Part II of this book) to manage and survive its penetrating disturbance. However, these emergency measures also deprive our experiencing ego of developmental opportunities accruing from hard psychical work to: come to terms with our judgemental and punishing reactions to our needs; integrate our id impulses into our experiencing ego; discover realistic ways to stabilise our narcissistic equilibrium by finding ways to engage with our social realities; develop our own moral function as integral to our sense of self (Rickman, 1951). We can only establish an autonomous mind capable of relating to our moral evaluations of ourselves and others, and assess their appropriateness to the circumstances, after facing the conflicting demands and needs emanating from within ourselves. As Reddish (2014; Chapter 2) argues, people lacking the ego capacities to engage with their archaic superego's threats and promises with an independent perspective feel permanently anxious about meeting their ideal expectations of themselves and petrified of catastrophe if they fail.

A clinical hazard of reifying the superego is of reinforcing a patient's sense of being 'done to' by a 'not me', alien authority-in-mind, unable to recognise that their imprisonment and suffering comes from their own morally righteous inclinations (Schafer, 1983). The therapist's role is to discern, behind a patient's deflated state, interventions from their self-punishing propensities which have crushed their experiencing ego's expansionary attempt to reclaim formerly disowned parts of self (Bouchard & Lecours, 2004). By recognising such processes, therapists can begin to put words to the patient's wishes and fears that conflict between aspects of themselves will be psychically fatal. With time and joint efforts, therapist and patient can notice and recognise formerly disclaimed parts of the experiencing self, bringing them into the ego's sphere of influence and choice. Such processes are mediated through the therapist's action as a tolerant, protective and understanding auxiliary superego (Horne Chapter 3; clinical chapters in Part II). By internalising the therapist's auxiliary superego function, the patient's judgemental and punitive attitudes towards their impulses are modified enabling them to gradually accommodate and integrate repressed and disowned needs into their experiencing self (Strachey, 1934 [1969]). As dissociated parts of the self become enacted in the therapeutic relationship they become available for recognition and affirmation by therapist and patient enabling their integration as part of the experiencing self (Bromberg, 2011).[5]

Having outlined the composition and dynamic workings of the superego in an individual's mind, I now turn to consider the moral pressures that social groups can exert on their individual members and the impacts on society when a citizen's superego malfunctions.

The moral interface where individual meets social expectation

For societies to function effectively, their members need to share certain core values to resolve conflicts arising between the rights of individual citizens and the state's responsibilities to society as a whole (Haidt, 2012: p. 17). Social order depends on the state to bring moral pressure to bear on those who cross socially accepted lines. Haidt identifies three ethical systems which inform the regulation of a society's conflicts. In most Western societies, when the health and safety of others is not at stake, individualistic cultures usually privilege individual rights and adjust for social needs accordingly.[6] In other societies, 'community ethics' hold sway, prioritising social relationship and communal needs over individual interests. Haidt also cites cultures regulated by 'divinity ethics' which subject both individual and community concerns to the values of 'divine purpose': the behaviours and relationships of group members are structured in terms of purity (and degradation), reflecting this 'higher' order. When an individual's priorities differ from their social community's dominant value system, they risk ostracism; for example a daughter, raised within a community ethic, who chooses a 'love marriage' over one arranged by her family; or homosexuals in Britain before the right to exercise their personal sexual preference was legalised and became culturally accepted. Naturally tensions between value systems become heightened for immigrants to communities with different ethical priorities. Globalisation and international digitalised communications expose societies to different value systems from their own which may be regarded as threats to their social orders e.g. digitised exposure to Western value systems prioritising individualism.

In Western societies, an individual's autonomy and rights to self-determination sometimes seem to acquire the force and weight of morality as a social regulating principle. Barnett (2007) observes such paradoxical phenomena in his analysis of the superego in post-modernist society when 'ought' is applied to a fallacious understanding of autonomy: 'you ought to be self-determining', including a sense of entitlement to have what is wanted, as and when it's wanted, perpetuated by consumer and popular culture. Barnett succinctly paraphrases this by reversing Freud's principle 'where id was there ego shall be' into 'where ego was there id shall be' (Barnett, 2007: p. 149). Such may be understood as powerful coincidences of internal and external pressures, when cultural and social phenomena activate strong regressive longings in individuals and prompt the ego to disconnect from superego restraints (Chasseguet-Smirgel, 1985). One example is found in the potential for digitised, disembodied communications, coupled with an individualistic 'ethic' privileging the individual's rights to self-expression, to lift restraints on venting hostile impulses towards others, regardless of the recipient's sensitivities (e.g. internet trolling). Another example might be the opportunities that such cultural and technological developments present to activate deep omnipotent longings to transcend realistic limits of time and space and bypass developmental needs to bear separations from others.

When social and cultural expectations coincide with a person's idealised view of themselves, the superego's enforcement of ego ideals gains additional leverage, intensifying internal conflicts between satisfying personal needs and consideration for others. Such conflicts in the minds of individuals may appear to find regressive solutions through joining political movements purporting to pursue social ideals which unconsciously satisfy narcissistic longings and primitive impulses. For example, political groups pursuing deeply rooted social values may activate unconscious longings for a conflict-free state of primary merger with mother. Such merger fantasies may feel realised when like-minded individuals join together and abdicate, to leaders and other group members, their personal moral responsibilities for assessing the means by which their personal and political ideals are pursued (Chasseguet-Smirgel, 1985). Nazi Germany and fundamentalist extremisms may be salutary examples of this dangerous eventuality.

Just as social and cultural phenomena impact on individuals so the behaviours of individuals may impact on societies: an individual's malfunctioning superego can generate an unbalanced mind which 'may result in serious problems for the individual, and for society as a whole' (Barnett, 2007: p. 154). Individuals with weakened egos may find conflicts between their personal and social needs are unsustainable, prompting resort to extreme solutions – in the direction of self-sacrifice or self-preservation – to rid their minds of conflict. Individuals fearful of expressing their sexual and aggressive impulses may choose self-sacrifice to protect their own psychic equilibrium and their significant others from anticipated harm. Extreme examples of such desperate solutions may be those with fundamentalist mindsets, defending their egos from disturbing impulses by acute obsessional defences (Murdin, Chapter 9). Those who were severely neglected and abused within their maturational environment, may survive psychically by resorting to self-preservative behaviours (Glasser, 1996) regardless of consideration for others. The most extreme example of this desperate solution may be psychopathic individuals (Taylor, Chapter 8).

In private practice therapists may not encounter patients with severe and violent psychopathic disorders or patients with extreme fundamentalist belief systems. However these two extremes of superego dysfunction illustrate the underlying dynamics and possible aetiologies behind disorders which can wreak havoc in societies. These may also illuminate pockets of fundamentalist functioning in patients crippled by severe obsessional defences, driving fundamentalist zeal, to keep at bay a fanatical superego (Freud, 1913, 1923); or pockets of psychopathic functioning in patients who treat others in calculating, dehumanising ways in certain circumstances. Significantly survival in some institutional and corporate environments in our national and globalised world may perpetuate adaptive psychopathic dealings between people (Music, 2014): for example, when institutions and 'faceless' corporations (Sacks, 2005) operate from cultures based primarily on economic values and organisational-interests, squeezing out and trumping all other considerations and values (Sandel, 2013).

Those structuring their lives according to fundamentalist principles of divinity ethics sacrifice their personal and social needs to the primacy of 'divine purposes' and derive their self-worth from purifying themselves of all need.[7] Though inevitably speculative and partial, a psychoanalytic perspective offers possible understanding of malfunctioning superego processes behind fundamentalist extremisms. Freud suggested that obsessional beliefs in magical, omnipotent thinking, equating thought with action and fears of contagion by displacement, necessitate treating 'dangerous' impulses as taboos because 'any violation will lead to intolerable disaster' (Freud, 1913: p. 27ff). Extremist fundamentalists may feel morally justified in imposing their 'purifying' principles on those who allow themselves pleasure and impulse satisfaction, both to fulfil a mission to order the world in accordance with divine sanctity and to protect themselves from contagion by the infidel's degraded, decadent standards. Money-Kyrle's following description of a type of conscience might fit that of a fundamentalist: 'at once self-righteous and censorious. Their guilt is for export only. They deny it in themselves but see it more clearly in others on to whom they project their share as well. So, they live in a state of moral indignation with the scapegoats for their own offences' (Money-Kyrle, 1952: p. 232). The superego in a fundamentalist mindset both reinforces the experiencing ego's identification with his ideals and imposes these values on others with a moral zeal and fervour barely concealing the underlying unconscious aggression which thereby obtains satisfaction.[8]

Psychopaths treat others as objects in mercenary, calculating and manipulative ways, to serve their self-preservative interests (Taylor, Chapter 8). Psychopathic individuals may understand an other's feelings and actions but use that knowledge corruptly and ruthlessly to dominate and control them, thereby protecting themselves from becoming helpless in a threatening environment (Parsons, 2009). They maintain self-control, to avoid being exposed – to self or other – as 'weak' and powerless, by externalising their vulnerability in others, and exploiting that emotionally dangerous state in them. The formative early experiences which predisposed the psychopath's developmental trajectory varies. However, the psychopath's treatment of others, from a psychoanalytic viewpoint, suggests that as children they experienced themselves as their primary caregivers' narcissistic objects: their own needs overridden by their caretakers' needs of them, their own unfolding personhood unrecognised, leaving them overwhelmingly ashamed of who they were. To survive psychically, they treat others as they were treated in their primary relationships, controlled and dominated out of existence. In such speculated circumstances, social relationships would be experienced as threatening and a survival strategy found in a self-preservative safety ethic (Narvaez, 2014). The relationship of a psychopath with his conscience may be described as amoral: 'They do not consciously experience . . . guilt themselves and regard those who claim to be influenced by moral obligations or scruples as hypocrites or weaklings' (Money-Kyrle, 1952: p. 232). Clearly these two types of conscience, when applied to fundamentalism and psychopathy, may characterise that of anyone at different times, towards different people, in different internal and external circumstances. Between these two extremes are those with 'authoritarian' consciences to which the ego defers, as to external authorities, on pain of punishment and self-recrimination. Those with a more collaborative relationship between their ego and superego propensities, are motivated by concern to protect themselves, and others, from harm: their failures provoke remorse, sadness and reparative drives to make amends (Money-Kyrle, 1952).

Having considered the moral pressures that social groups can exert upon individual members; some regressive needs that cultural phenomenon can activate in individual's psyches; and the impacts on societies of individuals with malfunctioning superegos, I now turn to consider the importance of superego functioning in the consulting room.

Is the superego concept relevant in 21st-century psychoanalysis?

Sandler (1960) pronounced the 'apparent conceptual dissolution of the superego' confirming this conclusion thirty years later (1989: p. 298). He was not alone in doubting the continued clinical usefulness of the superego concept (Hinshelwood,

Chapter 1). Sandler (1960, 1989) argued that contemporary practitioners have found it more clinically useful to ascribe the aggression driving superego activity to raw impulses emanating from the id; identifications comprising superego formation and content to the ego; and to work with the externalisation of the patient's internal object relationships within the transference and counter-transference. He suggests that 'conceptualisation in terms of internal object relations [rather than so-called superego-anxiety] allows us much greater scope to think and interpret in terms of a far wider range of affects than in the past' (Sandler, 1989: p. 306). Might we speculate that Freud himself presaged the redundancy of the superego concept when he chose to debut it in a paper titled 'The Ego and the Id' (1923)?

Naturally, I beg to differ and regard this book as testament to the continued relevance of the superego concept in psychoanalytic treatment. Human beings are 'ethical primates' (Midgley, 1994), social and therefore moral creatures: the exception, psychopathic individuals, prove the rule because they lacked the necessary maturational environment in which to develop their incipient sociality. The superego's psychical speciality resides in its representation of human 'moral function' (Rickman, 1951) and offers a unique dimension to our understanding of mental conflict and clinical work.

I have presented a case for regarding sociality and individuality as interwoven, each arising from the other, integral to human psychology, deeply rooted in our minds, brains and bodies. We are social beings. Our social relationships matter to us. We secure our reputations with ourselves and others by regulating our relationships with moral values encoded in social rules. However, our sociality also makes us susceptible to pressures emanating from our social world without and superego within. Doing 'the right thing', especially by others, has unquestionable imperative force as Britton captured when he wrote that even if we concur with Nietzsche that 'God is dead', '[h]is internal representation – the superego – is not' (Britton, 2003: p. 71). The superego conveys the authority of God, the childhood parents and those 'above' us in the social hierarchy, throughout life. In short, superego dispositions exercise a powerful hold over the individual's mind.

The constituents of the superego originate in different aspects of the individual's psyche acquiring a specialised moral function as contributors to superego activities. Aggression recycled from the id, deployed by the superego, is given moral force when disguised as morally justified self-judgement and self-punishment (or criticism when directed at others). Equally, the ego functions deployed by the superego – monitoring, perception, observation, reflection, evaluation, making judgements, regulating relationships with self and others – are all conducted through a morally augmented view of reality: 'The ego observes itself in a realistic light, the superego in a moral light' (Britton, 2003: p. 72). Often people experience their morally infused perceptions of reality as self-evidently imperative unlike Hamlet, who, in a moment of clarity declares, 'for there is nothing either good or bad, but thinking makes it so' (Shakespeare, n.d., p. 1141). Similarly, their well-being and positive self-regard depend on living up to their ideals (however unrealistic). Failures to fulfil those ideals are underwritten by fears for survival if (m)other's love is thereby lost (Freud, 1923: p. 58; Harding, Chapter 5). This narcissistic imperative may carry the moral weight of 'badness' equated with moral unacceptability (see Hinshelwood, Chapter 1; Harding, Chapter 5), captured here by Bromberg (2011):

> The child's healthy desire to communicate her subjective experience to a needed other is infused with shame because the needed other cannot or will not acknowledge the child's experience as something legitimately "thinkable". The attachment bond that organises self-stability for the child is now in jeopardy. She feels, not that she did something wrong, but there is something wrong with her self, that is, something wrong with her as a person.
>
> (p. 43)

The superego acquires moral force as the internalised representative of society-in-mind (Rickman, 1951) which a fragile ego may feel unable to question. Our sociality is fundamental to our human beingness, therefore ex-communication from society is dangerous for all those who care about their good-standing with self and others. Transgressing values upholding the social order places individuals outside the securities and benefits which society accords. Once we appreciate that sociality is an integral part of human psychology we can better understand an individual's susceptibility to the moral pressures exerted by their superego propensities.

As Reddish suggests (Chapter 2) when the 'archaic' superego has outlived its early organising and guiding function and acquired the moral overlay of the Oedipal superego, it can exercise a stifling hold on an ego petrified of developing independently of superego constraints. For others, their ego becomes deformed and weakened by defences developed to protect them from the shame and guilt meted out by their superego. Some of these defensive consequences for individuals' ego development are explored in Part II of this book. In Chapter 5, Harding explores the internal predicament of depressed patients who capitulate to the ruthless, harsh, self-punishment and self-loathing of their superego proclivities, leaving then feeling worthless, hopeless and helpless. In Chapter 6, Wood explores a place in the perversely organised mind for a variety of superego figures playing differing roles in the ego's survival strategies against core complex anxieties (Glasser, 1996), helplessness and profound depression. In Chapter 7 Nathan explores the inevitable exposure to not only the patient's, but also the therapist's elemental superego, when working with patients in borderline states of mind. In Chapter 8 Taylor explores psychopathic states of mind in which the ego, severely deformed by having had to direct all its energies into self-preservation in early relationships, switches off its superego, to mercenarily control and dominate others. In Chapter 9 Murdin explores patients with fundamentalist mindsets as their egos deploy obsessional defensive reaction formations, to survive their self-accusatory and self-punishing attempts to control their murderous and incestuous impulses.

Patients need their therapist's help to own, and liberate themselves from being in thrall to, their superego inclinations (see Harding, Chapter 5). First, to enable them to internalise a protective and loving superego (Schafer, 1960) from their therapist's auxiliary superego function (Strachey, 1934 [1969]). Second, to set aside the moral overlays they impose on their observations of self, others and reality, in order to explore their realities as they are, for what they are. When patients discover the personal meanings of their realities, they are then enabled to consult their superego judgements and make truly autonomous decisions about the moral stance they deem appropriate to their circumstances. Third, with such strengthened ego capacities they are equipped to develop a personal moral function (Rickman, 1951). With consciences fully integrated into their personalities, individuals may be less swayed by social pressures, or moral blackmail (from their own superego propensities or those of others) and less susceptible to switching-off their autonomous moral judgements and superego to merge 'mindlessly' with groups and leaders (Freud, 1921; Chasseguet-Smirgel, 1985). I therefore suggest that the concept of the superego, for all its conceptual, clinical and developmental complexity and difficulties, can help therapists to appreciate the measure of their task; can facilitate their patients to liberate themselves from their moral imperatives and their anxieties about daring to make autonomous moral judgements *and* can provide therapists with a template to focus this endeavour.

* * * *

In Part I of this book, we examine some theoretical and developmental perspectives of the superego and ego ideal, and the formative influence of the maturational environments in which individuals develop their moral sensibilities.

Part II explores a range of defences and mental organisations which an ego develops when caught between superego restraints and id impulses, and the impact these have on those individuals and their relations with their social worlds. The reader will observe that sometimes it is psychically impossible for a person to sustain and resolve mental conflicts within their own minds and with others. When engagement with others threatens their inner equilibrium they may resort to psychological strategies to cope which are then externalised in their relationships. In psychoanalytic treatment these self-preservative measures can be incarnated between therapist and patient in the hope of understanding and resolution. The reader is offered insights into ways of psychologically surviving persecuting, self-destructive superego demands and ego ideals, states of mind readily recognisable to anyone who experiences conflicts between meeting their own needs and those of others.

Part III considers the role of superego processes and functions in the context of professional psychoanalytic relationships. Driver explores the role of the superego during clinical training (Chapter 11); Colman explores the analyst's relationship with their analytic superego with which they must come to terms, in the course of their career, in order to relate effectively with their patients (Chapter 12); finally Harding explores the role of the therapist's superego in their conduct of an ethical attitude underpinning their analytic attitude towards their patients (Chapter 13).

Notes

1 Barnett, 2007 provides a thorough survey of the development of the superego concept in psychoanalytic theory.
2 Music (2014) provides a detailed overview of interdisciplinary evidence for the inherent sociality of young children.
3 The earliest forms of superego are ruthlessly harsh, according to the principles of talion law or paranoid-schizoid processes in Kleinian terminology (see Hinshelwood, Chapter 1; Caper, 1999). In this book, contributors refer to primitive superego functioning variously as 'archaic', 'primitive', 'elemental'. The concept of 'archaic superego' in Reddish's theory (2014, Chapter 2) has a particular developmental trajectory and functioning.
4 See Narvaez (2014, Chapter 5) for an overview of areas of the brain activated by the social, cognitive and emotional neural networks and circuits involved in moral thought and action.
5 In the interests of brevity the author will continue to refer to superego, ego and id whilst encouraging the reader to translate this 'shorthand' into the 'action terms' of an experiencing and acting self, as much agent as recipient of superego proclivities.
6 Groups within 'individualistic' societies may be regulated by norms to which individual members are expected to subject their personal needs and wishes (see Trollope, 2012). See Joanna Trollope's novel, The Soldier's Wife, for a fictional example of the impact of a military organisation's values on the lives of their serving officers and their families.
7 An unconscious paradox of self-sacrificial defences for the benefits of others, or to fulfil 'divine purposes', are that adherence to these procures the approval of the ego ideal, a source of narcissistic well-being.
8 See Carys Bray's novel, A Song for Issy Bradley for a moving fictional account of a Mormon family in crisis, their needs as individuals and a family subsumed to fundamentalist 'divine purposes' (see Bray, 2014).

References

Barnett, B. (2007) *"You Ought To!" A Psychoanalytic Study of the Superego and Conscience*. London, Karnac Books.
Bouchard, M. & Lecours, S. (2004) Analysing forms of superego functioning as mentalizations. *International Journal of Psychoanalysis*. 85, 879–896.
Bray, C. (2014) *A Song for Issy Bradley*. London, Penguin Books.
Britton, R. (2003) *Sex, Death and the Superego*. London, Karnac Books.
Bromberg, P.M. (2011) *The Shadow of the Tsunami and the Growth of the Relational Mind*. London, Routledge.
Caper, R. (1999) *A Mind of One's Own*. London, Routledge.
Chasseguet-Smirgel, J. (1985) *The Ego Ideal*. London, Free Association Books.
Eagleman, D. (2016) *Incognito: The Secret Lives of the Brain*. London, Canongate.
Fairbairn, W.R.D. (1952) *Psychoanalytic Studies of the Personality*. London, Routledge & Kegan Paul.
Fonagy, P. (2003) Towards a developmental understanding of violence. *British Journal of Psychiatry*. 183, 190–192.
Fonagy, P. & Target, M. (1996) Playing with reality1.: theory of mind and the normal development of psychic reality. *International Journal of Psychoanalysis*. 77, 217–233.

Freud, S. (1905) The essays on sexuality. In: *The Standard Edition*. Volume VII. London, Hogarth Press.
Freud, S. (1913) Totem and taboo. In: *The Standard Edition*. Volume X1. London, Hogarth Press.
Freud, S. (1914) On narcissism. In: *The Standard Edition*. Volume XIV. London, Hogarth Press.
Freud, S. (1917) Mourning and melancholia. In: *The Standard Edition*. Volume XIV. London, Hogarth Press.
Freud, S. (1921) Group psychology. In: *The Standard Edition*. Volume XVIII. London, Hogarth Press.
Freud, S. (1923) The ego and the id. In: *The Standard Edition*. Volume XIX. London, Hogarth Press.
Freud, S. (1930) Civilisation and its discontents. In: *The Standard Edition*. Volume XXI. London, Hogarth Press.
Freud, S. (1933) New Introductory lectures on Psycho-Analysis. In: *The Standard Edition*. Volume XXII. London, Hogarth Press.
Glasser, M. (1996) Aggression and sadism in the perversions. In: *Sexual Deviation*. 3rd Edition. Oxford, Oxford University Press.
Haidt, J. (2012) *The Righteous Mind: Why Good People Are Divided by Politics and Religion*. London, Penguin Books.
Hartmann, H. & Loewenstein, M.D. (1962) Notes on the superego. *Psychoanalytic Study of the Child*. 17, 42–81.
Klein, M. (1937) Love, guilt and reparation. In: *Love, Guilt and Reparation and Other Works 1921–1945*. London, Virago Press, 1988.
McGilchrist, I. (2009) *The Master and His Emissary*. London, Yale University Press.
Midgley, M. (1994) *The Ethical Primate: Humans, Freedom and Morality*. London, Routledge.
Money-Kyrle, R.E. (1952) Psycho-analysis and ethics. *International Journal of Psychoanalysis*. 33, 225–234.
Music, G. (2014) *The Good Life*. London, Routledge.
Narvaez, D. (2014) *Neurobiology and the Development of Human Morality*. London, W.W. Norton & Company, Inc.
Novick, J. & Novick, K. (1991) Some comments on masochism and the delusion of omnipotence from a developmental perspective. *Journal of the American Psychoanalytic Association*. 39, 307–331.
Parsons, M. (2009) The roots of violence, theory and implications for technique with children and adolescence. In: M. Lanyado & A. Horne (eds.) *The Handbook of Child & Adolescent Psychotherapy: Psychoanalytic Approaches*. 2nd Edition. London, Routledge.
Reddish, E. (2014) *The Petrified Ego*. London, Karnac Books.
Rickman, J. (1951) The development of the moral function. In: P. King (ed.) *No Ordinary Psychoanalyst*. London, Karnac Books, 2003.
Sacks, J. (2005) *To Heal a Fractured World: The Ethics of Responsibility*. London, Bloomsbury, 2013.
Sandel, M.J. (2013) *What Money Can't Buy: The Moral Limits of Markets*. London, Penguin Books.
Sandler, J. (1960) On the concept of the superego. *Psychoanalytic Study of the Child*. 15, 128–162.

Sandler, J. (1963) The ego ideal and the ideal self. *Psychoanalytic Study of the Child.* 18, 139–158.
Sandler, J. (1989) Guilt and internal object relations. *Bulletin of the Anna Freud Centre.* 12, 297–307.
Schafer, R. (1960) The loving and beloved superego in Freud's structural theory. *The Psychoanalytic Study of the Child.* 15, 163–188.
Schafer, R. (1983) *The Analytic Attitude.* London, Hogarth Press.
Schore, A.N. (1991) Early superego development: the emergence of shame and narcissistic affect regulation in the practising period. *Psychoanalysis and Contemporary Thought.* 14,187–250.
Schore, A.N. (1994 [2016]) *Affect Regulation and the Origin of the Self.* London, Routledge.
Schore, A.N. (2012) *The Science and the Art of Psychotherapy.* London, W.W. Norton & Company, Inc.
Shakespeare, W. (n.d.) *The Complete Works of Shakespeare.* London, Odhams Press Ltd.
Strachey, J. (1934 [1969]) The nature of the therapeutic action of psychoanalysis. *International Journal of Psychoanalysis.* 50, 275–291, 1989.
Trollope, J. (2012) *The Soldiers Wife.* London, Transworld Publishers.
Wright, K. (1991) *Vision and Separation Between Mother and Baby.* London, Free Association Books.
Wurmser, L. (2004) Superego revisited: relevant or irrelevant. *Psychoanalytic Inquiry.* 24, 183–205.

Part I
Theoretical and developmental considerations

Part I

Chapter 1

The good, the bad and the superego

From punishment to reparation[1]

R. D. Hinshelwood

Freud's 'discovery' of the superego in 1923 gave psychoanalysts a clear, and intensely useful conception. Though the idea of a moral conscience is timelessly old, Freud gave a perspective on the origins of that mental agency in the course of development of a child's mind. He drew on the almost limitless possibilities of the Oedipus complex which he had been exploiting conceptually for 25 years. In a subtle way Freud created a non-evaluative function for the capacity of humans to evaluate everything.

The concept however was not without criticism. Ernest Jones, as soon as 1926, raised a number of questions, including the curious issue that if the superego was an internalisation of the loved primary object, the mother for the little boy, how come it had the characteristics of a harsh, castrating father? In a nearly lost paper by Karen Stephen (1945) written in the 1940s, she queried how the supremacy of the reality principle, which entailed foregoing the Oedipal love, led to some agency based on the extremely unrealistic fear of castration, since few little boys have witnessed (or experienced) castration *in reality*. Nevertheless, the clinical usefulness of the concept was very considerable as it brought morality and ethics within the purview of psychoanalysis. Heinz Hartman (1960), a central figure in the development of classical psychoanalysis, ego-psychology, admired the concept for this reason. It was essential, he claimed, to distinguish the neutral attitude of the scientific psychoanalyst from the evaluation a patient makes as a moral person. Lack of such a distinction

> is bound to create confusion in the evaluations of mental health. It promotes a greater arbitrariness in these evaluations because it burdens the concept of mental health with a great many extraneous valuations, moral or even political.
> (p. 248)

To this end, Hartman meticulously detailed characteristics of mental health which he regarded as morally neutral – capacity for enjoyment and work, absence of pathology, rationality, adaptation, reality-testing, integration, autonomy, ego-strength.

This materialist aspect of the theory of the superego had attracted the attention of C. H. Waddington (1942), a Nobel Prize–winning biologist. He was so impressed by Freud's theory that he organised a book of commentaries and criticisms, from philosophers, theologians and psychoanalysts – the psychoanalysts being Karin Stephen (1942) and Melanie Klein (1942). The intriguing possibility for him was that Freud explained how morality evolved biologically. It is a product of nature, and not from divine counsel, or philosophical endeavour. Freud's theory seemed to support an argument for a *natural* ethics. That is, ethical conduct arises in nature itself, through evolution and in personal biological development. It is the capacity to embrace morals and ethics at all which has been the evolutionary achievement; although, to be sure, specific moral and ethical principles are instilled into that capacity by the society in which the person is brought up. Not surprisingly the authors of the critiques Waddington (1942) gathered came to no general consensus at all! Neither theologians nor philosophers liked it much.

For quite unrelated reasons, shortly after the description of the structural model in 1923 psychoanalysis began to take a different course in London, compared to Vienna. The odd and rather Spartan form of upbringing of children in the English upper middle classes, from which most British psychoanalysts then came, led to a significant interest in child development amongst the members of the British Psychoanalytical Society, and it led to the invitation to Melanie Klein to visit and settle in London. Klein was an early exponent of child psychoanalysis, inventing her 'play technique'. She was not shy to present new observations and theories, and to stand by them with a determined vigour. She argued that the development of children could be better understood by the analysis of children. That is, we can observe better during the time when their development is actually happening, rather than inferring back to childhood from work with adults.

One of Klein's boldest revisions in the 1920s was completely to rewrite the origins of the superego. Because she was unwilling to be branded a dissident as Jung, Adler and Rank had been recently, she rather tactfully implied that her reconceptualisations were minor adjustments to Freud's established theories. Her tact was probably fairly quickly seen through but after she moved to London in 1926 she had the firm patronage of Ernest Jones. So, she described Rita thus:

> As early as her second year, those with whom Rita came into contact were struck by her remorse for every naughtiness, however small, and her hyper-sensitiveness to any sort of blame.
>
> (Klein, 1926: p. 132)

Rita was only 2¾ years of age, very young on Freud's timetable of development; but 'her inhibition in play proceeded from her sense of guilt' (p. 29). But for Freud, the Oedipus complex develops in the third year of life, the genital phase; and it is only after that, as a resolution to the Oedipus complex, that the Oedipal parents are given up and introjected. That is, the superego and the guilt it provokes come later, after the Oedipus complex has arisen and declined. The superego is, as Freud said, the 'heir' to the Oedipus complex.

However, Klein was finding differently:

> [Rita] did not dare to play at being the mother because the baby-doll stood for her amongst other things for the little brother whom she had wanted to take away from her mother, even during the pregnancy. But here the prohibition of the childish wish no longer emanated from the real mother, but from an introjected mother, whose rôle she enacted for me in many ways and who exercised a harsher and more cruel influence upon her than her real mother had ever done.
>
> (p. 132)

So, it was clearly a matter of guilt, and therefore of that internal moral agency. Moreover, the symptoms Klein traced to the Oedipus complex had arisen even earlier than the analysis:

> One obsessional symptom which Rita developed at the age of two was a sleep-ceremonial which wasted a great deal of time. The main point of this was that she insisted on being tightly rolled up in the bed-clothes for fear that 'a mouse or a butty might come through the window and bite off her butty (genital)'. Her games revealed other determinants: the doll had always to be rolled up in the same way as Rita herself, and on one occasion an elephant was put beside its bed. This elephant was supposed to prevent the baby-doll from getting up; otherwise it would steal into the parents' bedroom and do them some harm or take something away from them. The elephant (a father-imago) was intended to take over the part of hinderer.
>
> (p. 132)

If the play is seen as a display of the internal world of unconscious phantasy, father (elephant) stood for the inhibiting superego:

> This part the introjected father had played within her since the time when, between the ages of eighteen months and two years, she had wanted to usurp her mother's place with her father, to steal from her mother the child with which she was pregnant, and to injure and castrate the parents. The reactions of rage and anxiety which followed on the punishment of the 'child' during such games showed, too, that Rita was inwardly playing both parts: that of the authorities who sit in judgement and that of the child who is punished.
>
> (p. 132)

Clearly, the 'part the introjected father had played within her' had begun at that earlier period of development (between 18 months and two years). If this threatening father was inside her, then the internalisation of the Oedipal parents had occurred before the accepted moment in the third and fourth years when the Oedipus complex resolves. So, the damaging rage and its inhibition are both parts of mental life inside the child as far back as 18 months. And thus, the child already has an inhibiting figure (felt as father) way before Freud said the Oedipal conflicts come into play. Rita was a patient in 1923 (when Klein was still in Berlin; Frank, 2010), precisely the same year as Freud's *The Ego and the Id* when he first postulated the superego and the classical structural model.

So Klein was finding from early on that the superego existed prior to Freud's resolution of the Oedipus conflict. And this turned Freud's theory on its head. In fact, Klein went on to postulate that the superego formed even earlier, and indeed she eventually (1932) used Freud's theory of the death instinct (despite her rather eccentric understanding of instincts). She drew on Freud to the extent that the death instinct is the origin of the negative feelings towards threatening objects, and is the origin of erotic masochism when fused with the libido; but she then claimed:

> It seems to me that the ego has yet another means of mastering those destructive impulses which still adhere to the organism. It can mobilize one part of them as a defence against the other part. In this way the id will undergo a division which is, I think, the first step in the formation of instinctual inhibitions. . . . We may suppose that a division of this sort is rendered possible by the fact that, as soon as the process of incorporation has begun, the incorporated object becomes the vehicle of defence against the destructive impulses within the organism.
>
> (pp. 183–184)

This is the first of the rare occasions when Klein uses the concept of the death instinct. She keeps close to Freud's ideas of deflection outwards (projection) and fusion; but then describes something absolutely new – a split in the id, which is a completely different view of the origin of the superego. There is no reason given as to why the id divides in order to combat its deflected rage, and as we shall see Freud was not too happy about that. But, it did present a possible solution to a problem with Freud's views which he had not solved – and he did acknowledge her solution.

The problem that Freud had noted is that the superego is not a simple internalisation. The introjected parents, once they function as internal inhibitors, are much harsher than the actual parents ever were – the point Karin Stephen (1945) had noted. Internally Father is a castrator, but in actuality Father probably never did such things. So Klein's solution was that the very beginnings of the superego are a hang-over from the self-directed destructiveness of the death instinct; it is that self-destructiveness which aims to bring the ego to death. Part of that instinctual self-harm forms a root from which the superego develops.

Freud noted Klein's idea, in the three brief mentions of Melanie Klein in his published work (Freud, 1930; p. 130n, 137n; Freud, 1931: p. 242), and acknowledged this as a possible cause of the curious added harshness. However, Freud recognised this, correctly, as a major re-writing of the classical development of the child:

> This dating of [the origins of the superego], which would also necessarily imply a modification of our view of all the rest of the child's development, does not in fact correspond to what we learn from the analyses of adults.
>
> (Freud, 1931: p. 242)

He hesitated to accept it completely. Nevertheless, he did seem slightly concerned about sticking with the evidence from adults.

The early positions and the reality principle

Klein however maintained the continuity between the very early 'bad' internal objects, 'even the earliest incorporated objects form the basis of the superego and enter into its structure' (Klein, 1935: p. 151). She graphically described this inner persecution,

> If we accept this view of the formation of the superego, its relentless severity in the case of the melancholic becomes more intelligible. The persecutions and demands of bad internalized objects; the attacks of such objects upon one another (especially that represented by the sadistic coitus of the parents); the urgent necessity to fulfil the very strict demands of the 'good objects' and to protect and placate them within the ego, with the resultant hatred of the id; the constant uncertainty as to the 'goodness' of a good object, which causes it so readily to become transformed into a bad one – all these factors combine to produce in the ego a sense of being a prey to contradictory and impossible claims from within.
>
> (p. 151)

This is from her paper that introduces the depressive position, but she elaborated it ten years later when she described the paranoid-schizoid position and the schizoid mechanisms. The picture is that in both depressive and schizoid states the person at first feels very persecuted, to the point of paranoia. Klein's deduction from this is that severe mental health conditions imply a hang-over of very early functioning. For Klein, it is not so much about the direction the libido is aimed at, but in her terms, it is the value of the object, its intentions towards the early self/ego, and the intensity of their intentions.

In other words, the infant begins life with considerable potential fears, which the primitive ego has great difficulty dealing with. This is the paranoid-schizoid position where objects are all-good or all-bad, and swiftly mutate from one to the other. So, at the beginning of life the infant does not recognise reality very clearly, in part because the real world is unknown to it, and it has yet to master its distance perceptions to survey the actual others; and it is partly because it needs to distort reality in order to cope with its fears. For Klein this primitive world is not just that of the severely mentally ill, but the most significant elements, especially the paranoia and the unreality, are usual enough for all humans at that stage. It is just that they hang over for some of us as the torturing condition of mental illness. And also in the form of the superego.

Psychotic anxieties and defences

It is clear that the reality of others is potentially distorted at, and from, the beginning. The infant ego has to employ its defences to cope with such experiences, and as Klein described in 1946, these include various forms of splitting, projection and introjection. Such processes do not enhance the capacity to see reality, but are aimed at constructing a more comfortable 'reality', and indeed the reality of the self and one's identity. They ignore or distort reality, because they involve phantasies of an omnipotent kind (see Freud, 1909 and his description of 'the omnipotence of phantasy', in the Ratman case). It is the tampering with reality which gives rise to the term 'psychotic', because a break with reality is the hallmark of psychosis.

Those phantasies tend to see extremely or completely 'good' things, or the opposite, extremely 'bad' objects. More than that the ego tends to see itself in similar ways, extremely good or extremely bad in itself. Good and bad are initially experienced in terms of comfort and discomfort at a bodily level. However, that bodily initiative, in the form of the superego, transmutes into a moral evaluation as time goes on. The sense of being under attack in the hands of a bad object which threatens life is first of all inborn in the biology, according to Klein, and only later do family patterns of behaviour adhere to the superego.

Equally inborn is dependence on the wonderfully good object which typically the infant sees as counteracting the bad one, especially at first in the form of the feeding breast. So, the blissful taking in of milk, is more than just bodily feeding: Klein described how the infant indulged in a phantasy that by feeding, and taking in good milk, the baby believed all bad things were dispelled, discharged or evacuated from inside itself. It has long been known by doctors and mothers that a feeding infant will almost immediately discharge faeces after ingesting milk, the gastro-colic reflex, which may well represent in a bodily way the blissful experience of purging the self as well as the body of all bad things.

Of course, this emotional tone to these bodily functions is quite unrealistic, and for the infant it pictures a world of extreme good and bad things which have to be manoeuvred so that the good things remain inside and accumulate there for as long as possible, and the bad things are distributed around outside the self/ego. And incidentally this separation of all good things within the self, is Klein's version of what Freud regarded as the initial narcissistic state of the ego.

These kinds of experiences and primitive (and imagined) manoeuvring of things is the description of the paranoid-schizoid position (Klein, 1946), and also the beginnings of an understanding of how psychotic states occur. There is not a superego here that resembles Freud's descriptions of the development in the phallic/genital phase around the third year of life. The infant certainly feels under attack, and it is in that state of vulnerability and persecution that the superego arises and is constituted initially of primarily destructive rather than moral objects.

The big disadvantage is that it is completely unrealistic. The real world has its own version of where good and bad, fears and satisfactions, lie. In the course of development Klein described how quite quickly the infant has to come to terms with this discrepancy between its phantastical reconstructions, and the reality of the world as it is.

The reality principle

The success of the paranoid-schizoid position is to re-arrange the world into well-intentioned comfortably close – good inside and nearer; evil outside and away. What disturbs this convenient existence is that the world is not like that. But for most infants the real world, reality, comes knocking, and is slowly bit-by-bit allowed to exist in the baby's mind. Although, of course for some infants, those destined to become psychotic, the reality principle (Freud, 1911) never fully gets a hold.

Reality for the infant is the gradual interference of the real world of other people in the constructions of his paranoid-schizoid position. The world is realised cautiously, and requires him to give up his early convictions. He is pushed to recognise the world is not a happy separation of frustration from satisfaction, good from bad. It is in the end a mixture – nothing in reality is all-good, and nothing, actually, is all-bad. Even the best has snags to it, and it is a hard task-master, and it calls forth some degree of frustration together with appreciation. The mixture of those poles of feelings must, for the earliest ego, feel like a confusion and only slowly mastered as a developing discrimination into accurately identified qualities of good and bad. This requires the beginnings of mental work, and sets up a lifetime of careful and increasingly accurate kinds of discrimination. It is a new ego function that has to start up to dismantle the convenience of the primitive good-bad distinctions, and the internal benign and external malign attributions. Such a dismantling respect commanded by the reality principle is the depressive position. It is a process as much as a state of mind.

The good, the bad and the superego

The depressive position is, in part, a process of healing the artificial divisions between good and bad constructed in the very primitive and very vulnerable beginning. What is bad, or good, at the early stages is not a set of moral qualities. The infant feels something good according to a feeling of satisfaction, the sense of bodily satiation. And the matching contrast for bad things, which prevent satisfaction, and thereby cultivate and intend painful feelings, sensations, perceptions and states of mind. At some point these visceral goods and bads, with their imagined intentional states of the object transmute into moral qualities of blessedness and evil. Or rather, at some point the effect of objects having a noxious effect, becomes implicitly, an *intention* to cause bad states. For Klein this attribution of intention to an object is probably innate. The object as an animate, and intending being, is seen in terms of the self. This is a defining characteristic of an object-relations approach as understood by Klein. It contrasts with Freud's 'object of an instinct', which is a more passive thing; the aim of an instinct finds an object to comply in providing the satisfaction desired.

In the paranoid-schizoid position, the superego is an object that seems to threaten (and intend) the pain of death. At this primitive phase, these moments, dominated by hate and being hated, gain evidence from actual unpleasant bodily sensation – shall we say hunger pains in the tummy. Then the crisis is constituted by those sensations, showing that this evil object is now *inside* the self, and so intentionally threatening death from within.

This is the critical moment to be considered the origin from which the superego will emerge, and its original sanction is the death penalty. It is not a long step to a potentiality for a morality – but what a morality. It is a cruel and unforgiving morality, an-eye-for-an-eye. A morality that demands the all-good, and insists on perfection. Imperfection in any respect is an unforgivable sin. Then reality can function as a rescuing lifeboat. As perfection is slowly given up on the journey through the depressive position, these demanding superego objects of the paranoid-schizoid position become less demanding. Then it is precisely because the actual parents are not so harsh that external reality can come to the rescue, providing more conciliatory response to transgressions. And indeed in psychosis when reality is given up (for other reasons) the ego loses the assistance of reality which is described here.

The real parents have the chance to provide a different morality. Not an eye-for-an-eye. As reality takes shape, senses and perception increasingly 'see' nuances. Feelings become mixed, and complex, and punishments are less extreme, and fit the crime. But in addition reality presents an increasing rainbow of emotions. Not just hatred, but a variety of negative feelings involving greater or lesser destructiveness.

Ultimately the depressive position brings to the fore a sense of the damaged good object. It is loved for its devotion to the infant, but also hated for its inevitable imperfections and failures. The outcome is a qualitative change, preservation of the loved one takes over or, as it is termed, 'reparation'. The loved one needs repair and restoration as a part of the love and devotion it inspires; and a new response can be felt in relation to the moral object – not only does the damaged loved one need restoring, a process begins to develop which we call forgiveness.

In short, I have described a long slow journey of the developing infant, and its superego. Starting from a pre-moral origin in bodily sensations which are experienced as mutual hatred and punishment, the developmental steps move on to a much less severe and less deadly compelling agent. The actual parents are important, and their capacity to refrain from punitive assaults is important. Their capacity is a potential navigational guide. Imperfection is tolerable, and a new quality of emotion, forgiveness, begins to enter the stage. Ultimately elements of a forgiving agency are added to the superego which gradually demands restorative efforts and not punitive suffering, and in the end the emergence of a self-forgiveness. This journey is never perhaps completed in a lifetime. And indeed, it may also show remarkable retreats in periods of stress and hardship. But we need to consider the superego as a process, it is a journey from deathly punishments to forgiving reparation.

Progression and the reverse

Klein used the term position in order to get away from the idea of temporal phases, one succeeding the previous. She says, 'working through of the persecutory and depressive positions extends over the first few years of childhood' (Klein, 1946: p. 15). Now we would understand that it is a process that extends throughout life, as Bion (1963) and Britton (1998) have argued, using the symbol $Ps \leftrightarrow D$. Britton especially recognised that in the course of this oscillation there is some development in *both* the paranoid and the depressive position. For instance, one could say that the paranoid-schizoid position starts with deadly opposition and moves progressively to confrontation, and to healthy competition. Whilst in the depressive position, the superego transformation moves from a viciously punitive one at first to a reparative one, from moralising revenge to forgiveness.

There is thus a progression of the whole see-saw system; using Britton's notation, the system moves from

$$Ps \leftrightarrow D \text{ to } Ps_{(1)} \leftrightarrow D_{(1)}. \text{ to } Ps_{(2)} \leftrightarrow D_{(2)}. \text{ to } Ps_{(3)} \leftrightarrow D_{(3)} \& . \text{ To } Ps_{(n)} \leftrightarrow D_{(n)}.$$

Of course reversion can also rapidly take place depending on context. When conscripted into an army at war for instance, the states of mind of the soldiers quickly traverses back to deadly opposition and moralising vengeance, even though in civilian life a soldier may have been a loving and creative man, occupied in an ambitious career, and forgiving of those colleagues who may have been more successful. There has been a long history of description of the 'archaic superego' resurfacing at times (Fenichel, 1932; Brierley, 1932; Rosenfeld, 1952; Caper, 1999). And Melanie Klein acknowledged 'the part which such an overwhelming superego plays in schizophrenia [and hypochondriasis]' (Klein, 1958: p. 88). There is, as Isaacs and others argued in the Controversial Discussions long ago a continuous activity of these most primitive unconscious phantasy from the beginning and, at the deeper levels of the unconscious, all through life (see King & Steiner, 1991).

Conclusion

The superego is a bit of a puzzle as it is on one hand extraordinarily helpful clinically; and equally so in its form in ordinary language, the moral conscience, it is helpful in ordinary ways in child rearing, the law and education and so on. However, on the other hand it is a conception that has been the focus of anomaly and disagreement as described. The contentions are no longer much debated, though its dynamics are not agreed. Perhaps its importance lies in the fact that it is an easily identifiable entity within the psychic, rather than its origins.

The theoretical debates and disagreements about the superego stretching back for the best part of a century have been exhausted, and without resolution. So, there is less interest today. More interest is directed to in the destructive forces in the human personality, than the activity of the superego and its guilt-ridden condemnations which arise from that destructiveness. That is we analyse the origins of what makes us feel guilty, not the origins of the agency that delivers the guilt.

So, it is of interest that this volume of serious opinion I am contributing to, about the concept of the superego, is now about to appear. It can be put alongside the recent volume by Reddish (2014). Perhaps there will be a resurgence of interest in the superego, its dimensions, dynamics and debates. The very fact of a materialistic and non-evaluative understanding of the most evaluative function of the human mind should remain of continuing fascinating interest not just to psychoanalysts but to all mankind.

Note

1 Much of the material in this paper was included in a paper, unpublished, given to the Psychotherapy Section of the Scottish Division of the Royal College of Psychiatry, at Pitlochry in 2001, and titled 'Has the concept of the superego run out of usefulness?'

References

Bion, W.R. (1963) *Elements of Psycho-Analysis*. London, Heinemann.
Brierley, M. (1932) Some problems of integration in women. *International Journal of Psycho-Analysis*. 13, 433–448.
Britton, R. (1998) *Belief and Imagination*. London, Routledge.
Caper, R. (1999) *A Mind of One's Own: A Kleinian View of Self and Object*. London, Routledge.
Fenichel, O. (1932) Outline of clinical psychoanalysis: chapter 3. *Psychoanalytic Quarterly*. 1, 545–652.
Frank, C. (2010) *Melanie Klein in Berlin: Her First Analyses of Children*. London, Routledge.
Freud, S. (1909) Notes upon a case of obsessional neurosis. In: *The Standard Edition of the Complete Psychological Works of Sigmund Freud*. Volume X. London, Hogarth Press, pp. 155–249.
Freud, S. (1911) Formulations on the two principles of mental functioning. In: *The Standard Edition of the Complete Psychological Works of Sigmund Freud*. Volume XII. London, Hogarth Press, pp. 213–226.
Freud, S. (1923) The ego and the id. In: *The Standard Edition of the Complete Psychological Works of Sigmund Freud*. Volume XIX. London, Hogarth Press, pp. 13–66.

Freud, S. (1930) Civilisation and its discontents. In: *The Standard Edition of the Complete Psychological Works of Sigmund Freud*. Volume 21. London, Hogarth Press, pp. 64–145.

Freud, S. (1931) Female sexuality. In: *The Standard Edition of the Complete Psychological Works of Sigmund Freud*. Volume XXI. London, Hogarth Press, pp. 221–244.

Hartmann, H. (1960) *Psychoanalysis and Moral Values*. New York, International Universities Press, Inc.

Jones, E. (1926) The origin and structure of the superego. *International Journal of Psycho-Analysis*. 7, 303–311.

King, P. & Steiner, R. (1991) *The Freud-Klein Controversies 1941–45*. London, Routledge.

Klein, M. (1926) The psychological principles of early analysis. In: *The Writings of Melanie Klein*. Volume 1. London, Hogarth Press.

Klein, M. (1932) *The Psychoanalysis of Children: The Writings of Melanie Klein*. Volume 3. London, Hogarth Press.

Klein, M. (1935) A contribution to the genesis of manic-depressive states. *International Journal of Psycho-Analysis*. 16, 145–174. Republished (1975) In: *The Writings of Melanie Klein. Vol. 1: Love Guilt and Reparation*. London, Hogarth, pp. 262–289.

Klein, M. (1942) A comment by Mrs Melanie Klein. In: C.H. Waddington (ed.), *Science and Ethics*, pp. 83–87. London: George Allen and Unwin. In: *The Writings of Melanie Klein*. Volume 1. London, Hogarth Press, pp. 320–323.

Klein, M. (1946) Notes on some schizoid mechanisms. In: *The Writings of Melanie Klein*. Volume 3. London, Hogarth Press, pp. 1–24.

Klein, M. (1958) On the development of mental functioning. In: *The Writings of Melanie Klein*. Volume 3. London, Hogarth Press, pp. 236–246.

Reddish, E. (2014) *The Petrified Ego: A New Theory of Conscience*. London, Karnac Books.

Rosenfeld, H. (1952) Notes on the psycho-analysis of the superego conflict of an acute schizophrenic patient. *International Journal of Psychoanalysis*. 33, 111–131. Republished (1965) In: Herbert Rosenfeld *Psychotic States*. London, Hogarth. And republished (1988) In: Elizabeth Spillius (1988) *Melanie Klein Today*. Volume 1. London, Routledge.

Stephen, K. (1942) Letter from Dr Karin Stephen. In: C.H. Waddington (ed.) *Science and Ethics*. London, George Allen and Unwin, pp. 69–81.

Stephen, K. (1945) Relations between the superego and the ego. *Psychoanalysis and History*. 2(1), 11–28, 2000.

Waddington, C.H. (1942) *Science and Ethics*. London, George Allen and Unwin, pp. 69–81.

Chapter 2

A new theory of conscience
The petrified ego

Elizabeth Reddish

> *And yet they, who passed away long ago, still exist in us, as predisposition,*
> *As burden upon our fate, as murmuring blood*
> *And as gesture that rises up from the depths of time*
>
> – Rainer Maria Rilke (1934)

Introduction

Whilst Freud's concept of the superego, 'the heir to the Oedipus complex' remains a cornerstone concept of psychoanalytic theory, a contradiction in its formulation was noted soon after publication in 1923. The implication that a healthy conscience evolves from the ego's subjugation of its own values to those of the superego and the corollary, that superego values are, by definition, 'good', was at odds with Freud's concept of ego maturity. Morality by this definition is a morality of fear, not of ego maturity (Stephen, 1946: p. 27; Money-Kyrle, 1952).

In 2003, the Kleinian psychoanalyst Ronald Britton went some way to resolving the contradiction by pointing out that according to his clinical observations, ego maturity was marked not by the moment when the ego subjugated itself to superego judgement but rather the opposite, by the moment when he discerned his patients beginning to *subject their superego to evaluation;* to challenge its judgements. The present chapter is about the earlier superego that is implied by this definition of ego maturity and the function it performs. As early as 1925 Franz Alexander observed an earlier version of the superego that was not an arbiter of morality but performed a quite different function. Alexander understood this earlier superego to be performing an 'affect-regulating', 'pattern-seeking', predominantly structuring function. His theory was that it protects the ego in its embryonic form until such time as the ego is sufficiently robust as to forge its own, unique perspective on reality (courtesy of the Oedipal superego). My research has shown that Alexander's observations have been repeatedly observed over the ensuing decades by psychoanalysts across a broad theoretical field (Reddish, 2014).

I argue that Freud's 1923 formulation conflates what we nowadays see clearly as two distinct types of morality the first, primal/survival morality, concerned with differentiating 'safe' from 'threatening' objects; the second, Oedipal morality, characterised by the capacity to contemplate 'right' and 'wrong' independently of threat to the self. It should be clear that the developmentally earlier, archaic superego is not rendered obsolete by the emergence of the Oedipal version, it merely loses its dominance, marking a shift in the power relationship between the ego and the superego. The archaic superego will rise again to dominance under severe ego stress. In this last respect it has been described as:

> a safety device of the highest order, which protects the self from dangerous internal instinctual stimuli. . . . [and] from dangerous external stimuli.
> (Jacobson, 1954: p. 75)

The important point is that survival morality is much earlier, in evolutionary terms – part of our phylogenetic legacy – and has little to do with cognition and thinking. It has to do with the instinctive flight from danger and is a core aspect of 'herd' mentality. Interestingly, neuroscientists have located the 'fight/flight' response in an evolutionarily older part of the brain. Oedipal morality by contrast – the considered attribution of 'right' and 'wrong' independent of threat to the self – is an aspect of individual psychic development. Interestingly, Freud makes reference to this developmentally earlier morality in 1895, twenty-eight years before his formulation of the superego: "the initial helplessness of human beings is the primal source of all moral motives" (p. 317). He progressed this thinking in *Totem and Taboo* (1912–13), but in 1923 chose not to incorporate it into his theory of superego generation (1923).

In *Totem and Taboo* he identified "two taboos of totemism with which human morality has its beginning" (Freud, 1912–13: p. 143). The first regarding food and warmth (matriarchal) and then those that originated in the primal horde regarding incest and murder due to threat to the social order (patriarchal). This would accord with the two stages of superego development proposed in the present chapter. However, oddly, his formulation of the superego makes no reference to the first of these and Freud does not say why. In a footnote to "The Ego and the Super-Ego (Ego Ideal)" (Freud, 1923: p. 28) he notes that he has been mistaken in ascribing the function of reality-testing to the superego and attributes it to the ego. In the 1923 formulation there is no reference to this primal world underpinned by fear of death by starvation or disease. Does this suggest that in the earliest stages of psychic development reality and morality are undifferentiated and by inference, apprehension of Oedipal anxiety signals the cognitive capacity for their distinction?

One might put the case that if, in its earlier form it is not an arbiter of morality, it is not, by definition, a superego. The counter-argument, evidenced by my clinical research, is that it is through challenge to the archaic superego (by the ego) that the Oedipal superego is forged/given form. If it remains un- challenged by the ego, it turns and criticises (the defining feature of a superego) the ego. Indeed, to the point where it becomes 'ego-destructive'.

This new theory and understanding of conscience began with a clinical puzzle that I observed in a particular profile of patients in treatment with me. These patients were successful professionals, and in more cases than not, also successful in their relationships. Nevertheless, they lived in a state of high anxiety. Their capacity for reality-testing (Freud's definition of ego maturity) appeared to be highly developed and yet their sense of self and identity was held together by only a thread, constantly threatening to unravel and subject to the running commentary of a superego that belittled and criticised them. Despite holding in some cases very senior positions at work, they had no sense of cumulative success, stability or continuity. Each day they began again – surviving, as they experienced it, just on their wits and drive. What was going on? My research led me to eventually conclude that their egos had remained in an embryonic state: atrophied and 'petrified': incarcerated within an archaic superego that had never been challenged, whose judgement had always been accepted, as reality. These patients' sense of self and identity was not rooted in their ego, but formed of identifications with this over-harsh superego – played out against the backdrop of an internal sado-masochistic dialogue.

A call for differentiation between the archaic superego and the oedipal superego is the essence of the argument presented in this chapter. Why is this important? There are two reasons. The first reason is that a healthy relationship within the individual's mind between their ego and superego is essential for the development of their autonomy and individuality. If the analyst mistakes primal anxiety for Oedipal anxiety, for example, interprets attacks on the analysis arising from Oedipal anxiety when the anxiety is primal in origin, irrevocable psychological damage may ensue.

The second reason has to do with the psychoanalytic understanding of the superego as the part of the mind that mentally bridges the individual with society and regulates relationships between the individual and their social world. In the period of years that I have been absorbed in thinking about the superego and its relevance today, quite a bit of literature has emerged regarding the application of psychoanalytic thinking to political and social issues. I argue that the archaic superego concept has particular relevance to our thinking about, and understanding of politics and society. The superego has emerged as a highly potent concept in this regard. It is a concept which can help us to understand the social problems which give rise to 'survival anxiety dominance', offering insight into the unconscious psychological and social dynamics between individuals and groups. For a world increasingly under siege from the religious, racial and political violence which results from 'moral certainty', (the hallmark of archaic superego dominance, where reality and morality are undifferentiated), the importance of this is beyond debate.

The concept of a part of the mind that demands 'absolute loyalty', thereby holding ego development and independent thinking hostage (such as I saw in my patients), has its external correlate in group psychology. Overtly, in nations led by dictators or autocrats; covertly, in the unconscious trans-generational transmission of ideology and other forms of shared narrative.

A recent book by Vamik Volkan argues that psychoanalytic ideas are essential for understanding and resolving international conflict i.e. the largest-scale human interactions. He is a Turkish-Cypriot psychoanalyst with extensive first-hand experience of working with diplomats and statesmen on the resolution of major conflicts in many of the trouble-spots of the world. Coining the term 'Large-Group Psychology' (Volkan, 2014), he argues for including an unconscious psychoanalytic dimension in any analysis of ethnic, national and international conflict.

> Long standing national and ethnic conflicts cannot be fully understood by focussing on real-world factors such as economic, military, legal and political circumstances. Real-world issues are highly psychologised, contaminated with shared perceptions, thoughts, fantasies and emotions both conscious and unconscious pertaining to past historical glories and traumas, losses, humiliations, mourning difficulties, feelings of entitlement to revenge, and resistance to accepting changed realities.
> (Volkan, 1997: p. 117)

In order to understand the aspects of human interaction that Volkan describes, and most topically, radicalisation, fundamentalism and terrorism, we need the concept of the archaic superego. Here we can see a direct correlation between individual and collective psychosis. (I am defining psychosis as the loss of capacity to be in touch with reality). For our ancestors, ostracism meant loss of protection by the tribe, not least for violating incest and patricidal taboos and therefore physical death through starvation or being killed by wild animals. These ancient facts of life have their contemporary correlates in circumstances where the assertion of an independent perspective can be fatal.

Closer to home, Korean-born German philosopher Byung-Chul Han (2015) puts forward a chilling case for the idea that neo-liberalism, by turning the worker into a free contractor – an 'entrepreneur of the self' – has rendered rebellion obsolete. In his article 'Why Revolution is no Longer Possible', he argues that nowadays it is commonplace for someone who 'fails to succeed', to blame themselves, seeing themselves, rather than society, as the problem. In psychoanalytic terms, the unjust superego, in the form of a boss or politician, is no longer the enemy suppressing freedom that one might resist, using independent thought to make the arguments, but rather a leader whom one has failed.

The clinical work – part one

My research began with a clinical challenge: that of engaging certain of my patients in their treatment. The difficulty lay in the 'absolute' nature of their moral values which constantly stymied my attempts to engage them. If I interpreted their difficulty as arising from their attacks on their objects, external and internal, my would-be patients would accuse me of being immoral to suggest such a thing. In terms of their moral universe I came to realise that this was true and it provided me with the first clue to understanding them sufficiently to be helpful. I noticed that alongside moral certainty, this group of patients also shared the (unconscious) belief that if they were to stray from fixed ways of thinking and behaving, a psychological catastrophe would result. That is to say, morality and reality were conflated, or rather, as yet undifferentiated.

None of these patients had consulted psychiatrists although nine had been prescribed anti-depressants at various points in their lives. I want to be clear that these were *not* people whom psychiatrists would describe as presenting with predominantly psychotic functioning. Neither social nor professional acquaintances would describe them as being 'out of touch with reality'. There were fifteen patients with this profile: nine women and six men aged between twenty-nine and forty-eight. I have two additional such patients in treatment as I write. They had successful professional careers, earned a good living, were hard-working and sociable, and in ten cases, had a long-term partner and children. Their professions included academia in science or humanities; senior civil servants; operations and information management directors in the public sector and a private company; a hospital doctor and two lawyers. They came for treatment presenting with generalised anxiety, in seven cases having self-harmed in the recent past. They said that they felt self-indulgent and embarrassed seeking help, because they knew that 'other people suffer far more than I do'. It soon emerged that they were actually in a parlous state; their suffering continuous and intolerable. From a theoretical perspective, I was puzzled by their apparent success at managing and adapting to reality, as this would suggest ego-strength, but on beginning treatment it became clear that they had little to no ego-strength. Their sense of self was seemingly made up of identifications with a superego which consistently crushed and mocked any attempt at ego emancipation. (What I have termed a 'Petrified Ego' (Reddish, 2014): an embryonic ego that has long ago ceased to breathe its own air, incarcerated and fearful).

I made a list of the symptoms these patients had in common.

- *Absolute moral values, moral certainty and rectitude*

"I feel as I have moral synaesthesia. I think about *everything* in terms of whether it is right or wrong"; "Although at school, another girl might bully me by sticking a pair of compasses into my arm, I would remain calm and say nothing, knowing that I had the moral high ground"; "I realise that I feel directed by an authority – then I realise when I think about it, that it's me!"; "I realise that although I don't respect my boss, I crave her praise and fear her disapproval".

- *Ongoing physical and mental exhaustion, no sense of achievement or meaning. Fear of missing something vital*

These patients work long hours and even when not at work, feel driven to achieve. Typically, they never take time off work for sickness or holidays. "I feel that I am running on empty"; "I feel I'm holding onto something very tightly, but I don't know what it is"; "I'm afraid if I file a piece of information falsely at work, the whole company will collapse"; "I realise that what I'm doing all the time, in all my relationships, is managing my mother"; "I feel as if every day is Ground-hog Day".

- *A sense of being fraudulent; that they will be found out at any moment*

The sense of something life-threatening just about to happen, was more or less constant. All of the patients initially expressed fear of being a fraud, in coming for treatment which they "didn't really need". They feared being found out with regard to their professional lives. At the same time, they felt neither alive, nor entitled to be. "I know I'm afraid of being a fraud so I seek out punishment".

- *A sense that they are somehow 'bad': their problems are their fault*

"I am my own suicide bomber"; "My own brain is working against me"; "My mother was depressed because *I* did something wrong"; "If I take in what you say, I shall be collaborating, like a double agent"; "I have the feeling that what I'm talking about has no relationship to what I'm thinking about"; "I feel bad, I have to do something to make myself feel better, which I'm ashamed of, so that proves that I *am* bad"; "I'm not allowed negative feelings, I never have been. If I do have them, then I don't feel it's *me*".

- *Dreams of physical and psychic dereliction*

Two types of dream: the first type: difficulty accessing a toilet or food and of walls or floors that are collapsing; the second type: physical dependence on mindless objects. Being in the presence of people who have control over the patient, but no mind; people with mouths but no eyes or 'zombies' – mindless savages with no remorse or sense of consequence.

- *Obsessional thinking – often of a suicidal nature*

All of these patients suffered from obsessional thinking, in which they describe a running loop of the same thoughts ad infinitum in their minds. It is distinct from obsessional compulsive disorder which typically identifies (visible) behaviour. However it performs the same function: to keep feelings (which are hugely feared) at bay. Eleven of the patients' obsessional thoughts constituted planning suicide or self-harm, and seven regularly did self-harm.

Can anything be inferred from this clinical material about the pre-verbal environmental development of these patients; about the relationship to the maternal object? Is it possible that due to sustained breaches in the mother's role as, what Freud called, 'the protective shield' during the pre-verbal stage, an archaic superego holds the psychic structure together, at the cost of these symptoms? Masud Khan (1964) wrote about cumulative trauma through disturbance of the mother's role as protective shield (p. 271). If the mother's failure to protect the child is perceived (by the child) as not just an absence of protection but as punishment: i.e. "the reason I do not protect (love) you is because you are (morally) bad. Therefore it is your fault that you suffer", this would account for the primal guilt, sense of being 'bad' and also the precariousness of their mental states, despite being so apparently robust.

What do others have to say about the archaic superego?

The archaic superego: research into origin and function

As a next step, using an electronic psychoanalytic database, I resolved to find out what other practitioners had observed, to see if they had answers. To this end, I researched clinical observations of psychoanalysts across different schools over the past few decades (who worked with infants and adolescents as well as adults) and discovered a great deal of evidence of what they understood to be an early form of the superego. Broadly this was seen to be performing two distinct but related functions. The first was to organise pre-verbal experience by recognising experiential patterns and establishing 'models' of reality, thereby establishing predictability and hence continuity of, experience. In the earliest infant stages, this was sensory. The second function was to regulate feelings: that is, to re-establish psychic equilibrium when over-aroused.

A summary of these findings:

- *The archaic superego as the earliest organiser of experience through pattern recognition and modelling*

A broad range of terminology, spanning eighty years, was used to describe the organising of experience attributed to early superego functioning. Many practitioners treating children used the term 'pre-oedipal phenomena', which they saw organising and protecting against disintegration of the psyche. Rene Spitz (1958), working with children under two and observing 'organisational' elements of an early superego speaks of 'primordia' and 'roots of the superego'. Sandler (1960) offers the term 'Pre-autonomous superego schema' to describe the conflicting aspects in the mind of a child between approving and permissive, as well as prohibiting and restraining features. A 'loving, beloved and/or protective superego', one that promotes self-esteem, is identified by Jacobson (1954); Schafer (1960); Schecter (1979); and Eisnitz (1980). Grotstein (1990) identifies the 'Pre or A-moral superego' that is 'a counterpoint to chaos'. Schecter (1979) describes 'Pre-autonomous superego forerunners'. Caper (2008) identifies an 'archaic superego'.

The common element in what these practitioners describe is a pre-Oedipal superego that models and organises experience in support of an embryonic ego. In providing a 'counterpoint to chaos', this structure enables differentiation of safe from threatening experiences and at later stages in development (such as puberty), provides a temporary retreat in the form of a defence against disintegration.

With regard to specifically sensory experience, in 1925 Ferenczi had coined the term 'sphincter-morality' to describe the following phenomenon: "The anal and urethral identification with the parents . . . appears to build up in the child's mind a sort of physiological forerunner of the ego-ideal or super-ego. . . . it is by no means improbable that this semi-physiological morality forms the essential groundwork of later purely mental morality" (p. 378). Spitz (1958); Kestenberg and Brenner (1986); and Hytinnen (2002) make an explicit link between physical restraint and superego development. Hytinnen (2002) draws together the work of Freud and Winnicott (in particular, the concept of the 'facilitating environment') in his observation of what he calls the archaic superego as a provider of shelter during the adolescent phase. He describes it as place of internal safety, which the adolescent returns to, during the difficult phase of searching for an identity. Hytinnen (2002) notes that this archaic superego is punitive, but nevertheless it allows the adolescent to maintain the integrity of his childhood whilst creating the new integrity of adulthood.

> It is the archaic superego which protects and guards each step of the development which the adolescent takes in order to grow towards his own autonomy.
> (p. 52)

It is unconditional and, as such, it is an organising activity that predates apprehension of the Oedipus complex.

- *The archaic superego as the regulator of affect*

The second function that these practitioners and theorists understand the archaic superego to be performing is functioning as an affect-regulator, protecting an embryonic ego from being overwhelmed by external and internal stimuli. Weissman (1954) notes that obsessional neurosis may be a symptom of predominance of the archaic superego and identifies two structurally distinct superegos. The first he calls an 'archaic superego', which threatens the ego with the loss of the love object, which he differentiates from the later 'developed', or 'mature' superego. It is the latter he says, which threatens castration and loss of self-esteem. Franz Alexander (1925) describes the archaic superego as a 'regulator of instinctive life'. Jacobson (1954); Weissman (1954); Beres (1958); Holder (1982); and Hytinnen (2002) make similar observations.

Unlike his ego-psychologist colleagues, Leon Wurmser (2004) continued to believe in the superego as a useful concept and observed primitive affect regulation to be an essential function of its earliest manifestation. He referred to it as providing a 'back-up system', which comes into play when trauma, having evoked the 'most profound sense of helplessness', causes a collapse of the more mature (ego-forged) functioning.

Implications for superego functioning in my patient group

The implication of the research for my patient group is that there has been no ego development. Instead a primitive form of the superego has provided a structure of 'pseudo-independence'; a framework for mental functioning. The price that is being paid for this apparently successful adaptation to reality is high levels of anxiety and a steadily building sense of purposelessness. What the new theory also implies is that unlike severely depressed or predominantly psychotic patients, the prognosis for these patients is good and that treatment may be relatively short. The reason being that embryonic ego has remained 'intact' within the protective shell of the archaic superego. At the same time it is undeveloped, incarcerated and 'petrified': both fearful and inert. The theory suggests that these patients are almost fully identified with their superego, living in a two-dimensional psychic reality where they feel they are only just coping and consistently fear annihilation. This annihilation will, according to the theory, be the collapse of the defensive structure, the protective shell. As early as 1925, Franz Alexander formulated his understanding of how the 'protective' archaic superego thwarts ego growth in the following powerful image. He describes it as like a 'frontier guard', whose task is to regulate instinctual life.

> The superego behaves like a dull-witted frontier guard who arrests everyone wearing spectacles because he has been told that one particular person is wearing spectacles.
>
> (p. 24)

In this way, ego challenge is constantly thwarted by the threat asserted by the superego.

These patients function in the world but at huge cost; nothing fresh or new can permeate the protective frontier and increasingly precariously, 'the centre cannot hold'. The quality of their relationships, on examination, is fragile and volatile. Career development has ground to a halt. These patients feel they are surviving by the skin of their teeth; paradoxically it is only by virtue of their illness that they are able to go on. Like Atlas, they carry the world on their shoulders and letting go will mean the collapse of their reality. The lack of purpose in their lives has become perilous. Many patients refer themselves around significant birthdays, usually near thirty or forty years old, suggesting that the reality of time passing breaks through the protective shell. The success in life that they *have* had, managing and adapting to reality, implies great strength in the structuring function of the superego, despite its ultimate limitation. It is due to this strength and the relatively 'intact' nature of the embryonic ego that once the patient can engage and the ego is accessed, psychic development is relatively swift. This means that these are very satisfying as well as interesting cases. Interestingly my patients worked in institutions such as the civil service, universities, hospitals and law firms, organisations that have clear and firm hierarchical structures.

The clinical work: part two

Returning to the symptoms listed earlier in the chapter. What light does the evidence shed on explanations for these?

- **Permanent sense of physical and mental exhaustion, no sense of achievement, of meaning, of cumulative experience**

This symptom could be due to an instinctive drive for ego development which is being constantly frustrated, causing it to be subsumed into ever more vigorous adaptation to, and accommodation of, the (perceived) archaic moral strictures of the object. Failure to satisfy others is attributed by the patient to not having tried hard enough and so they try harder. The fact that the other can by definition never be satisfied, completes a vicious circle of energy expended to no purpose. The patient is engaged in re-enacting what they perceive to be their original 'failure'. In addition the exhaustion of doing this is tolerated because it is punishing, and punishment is 'soothing' for someone who feels guilty. Also perhaps, fear of the loss of any kind of integrated mind because to challenge the status quo would be to risk disintegration.

- **Absolute moral values. Moral superiority and rectitude**

According to the theory, a feature of this illness is that the patients' structuring of psychic reality is determined by an archaic, phylogenetically inherited superego. This affords them a way of assessing their experiences in order to make sense of them and a sense of certainty which is essential, given how hollow they feel inside. At the same time this sense of certainty is not founded in ego-strength, meaning that the formation of satisfying, meaningful relationships is not possible.

- **A sense of being fraudulent and they will be found out at any moment**

This symptom is possibly due to an unconscious awareness that their psychic integration is precarious; that it is facilitated by a carapace and has no solid core or foundation. It is as if the modelling, organising capability of the early superego is fused with the social self, trapping the embryonic ego inside, terrified, in equal measure of being, and not being, 'found (out)'.

- **A sense that they are somehow 'bad', their problems are self-inflicted. False objectivity**

These patients cannot conceptually differentiate between being morally 'bad' and feeling 'bad' as in unhappy or unfulfilled. Put another way, they cannot tell the difference between a moral evaluation and a psycho-somatic experience because morality and reality are undifferentiated. Despite the very convincing impression of having the capacity for objectivity, these patients do not in fact have this perspective. One aspect of true objectivity is the capacity to contemplate and reflect without evaluation. For these individuals, 'To see is to judge'; there *is* no perspective, no seeing/observing, *without judgement*. The symptom also expresses unconscious awareness of the superego/ego relationship. They recognise that their problems *are* self-inflicted but they are compelled to continue, for fear of the perceived catastrophe if they stop.

- **Dreams of physical dereliction: crumbling walls, floors with holes. Physical dependence on 'mindless' objects**

This symptom suggests unconscious awareness of the deprivation by and cruelty of, the archaic superego which has long outdated its primary function. The coincidence of such dreams in individuals who appear to enjoy successful social adaptation is one of the most striking symptoms. Fear of insubstantial walls and floors can be understood as representing insubstantial internal structures. Physical dependence on mindless objects may show that somewhere the patient knows and fears the extent to which they themselves are engaged in rendering themselves 'mindless', undermining at each moment, the drive for mental space and growth and holding their embryonic ego hostage.

- **Obsessional thinking – often of suicidal thoughts**

These individuals are caught in a moral dilemma and obsessional thinking is a way of managing this. To think about, to imagine suicide, is soothing and comforting in the sense that it keeps the harsh internal critic at bay. They occupy a psychological world where to identify badness in other people, as opposed to in themselves is tantamount to betrayal, with almost biblical severity. A voice inside will say "how dare you?! Who do you think you are?" The patients are unable to identify badness outside of themselves because they believe that by doing so, they will cut themselves off from the source of their survival. To allow themselves to feel 'satisfied' or 'replete' would mean that they had deprived the other person of that experience. "Other people must come first".

How does the theory translate into guidelines for treatment?

1   The psychic reality of patients with a petrified ego is structured by the archaic superego. They are especially vulnerable to feeling they have done something wrong, and therefore feeling guilty. It is important to help these patients to feel psychically safe by building trust through stability and continuity and being mindful that until they feel sufficiently safe, they will not risk psychic change. It can help to refer to oneself, in a therapeutic role, as an 'ally'. You may well be the only person in their life who sees and understands the problem, as it is so effectively disguised.

2   This state of mind, despite being hard to bear, at the same time affords a sense of equilibrium and therefore anything which threatens the status quo is profoundly feared. Paradoxically, the patient is equally fearful of being seen/found and *not* being seen/found. This means that the therapist too, will sometimes find the work hard to bear, but the fact that the patient is coming for help is the clearest indication that they *are* open to it.
3   We can assume that because regulation of feelings (the crudest kind of 'holding together') has been internally achieved and managed, emotional dependence on another is an unknown experience. Once they *can* allow themselves to be emotionally 'touched' and risk (awareness of) dependence, this needs to be carefully and steadily nurtured. Keeping one's word with regard to the most practical details such as days and times of sessions is essential.
4   Despite emotional arrest, these patients are often cognitively sophisticated and quick-witted. This can be daunting for the therapist who may feel intellectually inferior. It will help to remember that the simplest of interactions in the consulting room can be helpful, as their capacity for mentalisation (a process of transformation that frees the psyche from overwhelming bodily pressures) will be limited. Bouchard and Lecours (2004) find that this limited capacity is co-incident with a punitive superego. Patients can become very frustrated as it all can feel 'too little, too late'. Patience is important as you wait for a sense of the petrified ego to make itself known, often initially through a dream, or through body language. Sometimes one glimpses the physical presence of a child in the face or body. It may come in the form of stories about young children or vulnerable animals. Once it has emerged, the therapist's work is to both encourage it and at the same time to help the patient to isolate and perhaps name the critical voice. Music (2015) writes about ways in which treatment of traumatised patients needs to be cognisant of the ways in which they use either their minds or bodies as objects, in the absence of a satisfactory external object.
5   Take care not to mistake compliance for a healthy working alliance. Punctual attendance at sessions and payment of bills may be unconscious communications of fear, of keeping the terrifying object from engulfing them. Every analyst is susceptible to a compliant patient and what can result is a pathological, sado-masochistic analytic couple that even supervision can easily miss.
6   Patient-centred interpretations suggesting how the patient might be feeling within themselves, rather than about the analyst, will be more successful (Steiner, 1994). For example acknowledge how alone and exhausted they feel, having to do everything for themselves, carrying this weight and never able to set down their load even for a moment. Interpret transference in very simple terms, more to the analytic space than to the analyst. 'Here is somewhere where you can leave thoughts and ideas and find it again when you return'. Or, 'you feel bad but you may mean that you feel unhappy – perhaps this is your way of telling me this'.
7   Encouraging patients to find words to describe their feelings and then using the same words, building up a language, is important. These are unlike

patients dominated by psychotic defences who are likely to experience this as frightening, perceiving the analyst to be a 'mind-reader' with super-natural powers. Encourage awareness of their internal dialogue and the language of the superego, the words and phrases that are used: "I'm bad to want help, I'm weak and despicable, I'm morally pathetic, who do I think I am?" These can be so swift – cascading in split seconds in the patients' mind – it is important to try to catch them.

8   As treatment progresses, an acute fear of dying may surface, perhaps in a dream. Care needs to be taken that sessions are of sufficient frequency during this period and to be aware of changes in the patients' physical health and important relationships. Encourage reporting of dreams, as sometimes the first indication of ego emancipation is a shift away from the 'dereliction' type of dream towards something hopeful. The patient's capacity to hold more than one reality in mind is evidence of development. Look out for material where the patient reflects on a past incident from a new perspective. This will indicate psychic growth and a lessening in fear of ego assertion: a lessening in the fear of 'having your own view'.

9   Once they can risk expressing a view which challenges a long-held belief, they will be encouraged to challenge *other* beliefs. The reason being that contrary to their expectation of increased anxiety and annihilation, they actually feel *less* anxious and more integrated. Alleviation of anxiety, transformed to more normal levels, frees up energy, dissipates the sense of fraudulence, of missing something and feelings of being bad. A sense of purpose and meaning to life will follow.

References

Alexander, F. (1925) A meta-psychological description of the process of cure. *International Journal of Psychoanalysis*. 6, 13–35.

Beres, D. (1958) Vicissitudes of superego functions and superego precursors in childhood. *Psychoanalytic Study of the Child*. 13, 324–351.

Bouchard, M., & Lecours, S. (2004) Analyzing forms of superego functioning as mentalizations. *International Journal of Psychoanalysis*. 85, 879–896.

Britton, R. (2003) *Sex, Death, and the Superego*. London, Karnac Books.

Byung-Chul, H. (2015) *Why Revolution Is No Longer Possible*. Available at: www.opendemocracy.net. [Accessed 23 October 2015].

Caper, R. (2008) *Building Out into the Dark*. London, Taylor and Francis.

Eisnitz, A.J. (1980) The organization of self-representation and its influence on pathology. *Psychoanalytic Quarterly*. 49, 361–392.

Ferenczi, S. (1925) Psycho-analysis of sexual habits. *International Journal of Psychoanalysis*. 6, 372–404.

Freud, S. (1895). Project for a scientific psychology (1950c). In: *The Standard Edition*. Volume 1. London, Hogarth Press, pp. 1–175.

Freud, S. (1912–13). Totem and taboo. In: *The Standard Edition*. Volume 13. London, Hogarth Press, pp. 1–161.

Freud, S. (1923). The ego and the id. In: *The Standard Edition.* Volume 19. London, Hogarth Press, pp. 1–59.

Grotstein, J. (1990) Nothingness, meaninglessness, chaos and the "black hole": 1 – the importance of nothingness, meaninglessness and chaos in psychoanalysis. *Contemporary Psychoanalysis.* 26, 257–291.

Holder, A. (1982) Preoedipal contributions to the formation of the superego. *Psychoanalytic Study of the Child.* 37, 245–273.

Hytinnen, R. (2002) The archaic superego: the guard of instincts from childhood to adolescence. *Scandinavian Psychoanalytic Review.* 25, 48–55.

Jacobson, E. (1954) The self and the object world – vicissitudes of their infantile cathexes and their influence on ideational and affective development. *Psychoanalytic Study of the Child.* 9, 75–128.

Khan, M.R. (1964) Ego distortion, cumulative trauma and the role of reconstruction in the analytic situation. *International Journal of Psychoanalysis.* 45, 272–279.

Kestenberg, J.S. & Brenner, I. (1986) Children who survived the holocaust – the role of rules and routines in the development of the superego. *International Journal of Psychoanalysis.* 67, 309–316.

Money-Kyrle, R. (1952) Psycho-analysis and ethics. *International Journal of Psychoanalysis.* 33, 225–234.

Music, G. (2015) Bringing up the bodies: psyche-soma, body awareness and feeling at ease. *British Journal of Psychotherapy.* 31(1), 4–19.

Reddish, E. (2014) *The Petrified Ego: A New Theory of Conscience.* London, Karnac Books.

Rilke, M.R. (1934) *Letters to a Young Poet.* Translated by M. D. Herter Norton. New York, W. W. Norton & Company, Inc., 1954.

Sandler, J. (1960) On the concept of the superego. *Psychoanalytic Study of the Child.* 15, 128–162.

Schafer, R. (1960) The loving and beloved superego in Freud's structural theory. *Psychoanalytic Study of the Child.* 15, 163–189.

Schecter, D.E. (1979) The loving and persecuting superego. *Contemporary Psychoanalysis.* 15, 361–379.

Spitz, R. (1958) On the genesis of superego components. *Psychoanalytic Study of the Child.* 13, 375–405.

Steiner, J. (1994) Patient-centred and analyst-centred interpretations: some implications of containment and countertransference. *Psychoanalytic Inquiry.* 14(3), 406–422.

Stephen, K. (1946) Relations between the superego and the ego. *Psychoanalysis and History.* 2, 11–28, 2000.

Volkan, V. (1997) *Bloodlines: From Ethnic Pride to Ethnic Terrorism.* New York, Farrar, Straus and Giroux.

Volkan, V. (2014) *Psychoanalysis, International Relations, and Diplomacy: A Sourcebook on Large-Group Psychology.* London, Karnac Books.

Weissman, P. (1954) Ego and superego in obsessional character and neurosis. *Psychoanalytic Quarterly.* 23, 529–544.

Wurmser, L. (2004) Superego – relevant or irrelevant? *Psychoanalytic Inquiry.* 24, 183–206.

Chapter 3

Reflections on the ego ideal in childhood

Ann Horne

We had been at a family funeral – the boys' great-grandmother. Joe was a very likeable and competent six-year-old, Harry a highly intelligent, unpredictable but always interesting four and Sam an utterly engaging and charming rising two. The stresses of funeral and extended family relationships had left a blanket of tiredness over everyone. Sam, sensing this uncomfortable atmosphere, nosed forcefully into his mother and grandmother, seeking a reaction, looking around everyone to see if he had gained one. 'Show us your tummy button, Sam!' – his mum, but the cry was taken up by several others, gently egging him on. Sam sought eye contact with us all, a little uncertain as to whether the mood had actually changed and he could perform his party piece. Harry turned to me and said firmly, '*I* have a tummy button but I'm *not* going to show it to you!' '*Everybody* has a tummy button', Joe commented. 'It's just that Sam really likes showing his off!' Sam checked out his audience, beamed and struggled to pull up his sweatshirt . . . to reveal . . . his vest. He laughed at finding himself still adored and loved as we all joined in. One could offer that Joe was already assured in his knowledge of social appropriateness – his superego was not burdensome and he lived up to his ego ideal of mature and understanding big brother; that Harry's ego ideal told him that he did not want to be babyish and that he found embarrassment in the notion of being so; and that Sam had some awareness that things permitted and not-permitted were being played with but his ego ideal was one where he could always find a happy engagement with his world.

Introduction

I have always rather delighted in the notion of the ego ideal and found it a very useful concept in psychoanalytic work with children and young people. That said, I admit to selectivity in my working definition of it. I appreciate Charles Rycroft's succinct view of the concept:

> *Ego ideal* – The self's conception of how he wishes to be. Sometimes used synonymously with the super-ego, but more often the distinction is made

that behaviour which is in conflict with the super-ego evokes guilt while that which conflicts with the ego ideal invokes shame.
(Rycroft, 1995: p. 45)

The axis of ego ideal/shame is an important one and one we shall return to. Where I would expand Rycroft's definition would be to add to the first sentence 'and the self's conception of how he would wish the world to see him': when we deal with shame and humiliation, we need also to have in mind gaze and being seen – the gaze that is necessary to contain and to mirror in infancy, and that can so easily instead become a gaze that fosters shame. Harry, in the opening vignette, was well aware of negative forces in relation to seeing and being seen; Sam checked that people were looking, assessed their mood – and was delighted to be seen.

There remains frequent debate as to just where Freud, latterly (1921, 1923), would have had 'ego ideal' fit into the superego constellation (as a separate instrument, as a sub-structure or simply as an alternative term for superego). Many contemporaries like Aichhorn, writing in 1925, were clear that it had been already subsumed into the superego, while leaving it open to be a sub-set of superego functions:

> In this chapter[1] the terms 'ego-ideal' and 'super-ego' are used synonymously. Among the majority of writers in psychoanalysis, 'super-ego' has gradually supplanted the older term, 'ego-ideal'. *Recently* there has been a tendency in psychoanalytic literature to use 'ego-ideal' to differentiate special functions within the 'super-ego'.
> (Aichhorn, 1925 [1935]: p. 211)

The term first appears in 'On narcissism: an introduction' (Freud, 1914) in the Strachey translation of the Standard Edition. I have chosen to follow the modern translation in 'On the Introduction of Narcissism' in *The Penguin Freud Reader* (Phillips, 2006) as it both gives credence to Freud's already having established the term 'narcissism' and makes the text a little clearer. Here, interestingly, we find him using both 'ideal ego' and 'ego ideal'. These seem to carry differing purposes and both to be something other than mere functions of the superego. The origins of the *ideal ego* – as he first outlines the concept – lie for Freud in the infant's early experience of narcissism.

> It is this ideal ego that is now the recipient of the self-love enjoyed during childhood by the real ego. The individual's narcissism appears to be transferred onto this new ideal ego which, like the infantile one, finds itself possessed of every estimable perfection.
> (Freud, 1914; Phillips, 2006: p. 380)

This ideal ego one could see as that which sustains us in daydreaming and fantasy, an omnipotence of a more illusory kind. However, in their experience of growing beyond infancy and encountering the exigencies of the real world – the process of disillusionment described by Winnicott, or the attainment of the Reality Principle in Freudian terms, or the achievement of the depressive position in the Kleinian idiom – most children salvage a functional and good-enough position with the establishment of the *ego ideal*, a compromise between narcissism and reality, omnipotence and parental introjects. Freud uses that concept in the same paragraph as his thoughts on the ideal ego (above) and concludes: 'What [human beings] project as their ideal for the future is a surrogate for the lost narcissism of their childhood' (*ibid.*).

These two – ideal ego and ego ideal – are important in our work with children and adolescents especially and the differing emphases matter. Sophie de Mijolla-Mellor (2005) compares these:

> Thus, the ideal ego could be seen as the nostalgic survival of a lost narcissism, while the ego ideal appears to be the dynamic formation that sustains ambitions towards progress.

I like this recognition of a dynamic formation and would agree with it. It resonates with Eigen who wrote that 'ideal states . . . often make intrinsic contributions to a growing sense of self, although they may also blur reality and work against growth' (Eigen 1993a: xxv). The ego ideal encourages a view of the developing self as one with possibilities, perhaps in contrast to the position of Freud and several subsequent theorists (e.g. Chasseguet-Smirgel (1974, 1975/85), also noted by Eigen who writes that they can be seen to be focusing on 'deciphering the pathological element in attachment to ideal states, relatively neglecting their healing aspect' (Eigen 1993b: 63). Joe and Anne Marie Sandler (1998) engage with this when they write that the ego ideal is in its basic form *the self that I would like to be* – 'the ideal self representation'. They add two divisions of the ego ideal – 'the ideal objects representation' (which is closer, perhaps, to the superego) and 'the ideal child representation' which is based on introjects and values of the parents, their wishes for the child. Together with 'the self that I would like to be seen to be', this is the ego ideal in health, the child in a state of aspiration and knowing his capabilities, a self with possibilities – it speaks of the latency child going out into the world, seeking mastery and outlets for his curiosity. Where the child's development has gone well enough, this is a resilient ego ideal; but not all children are allowed this experience.

Where early narcissism is failed

Freud introduces section III of 'On the Introduction of Narcissism' (where he first presents the ego ideal and ideal ego) with a caveat:

> There are certain questions that I should like to leave to one side for the time being since they represent an important area of study that has still not

been fully dealt with: questions as to what disruptions the primal narcissism in children is prey to, what reactions it displays in resisting them, and what paths it is forced along in that process.

(Freud, 1914; Phillips, 2006: p. 378)

We can turn to Winnicott (1968) for an assessment of what is necessary if the developmental movement beyond narcissism is not to become pathological. The *necessary* 'failure' of adaptation that leads to reality sense and a separate self is one that depends on the mother's intense early attunement to her infant's needs and capacities – the good enough mother, as Winnicott reminds us, provides a process of disillusionment, a gradual 'failure' of adaptation. After an early stage of omnipotence when his needs are anticipated and met, the infant is let down gradually from this position, in turn learning to temper that omnipotence and adjust to the needs of others and the real world. This one expects in normal developmental and familial experience and it happens at a pace that the infant can cope with, that does not create over anxiety in the child. Where there is a gross failure of maternal adaptation to the infant's needs, on the other hand, or where mothering is erratic and the infant can neither experience his object as reliable or child-centred nor gain any sense of his own narcissism, Winnicott writes, development is distorted. It may be that there results for the baby a privileging of the mind which can lead to False Self elaboration or precocity (Winnicott, 1960); the child may seek refuge in mindless states, or absence of imagination; and where body is split from mind, psychosomatic illness may result. Where violence and abuse have featured – not simply failure in adaptation but recurrent treating the infant as part-object – there may equally be a privileging of the body in the child for whom desperate bodily based defensive manoeuvres then come to be used to try to rid the mind of memories of humiliation and shame.

When we fall short of our ego ideal, shame stalks in. This is a necessary developmental process in childhood: shame, as Don Campbell has written (1994), provides us with a shield against the trauma of being found out not to be what we had hoped to be and hoped to present to the world. We cover our faces, flush, turn away; children will crawl behind or under furniture and people, they run off, taking themselves out of the spotlight of being seen as they do not wish to be seen. Our egos are bruised but, in normal development will recover and we will recall such incidents with embarrassment – or have them recalled for us by mischievous family members. But for the child whose experience has been that of being shamed and humiliated constantly – the child viciously abused, taunted, objectified – there is no safety in shame, only the accumulative trauma of yet another shaming. For such children and young people, there is greater likelihood of seeking the fantasy solace of an ideal ego, omnipotent and unreal, and who may offer potency instead of humiliation.

'In the absence of self-knowledge an identification with an ego ideal is substituted, which shrouds the person from self-knowledge.'

(Symington, 1986: p. 331)

Symington goes on to give as example Lacan who, he writes,

> 'was violently anti-authoritarian and declaimed against the International Psycho-Analytical Association, yet when he was in authority over his own society he was enormously authoritarian seemingly without knowing it' (*ibid.*) but the example could equally be the young person who *dare* not know himself, the introjections from his parents and environment according such a sense of humiliation.

It is not so long ago that the Government in the UK initiated a 'respect agenda', to operate in relation to bored and disaffected youth found drinking in town centres or engaged in delinquency. Unsurprisingly, politicians who had closed Youth Centres, cut funding to the Youth Service and left local authorities ill-financed to make provision for the young saw this in terms of the need for young people to respect their elders. . . . Not particularly charitable examples, then, for identification and the moderation of an ego ideal. For young people on the edges of violence, respect was also an issue – the absence of respect, a sense of disrespect or 'being dissed' which meant that the vulnerable, brittle ideal ego had to respond speedily to a felt insult to restore a position of omnipotence. The ideal ego can thus often be found where violent young people are found – and an identification with a highly delinquent or violent gang member can conceal one's own permanent sense of worthlessness and humiliation. Or we may note an identification with the violence itself, as we will see with Martin.

The ideal ego as a defence against humiliation

For many children there has not been an environment that has allowed them to develop that crucial ability to protect the self psychologically, grow a psychological skin and with it shrug off the lesser slights that we encounter in life; or the nature of the dysfunctionality is continuous, relentless, with no benign intervention – as we might find in across-generationally abusive families – and the child has 'little chance of developing a coherent and realistic picture of himself and his parents; his perceptual framework is built on shaky ground' (Lomas, 1967: p. 13). Lomas was writing of the early days of psychoanalytically based family therapy, working with families with schizophrenic family members, but the developmental damage can also be seen in many perverse family constellations. I would posit that the risk is highest where the child cannot be allowed to be a separate being, to be perceived and enjoyed as a self with integrity. Martin was such a child; *his* ideal became entwined with the instruments of violence which preoccupied his fantasies.

Martin

Resident in a specialist youth treatment centre, Martin at 14 years of age had attacked violently a staff member, a woman to whom he was close. The attack was said to have 'come out of the blue' (the referring team wrote, 'He has behaved in a very violent manner, including a serious unprovoked attack, when he was apparently calm and content'). The alarm system failed and no-one else was in the unit at the time. Martin shouted, 'Die, bitch, die!' amongst other verbal assaults during a prolonged onslaught. He received an 18-month Conditional Discharge for this offence and is said – as with many violent and delinquent boys and young men – to have 'shown no remorse'. Remorse, of course, represents a developmental achievement which encompasses a sense of self, other and superego attainment: this was not a position available to Martin.

He had arrived in the centre 2½ years previously, some three months before his twelfth birthday, having been given a sentence of five years for two counts of arson and two further counts of arson with intent to endanger life. He was 11 years old when he committed the offences.

In brief, Martin came from a cross-generationally sexually violent family. His experience before his reception into care age five is the most perversely abusive, incestuous and violent that I have ever encountered: sexual and physical abuse by his mother, step-father and their friends and forced abuse of his siblings to entertain the adults. He did not settle with any foster parent – understandably, given his history and what family and intimacy meant to him. He was admitted to a Children's Unit age six.

The Unit reports describe him as exhibiting sexualised behaviour towards adults and children. He had nightmares and sleep problems, was distrustful, destructive and ran away frequently. He was also enuretic by night – a symptom that only cleared up after the move to his adoptive parents. Therapy reports comment that he viewed adults as persecutory, had jealous and murderous feelings and fantasised about omnipotence – not surprising, really. Martin's sexualised behaviour arose in response, he thought himself, to feelings of being controlled. However much the professional teams suspected at this time, Martin remained resolutely silent about his past. The containment of a good placement, a good specialist school for children with emotional and behavioural difficulties, regular psychotherapy and a coherent care plan allowed him a settled period.

He moved to live with his adoptive family aged eight years, exactly two years after arriving in the unit. This entailed a considerable geographical relocation and the loss of his therapy. It was to his foster father that he disclosed his childhood abuse. He settled there for a few years but the terror of intimacy began to build and his fire-lighting began. In interview with a very good child psychiatrist he talked of needing to be away, fear of closeness and fear of what he might do as a consequence of this dread.

Despite clear recommendations in the psychiatric court report that no attempt should be made to force Martin to recall his abuse – rather, staff should only ever go at his pace and in response to his expressed interest – it was decided to undertake life story work and to approach his abuse. The early signs of his distress at this were not recognised: the violent attack ensued.

Martin had been used – treated as a part-object – by his mother with devastating impact on the essential development of the protective sense of shame. His vulnerability to the engulfing internal mother, and the split internal humiliating and abandoning mother, caused his acting-out to be directed against women and it was the need for and dread of closeness to them that triggered his rush to violence. Verbal abuse, often with very sexually disparaging language, was a common way of Martin's expressing his anxiety but the symbolisation of this was not sufficient *when the anxiety was not recognised as such* – and he then had to act.

On visiting the Centre, it became clear that during the period leading up to the assault Martin had attempted to secrete cutlery and to adapt furniture (which he broke) into weapons. He has also talked of sexually assaulting staff and spent long periods of time in the lavatory with pictures he had torn from a catalogue – pictures of knives and chainsaws. He was thought to masturbate to these. He talked of killing himself, cut himself superficially, pushed things into electrical sockets and threw water over the TV, hoping it would blow up and he would die. His threats to kill staff since then were taken very seriously and reported to the police.

It is not hard to see the serious decompensation resulting from Martin's being induced to recall and review the trauma and humiliation of his past. The establishment of a tight regime led to some settling – for the month after the attack he was involved in a violent incident each day. This settled during the following month with close monitoring and lessened even more after that.

When thinking of Martin and his masturbating to a catalogue, one concludes that the only position available to him at this lowest point appeared to be identification with objects of violence. He had become one too – the internal 'ideal image' as perpetrator mentioned by Parsons and Dermen (1999): 'The job of the child psychotherapist,' they continue, 'is to resist collusion either with the values of his ideal self (violence) or the demands of his harsh conscience (sadistic punishment); rather it is to understand his predicament, something he cannot do himself' (Parsons & Dermen 1999: 345).

Ferenczi (1933) first alerted us to this reaction to abuse: 'The [abused] child changes into a mechanical obedient automaton' (p. 163). The mechanical self becomes the only recourse available – an ideal ego of a kind. This is reminiscent of Cooper's comments on the core trauma in perversion and on 'dehumanisation', which he defines as a strategy to protect against human qualities of loving, vulnerability and unpredictability:

> the core trauma in many if not all perversions is the experience of terrifying passivity in relation to the pre-oedipal mother perceived as dangerously malignant.
> (Cooper, 1991: p. 23)

Martin had just been reminded – in a persistent way – of the dangers and horrors of feeling human. His violence had become something to cathect and to identify with: an ideal self.

Carlo

Carlo's mother had struggled with her ambivalence at having a male child whom she had dressed as a girl when he was a toddler and small child, and with what one might conjecture was a hatred of him, disguised as over-protectiveness that allowed him no friends and no life outside the home. He certainly lacked the admiring gaze and experience of omnipotence that the Winnicottian child claims as his right, and the affirmation of self, body and gender. Carlo's father seems to have been unavailable as a model for identification or a counter-weight to his mother. Carlo's consequent rigid 'masculine' thinking (his term) and mechanistic view of the world arose from atrophied curiosity, creativity and imagination; there had been no early experience of finding the space between reality and illusion where creativity grows. He had struggled in school, both with academic work and with friendships, and was now at a Further Education College, pursuing Computer Studies.

He had been referred at age 19 as he had expressed a wish to become female, perceived himself as transsexual and was extremely depressed and suicidal. Now living with his grandmother, away from parental criticism and humiliation, he could cross dress at ease in this home. I mention him briefly as it is also possible to view his perception of himself as offering an ideal ego of a mechanistic and illusory kind.

At our first meeting, Carlo was concerned that I understand just how conflicted he was and how serious he was in thinking about gender reassignment. He told me I had a year, then he would probably be off. He described himself as being like a computer where the male side and the female side access the hard drive in turn but not both at the same time. When his male side feels depleted, the female side will kick in and he will have to cross dress. He also described how he would become aroused by watching an erotic video or reading a magazine. His 'male side' patently felt potent and excited. Instantly, his 'female side' would insist, "You'd really like to *be* her, wouldn't you!" – denying and concealing the desire.

At the same time, he told me that it was very important for me to know that his female side did not want to kill off his male side when she took over; rather, the female side acted as a cloak, keeping the male side hidden. This felt more like the split, the deception, which we find in transvestism and seemed to carry some hope. We were able very briefly to think about his proposed gender reassignment operation as an attack in that context, but only very briefly.

I wonder if the mechanistic ideal self, for young people who have experienced hatred in the acts and the gaze of the other, is the only possible psychological construct available to them, not only because it is a minimalist identification without fear of human attachments and therefore humiliation, but also because it gives an illusion of control. It may be the only position to be found by the child for whom an experience of omnipotence has never occurred and could never be envisioned. We recall the child, described by Fairbairn (1946), who perceives himself as bad in order to sustain the idea of a parent who might love him – it is his fault, not the parent's, that he is hated. Having a computer-like ideal ego gave Carlo a safe, controlled, primitive arena in which to exist; it would take two years before we saw the development of a – fragile – ego ideal and self that could risk relationships, where he could view himself as a young man with attributes that *he* recognised were valued by others.

It is not an easy thing to mend a broken mirror: gaze and the ego ideal

Kate also made me think about gaze. We met a few days after her seventh birthday; we said our moving goodbyes 7½ years later. Kate had also come to the clinic because of concern that she had begun to act in a sexually inappropriate way – in her case with her younger brother, being compelled to encroach repeatedly into his bedroom in the middle of the night for sexual engagement and exploration. She had learning difficulties – global developmental delay, functioning on the first centile – was encopretic, still in nappies at night, and was neglected and waif-like.

Kate's family demonstrates once more the need to hold in mind several generations. Who the child is in the parent's gaze would seem to me to be one of the early steps or mis-steps for the child; can the child be held and be wanted would be the first; and is she held – and who is she – in the *mind* and gaze of the parent. These processes are affected cross-generationally. Kate's mother had been brought up in an atmosphere of domestic violence and sexual abuse. She married a violent and abusive much older man by whom she had a son, Richard, who disclosed, then retracted, his mother's sexual abuse of him. Her second husband, Mr Long, father of Kate and her three little brothers, had, like his wife, learning difficulties but was notably able to respond to distress in his daughter – this was evident on the rare occasions that he brought her to her therapy. I mention this as Kate's experience of violence at home was that of her mother to this overly mild father – and of her brother Richard who sexually abused Kate from her early months when ordered regularly by their mother to bathe her. This only ceased when she was five years old and he was removed from home. Mrs Long, however, seemed unable and unwilling to sustain the practicality of the Court's injunction against his visiting and he remained a threat.

I find Winnicott's term 'personalisation' useful (Winnicott, 1949, 1970): 'Personalization' is 'an in-dwelling of psyche in soma' (Winnicott, 1970: p. 10). We are thinking integration of body and mind: as he writes, this 'in developmental terms represents an achievement in health' (Winnicott, 1970: p. 7). I would posit that, for many children who use activity as a defence against painful memory, the body itself merely functions and 'is'; it is to be *not* thought about at all times. Part of the therapeutic process is to enable the child to entertain the body in mind, to have a body image and a concept of body in which s/he then can belong and which can also be included in the ego ideal.

In this we think of the child as a part-object to the mother – an extension of the mother, a psychological dustbin, a repository for uncomfortable emotions and unbearable thoughts – not a sentient being with integrity and individuality; and we recall Estela Welldon's formulation of the perverse female who turns inwards, to the body and the body products, in her annihilation of her internal, abusing mother (Welldon, 1988). For the child of such a parent Winnicott's comments on the development of the self are helpful:

> The self essentially recognises itself in the eyes and facial expression of the mother and in the mirror which can come to represent the mother's face.
> (Winnicott 1970: p. 16).

Mrs Long, Kate's mother, during the first four years of therapy when Kate still lived at home, would wait for her in the waiting room, headphones firmly attached, mouth filled with biscuits, or speaking extremely loudly on her mobile phone – rarely was she ready or receptive when Kate returned. Indeed, the taxi journey to the clinic was, she stated, *her* respite from the other three children and her husband – thus annihilating Kate as a being with her own needs.

Winnicott goes on to emphasise the role of parental expectations in modifying and forming the emerging self – and we recall Mrs Long's ambivalence about her daughter, her exposing her to the son whom she had abused. For the child who is a part-object, the formation of an ego ideal is a long way away. Yet there was a sense of hope right from our first meeting:

> A tall, extremely thin, fey looking child sat apart from her heavily pregnant mother in the waiting room. She had fine, mousey brown hair and a tremendous sense of lightness about her as if somehow she was not certain about having substance. Her grubby NHS spectacles sat aslant her face and were held together with elastoplast. Nevertheless, she placed herself before me as I introduced myself to both and stared, head on one side, with very direct curiosity. She hesitated as we came down into my basement room – possibly the due anxiety one would expect at a first encounter but I felt it more to be an uncertainty about what one did. Very soon the session theme of 'how do you get things right?' emerged. Already, it seemed, there was a child who was concerned about the state of mind of the object rather than in any way egocentric.
> (Horne, 2012: p. 390)

In that stance, right before me, I felt that I was meeting a child who could consider a new object, although her need to placate that object in our first meeting was telling: I thought it a flash of a self that saw possibilities but where equally a false self might be the outcome were she not to be helped to a different experience of herself in the world.

In therapy, throughout the first months Kate played very repetitively at hide and seek, longing and fearing to be found. In the counter-transference, hunting behind chairs, under the couch and in her favourite place beneath my desk (from which I often thought she emerged, brought into life, into a world where she was seeking to be perceived differently from the perception she saw in her mother's gaze) I felt she was also revisiting the dangerous drama of being found by her abuser. Heightened anxiety and adrenaline rush repeated the anticipatory body sensations of her infant self. My comments centred on the fear that I might be abusive, the wish that this now might be different, and the need constantly to repeat the good experience of being found by a good enough object. As with a small child, the emphasis was on the joy of finding – '*There* you are! How awful it felt not to find and see you!' – and the process of internalising a normal developmental engagement between adult and child. It is such a developmental achievement to know one can make the other person pursue one; how much more so when that grown-up's gaze can be trusted and the internalisation of both a benign object and a self that is worth pursuing is possible. Only then, I would think, can an ego ideal start to be a possibility.

Who the child is in the eyes of the incestuous and incest-permitting mother and of the incestuous partner becomes an important question. I am reminded of the Chinese proverb: It is not an easy thing to mend a broken mirror. The crack in the mirror remains visible and affects the reflection, altering how one perceives oneself.

The absence of any stage of what Freud would call 'primary narcissism' must be part of our construct. Nor is there the straightforward affirmation through gaze between mother and baby:

> Of course, the baby does see the mother's smiling face, but this, which is in reality her response to his smiles, reflects back to him his own aliveness: 'The mother is looking at the baby and what she looks like is related to what she sees there'.
>
> (Winnicott, 1967: p. 112; Wright, 1991: p. 12)

This calling-forth of the baby from a state of apperception to one of perception – being seen giving rise to seeing and perceiving as a real, separate being – is the final statement from Winnicott on the body-gaze-psyche continuum. The mother as mirror reflects back to her infant what she perceives when she sees him, 'giving back to the baby the baby's own self'. The reflection he sees in his mother's face is his own. When this process is absent, the infant gazing at the mother sees how *she* is feeling, not a reflection back of him, his own feeling state and being. That could be depression; it could be dislike or hatred; or perhaps the modern mother on the mobile phone is expressing indifference. Thus the baby's sense of feeling *real* is cultivated, or not, right at the beginning. Winnicott's earlier work (1949) on psyche and soma, mind in body, shows the importance to the infant of experiences of holding, handling and object relating. To 'holding' and 'handling' we should add, as we observe her, the mother's use of gaze to hold and to authenticate. Perhaps, too, we should keep in mind the consequences not simply of an absence of this affirming gaze but also of the presence of a gaze which is corrupt, the prelude to the infant as object used to contain the adult's perverse projections (not uncommon in referrals to our clinics today) and which leads to the privileging of the body as the only source of validation of a self of a kind that the child can find.

At our final session, seven years after our first meeting, gaze, seeing and the mirror were important:

> Kate walked slowly up to the door. My raincoat hung on a hook. There was a long mirror on the wall to the left of it. She reached out – again slowly as if ready to comply with any prohibition. I watched, not feeling any aggression in this move. She put on the coat. It fitted her perfectly at age 14½. She struggled to fasten the belt but persisted – her own containment – and looked in the mirror. We both felt great sadness. I found myself unable to speak, tears

in my eyes. When I could find words, I commented that she was trying out being me and having me wrapped around her in that way; perhaps, though we both would miss each other, we would also have each other inside our minds.

(Horne, 2012: p. 403)

Parts of her therapist had been introjected to inform her ego ideal and she could bear to see her real self and her self-held-by-therapist very honestly in the mirror.

Afterthought: training, analytic internal objects and the analytic ego ideal

One may well, as a child (and adult) psychotherapist, be oneself servient to a harshly punitive superego: the generally hierarchical structure of trainings has added to that likelihood as we engage with a tendency to idealise our teachers, analysts and analytic forebears and to institutionalise our own particular understanding of their theoretical and technical stances. It is particularly an issue for trainees. I have described this phenomenon, a little tongue in cheek, as 'the Great Child Psychotherapist in the Sky' (Horne, 2006), felt to be looking over one's shoulder as one works and learns, quickening a primitive and as yet untempered analytic internal object. How we develop our ideal analytic selves – our analytic ideals – is part of the process that leads to how we then understand and help structure the internal self/ego ideal of our child patients – and how we engage with the analytic ideal selves of those we supervise and teach. For training schools, it is essential that this process is known, discussed and its implications shared, and that there is genuine engagement of all those involved in the training with the trainees – keeping in mind a training process that takes place *between* people, co-created, not a process of doing something *to* the other, allows a more healthy and integrated analytic ideal self to emerge.

> In each baby is a vital spark, and this urge towards life and growth and development is a part of the baby, something the child is born with and which is carried forward in a way that we do not have to understand. For instance, if you have just put a bulb in the window-box you know perfectly well that you do not have to make the bulb grow into a daffodil. You supply the right kind of earth or fibre and you keep the bulb watered just the right amount, and the rest comes naturally, because the bulb has life in it.
>
> (Winnicott, 1949: pp. 27–28)

The trainee has the desire to be a therapist; the child has the desire to be a self of substance – for both, the environment and the nourishment ought to allow the development of a syntonic ego ideal that supports a flourishing, growing self.

Note

1 Aichhorn, A. (1925) Chapter 10 – Significance of the ego-ideal in social behaviour.

References

Aichhorn, A. (1925) *Verwahrloste Jugend*. Vienna, Internationaler Psychoanalytischer Verlag. Published in English in 1935 as *Wayward Youth*. New York, Viking Press.

Campbell, D. (1994) Breaching the shame shield: thoughts on the assessment of adolescent sexual abusers. *Journal of Child Psychotherapy*. 20(3), 309–326.

Chasseguet-Smirgel, J. (1974) Perversion, idealisation and sublimation. *International Journal of Psycho-Analysis*. 55, 349–357.

Chasseguet-Smirgel, J. (1975) *L'Idéal du Moi, Essai sur la Maladie d'Idéalité*. Paris, Tchou. Published in English in 1985 as *The Ego Ideal: A Psychoanalytic Essay on the Malady of the Ideal*. London, Free Association Books.

Cooper, A.M. (1991) The unconscious core of perversion. In: G. Fogel & W. Myers (eds.) *Perversions and Near-Perversions in Clinical Practice – New Psychoanalytic Perspectives*. London, Yale University Press.

De Mijolla-Mellor, S. (2005) Ego ideal/ ideal ego. In: A. Mijolla (ed.) *International Dictionary of Psychoanalysis*. New York, Macmillan. Available from Encyclopedia at: www.encyclopedia.com/psychology/dictionaries-thesauruses-pictures-and-press-releases/ego-idealideal-ego [Accessed 15 January 2018].

Eigen, M. (1993a) *The Electrified Tightrope*. London, Jason Aronson.

Eigen, M. (1993b) Instinctual fantasy. In: *The Electrified Tightrope*. London, Jason Aronson.

Fairbairn, W.R.D. (1946) Object relations and dynamic structure. *International Journal of Psychoanalysis*. 27, 30–37.

Ferenczi, S. (1933) On the confusion of tongues between adults and the child. In: *Final Contributions to the Problems and Methods of Psychoanalysis*. New York, Basic Books, 1955.

Freud, S. (1914) On narcissism: an introduction. In: *The Standard Edition*. Volume XIV. London, Hogarth Press, pp. 67–104. Translated as 'On the Introduction of Narcissism'. In: A. Phillips (ed.) *The Penguin Freud Reader*. London, Penguin Books, 2006.

Freud, S. (1921) Group psychology and the analysis of the ego. *The Standard Edition*. Volume XVIII. London, Hogarth Press, pp. 67–134.

Freud, S. (1923) The ego and the id. In: *The Standard Edition*. Volume XIX. London, Hogarth Press, pp. 13–63.

Horne, A. (2006) Interesting things to say – and why. In: M Lanyado & A Horne (eds.) *A Question of Technique: Independent Psychoanalytic Approaches with Children and Adolescents*. London, Routledge.

Horne, A. (2012) Entertaining the body in mind: thoughts on incest, the body, sexuality and the self. In: P. Williams, J. Keene & S. Dermen (eds.) *Independent Psychoanalysis Today*. London, Karnac Books.

Lomas, P. (1967) The study of family relationships in contemporary society – introduction. In: P. Lomas (ed.) *The Predicament of the Family*. London, Hogarth Press & Institute of Psychoanalysis.

Parsons, M. & Dermen, S. (1999) The violent child and adolescent. In: M. Lanyado & A. Horne (eds.) *The Handbook of Child & Adolescent Psychotherapy: Psychoanalytic Approaches*. London, Routledge.

Phillips, A. (ed.) (2006) *The Penguin Freud Reader*. London, Penguin Books.

Rycroft, C. (1995) *A Critical Dictionary of Psychoanalysis*. 2nd Edition, London, Penguin Books.

Sandler, J. & Sandler, A-M. (1998) *Internal Objects Revisited.* London, Karnac Books.
Symington, N. (1986) *The Analytic Experience – Lectures from the Tavistock.* London, Free Association Books.
Welldon, E. (1988) *Mother, Madonna, Whore: The Idealisation and Denigration of Motherhood.* London, Free Association Books.
Winnicott, D.W. (1949) Mind and its relation to the psyche-soma. In: *Collected Papers: Through Paediatrics to Psychoanalysis.* London, Hogarth Press, 1975.
Winnicott, D.W. (1960) Ego distortion in terms of true and false self. In: *The Maturational Processes and the Facilitating Environment.* London, Hogarth Press, 1965.
Winnicott, D.W. (1967) The mirror role of mother and family in child development. In: P. Lomas (ed.) *The Predicament of the Family.* London, Hogarth Press. Reprinted in: *Playing and Reality.* Harmondsworth, Penguin Books, 1971.
Winnicott, D.W. (1968) Communication between infant and mother, and mother and infant, compared and contrasted. In: D.W. Winnicott (ed.) *Babies and their Mothers.* London, Free Association Books, pp. 89–103, 1988.
Winnicott, D.W. (1970) Basis for self in body. *International Journal of Child Psychotherapy.* 1(1), 7–16, 1972.
Wright, K. (1991) *Vision and Separation: Between Mother and Baby.* London, Free Association Books.

Chapter 4

The neurobiological bases of human moralities

Industrial civilization's misguided moral development

Darcia Narvaez

How does conscience develop? Does moral virtue emerge from lived experience or does it require explicit teaching, even coercion? The idea of the superego-as-conscience typically assumes an otherwise ungovernable id. But ideas of the superego and id appear to emerge from industrial civilization, a place where humans grow outside their typical nest and away from their species-typical nature. This chapter examines two approaches to conscience development. Converging science suggests that industrialized nations have got things the wrong way round and created the problems they deplore. In my view, the enlarged ego and domineering superego apparent in industrialized nations come about from under- or mis-care in early life, which civilization does especially well. Under-care occurs when communities, families, and mothers forget or are pressed to deny the evolved needs of the child and fail to provide the developmental system or nest children need to grow well as human beings. This results in toxic stress for the child, leading to the need for extra defences to survive a cruel social environment that undermines species-typical psychosocial-neurobiological development.

In contrast with pre-civilized societies, it is often assumed in industrialized societies that punishment and coercion are needed to instil conscience and shape children into good members of the society (those with hierarchies, inequality, and anticipated rewards in the future). Civilized peoples often fear that humans will act like animals (id dominance) if not coerced and punished (to develop the superego). The fear of animality bears the markings of a misunderstanding of the nature of human nature and how it develops. This fear is no doubt rooted in the many dys-regulated humans that civilized nations foster by misguided child raising, perpetuating a cycle of mis-development and subsequent harsh reaction. Western civilization has a long history of fearing Nature (Plumwood, 2002) and of mistreating children (de Mause, 1995) that contrasts with pre-industrialized societies who partner with nature (Martin, 1999) and 'indulge' young children (Hewlett & Lamb, 2005), creating cooperative and self-controlled individuals (and in first nation societies, losing one's animal nature is considered dangerous). As will be described, neuroscientific studies show us how neurobiological and moral development are related.

What do children need to develop properly as members of the human species? Parents in industrialized nations are often very confused by this question, until they find an expert to guide them – e.g., government official, religious adviser, or parenting entrepreneur. Unfortunately, many of these authorities display confusion and ignorance themselves. For example, John Watson, former president of the American Psychological Association, wrote a parenting book, *Psychological Care of the Infant and Child* (1928) where he suggested that babies be treated like young adults – with little affection or attention – so they get used to such treatment from the start. Religious authorities from Augustine onward have argued that children need to be punished, their wills broken, in order for them to be obedient. Alice Miller (1983 [1990]) reviewed child raising manuals from recent centuries, including those of Nazi Germany, finding that similar advice was given for creating obedient children – punish them extensively before age three, because they won't remember it but will be completely controllable later through threats. Expectations for child, then adult, compliance support coercive treatment of children, which may be useful for supporting hierarchical, industrial structures that demand docility and submission to the machines of civilization. Such expectations are accompanied by ignorance about how to optimize human potential and result from the demands of industrialized social organisation on parents which undermine social processes of more naturally self-organised communities. It turns out that civilization represents only 1% of human genus history. Human nature and morality in the 99% of human history, pre-civilization, is a different story. All over the world, as documented by scholars, those living like our 99% behave quite differently from those in civilized nations. One might think that the id runs wild. Certainly, for a prudish viewer, sexual freedom might seem like the rampant id at work. But societies of the 99% show great cooperation, self-control, and minimal aggression, not the aggressive selfishness assumed to characterise the id. In fact, there is little evidence of the many psycho-pathologies apparent in civilized nations, perhaps because there is little cause for them, not just because of sexual freedom but because of the nurturing care provided in critical periods – the nurturing humans evolved to need. Humanity's 99% represents the time period of species-typical child raising and social living. The divided self (id, ego, superego) is less apparent in these societies, and yet there is high cooperation and minimal conflict – without coercion. Instead, it appears that the obedience-demanding superego and the wild id are a result of species-atypical childhoods. But that is getting ahead of the story.

Species-typical childhoods

Human beings are biosocial becomings (Ingold, 2013). Most importantly, humans are biosocial *constructions*. This means our biology is shaped by social experience, especially in early life when the brain is highly immature and growing rapidly, dependent on experience for the setting of parameters and thresholds for multiple systems. It also means that our sociality is highly influenced by our biology – i.e., how well our neurobiological systems function influences how well we get along with others. In fact, humans are much more epigenetically shaped after birth than our primate cousins (Gomez-Robles et al., 2015). The nature of self and personality begins in early life with the layered biological systems that are shaped by early experience through epigenetic and plasticity effects (e.g., number and functionality of neurotransmitters, thresholds and parameters for such things as the stress response and vagal tone). These systems are co-constructed by the dynamic interactionism between maturational schedule and life experience. The dynamism of development, with the child's brain systems developing rapidly (thousands of synapses a minute), means that experience is shaping the layers of foundational capacities for personality and intelligence (for reviews, see Lanius et al., 2010; Narvaez et al., 2013, 2014, 2016a). Humans have a set of evolved basic needs that when met optimize their development in a species-typical direction.

How do we know what needs to be provided to a helpless infant? Every animal has a nest for its young that optimizes normal development. Humans also have a nest. Humans evolved with a developmental system that matches up with the maturational schedule of the child. Humanity's nest is particularly intense because of the young child's immaturity and it lasts a good while because of the time it takes a human to reach adulthood (the longest of any animal – till age 20 for physical growth and nearly age 30 for brain development). A species-*typical* 'nest' for humans is rooted in ancient social mammalian parenting practices that match up with the maturational schedule of the child. The evolved developmental nest or niche includes extensive, on-request breastfeeding; extensive affectionate touch; responsiveness to needs to avoid distress in babyhood (before age three) and synchronized social experience; free-play in nature with multiply-aged mates; soothing birth experiences; multiple responsive adult caregivers; positive social support for mother and child. All these components are related to neurobiological development and a body/brain system that works optimally (e.g. Narvaez et al., 2013). They also bear on the development of the self and morality.

Observers have noted that small-band hunter-gatherers (SBHG; the type of society that represents 99% of human genus history) provide the species-typical nest and at the same time display calm, generous, cooperative, open, compassionate personalities in adulthood. We can see that the evolved nest provides the type of care that fosters the self-regulation, empathy, and social fittedness that underlie these personality dispositions. Through lived experience, those in SBHG societies develop a self-fitted for social and moral life.

Development of the self

The self is formed first in experiences with caregivers, through somatosensory experience internal and external to the body. The evolved nest provides full sensory experience for a baby as physical contact is nearly constant and involves smelling, tasting, hearing, sharing touch and communications with mother. Then gradually, sensitively, the 'good-enough' mother introduces the infant to others 'in small doses . . . because of the devotion she feels for her own baby' (Winnicott, 1957: p. 58). The caregiver must be present in her own body to 'hold' the baby well. Skin-to-skin contact with an emotionally and psychically present caregiver promotes optimal development (e.g., stress response systems). The infant is kept content and in the middle of community activities, with every need met (caregivers grant 'infant omnipotence'; Winnicott, 1957). Enjoyment of being with the child and meeting the child's needs gladly convey the love and attention a baby needs to proceed on a pathway towards flourishing. Of course, with maturation, the child will need to learn to deal with unexpected stress, but any extensive distress should be avoided until basic systems are established after early childhood.

The child's early experiences bring about capacities for non-verbal social communication, including intersubjectivity and synchronicity. The interpersonal dynamics of synchronizing motives, intentional states, and behaviours with another – the forming of a duet of 'being with' the other person by participating in the dynamic flow – can be described as a *communicative musicality* (Trevarthen, 1999) or 'vitality contours' (Stern, 2010) learned in early life. Stern describes the many months of learning non-verbal communication (before language interferes) which includes mutual eye gaze practices (how, how long, with whom), how to read postures, how to solicit others for needs like food or play, 'rules' of games, turn taking, greetings, joking, expressing affection, making friends, and much more. Through these close care experiences babies experience and practice empathy, perspective taking, and resonance. Jessica Benjamin (1988) notes that intersubjectivity is the way children learn mutual recognition:

> To affirm, validate, acknowledge, know, accept, understand, empathize, take in, tolerate, appreciate, see, identify with, find familiar . . . love. . . . What I call *mutual recognition* includes a number of experiences commonly described in the research on mother-infant interaction: emotional attunement, mutual influence, affective mutuality, sharing state of mind.
>
> (pp. 15–16)

For Loewald (1979) (quoted in Shaw, 2014: p. 387), caregivers hold and mediate for the child a hopeful vision of the child's potential, 'a vision based in the empathic, loving, and respectful recognition of the child's emerging identity,' evoking, nourishing, and protecting the child through the sacred bonds of parent and child.

In care-giving that provides the evolved nest, the child develops holistically, with an embodied unity of thinking and feeling (heart-mind), guided by mother and allo-mothers. The proto-self is largely unconscious and emerges from birth, when infants are ready for communication with others, even showing playful deception in the early months of life (Reddy, 2008). The proto-self manifests creativity and imagination in social relations. In the first five months of life, face-to-face affective communication and shared signalling play a primary role in the development and exercise of emotion (Beebe et al., 1997; Tronick, 1989). Life is social and it is pleasurable.

> Keeping faith in a developing child's potential to grow; encouraging the potential to develop meaningful ways of expressing her subjectivity; supporting

the expansion of meaning and pleasure in intersubjective relatedness; and steadfastly committing to honouring the developing child's need for safety, especially from exploitation – these are the conditions that we know support healthy growth and development.

(Shaw, 2014: p. 144)

However, it is not enough to only receive care: the child's gift of love must also be received in return. 'Frustration of his desire to be loved as a person and to have his love accepted is the greatest trauma that a child can experience' (Fairbairn, 1952: p. 39). Reciprocal relations of intersubjective sharing and social gifting is fundamental to building a confident and trusting core self.

As noted, small-band hunter-gatherers (the type of society that represents 99% of human genus history) provide the species-typical nest (see Narvaez, 2013, for reviews). These societies would be places where no transitional object is expected or required as the mother or others are always present and available. Co-sleeping occurs for all community members. Adults display calm, generous, cooperative, open, compassionate personalities in adulthood. This is not surprising if one understands the interrelation of the nest to neurobiological development and the growth of personality. When babies and young children receive what they need, their goodness or virtue develops naturally, from the ground up (Narvaez, 2015, 2016a). Their many biological systems are well self-regulated and coordinated, tuned up to normal-optimal development. Moral capacities build on basic physiological functioning (e.g., stress response) which shapes the moral personality signature a person carries into adulthood. Moral capacities are built on social experience. The experiences of recognition, resonance, and respect develop a propensity for relational attunement (what I call the Engagement Ethic; Narvaez, 2014). Relational attunement gives space to the other and to the self to make joint decisions, to be spontaneous with one another. The evolved nest nourishes the roots of empathy and the self-efficacy to express it (empathic effectivity roots). Relational attunement and empathic effectivity roots might be called moral subcomponents (Kupperman, 2005), specifically, of an engagement ethic, a moral orientation guiding behaviour later in life. Both are fostered in the evolved nest.

Superego as practical wisdom

Early dynamic experiences undergird our expectations and sensibilities for social life. 'Dynamic forms of vitality are part of episodic memories and give life to the narratives we create about our lives' (Stern, 2010: p. 11). Episodic memories are rooted in our neurobiologically grounded 'narratives' or schemas for the self: 'I am good and competent and the world is to be trusted' vs. 'My urges are bad and the world is to be distrusted' (Narvaez, 2011). These then shape the superego that guides life. Let's examine these ideas more closely.

Early experience (and subsequent significant experience) shapes social and moral affordances (what we perceive as action possibilities) and the rationales we provide for our actions. That is, our neurobiological narrative (how our body reacts to events) and social capacities that are built initially in early life lead to personal life narratives of justification, which are flavoured by our culture. Early life sets up the narratives – neurobiological and personal – that guide actions, dispositional patterns of Being (person by situation consistency). The companionship care of the evolved nest fosters open heart-mindedness – it is nurtured by an empathic lifestyle and expected of the child as she[1] matures. Under natural conditions the newborn begins life with a feeling of being real and alive and a '*sense* of being an entity' (Laing, 1959 [1990]: p. 41). When a young child's evolved needs are met through companionship care, including experiences of ongoing intersubjectivity with familiar, loving others, cooperation with self and others becomes an intuitive baseline for life (Narvaez, 2014; Trevarthen, 2005). A healthy person has 'a sense of his presence in the world as a real, alive, whole,' allowing the child to experience others 'as equally real, alive, whole, and continuous' so that when this 'basically *ontologically* secure person' encounters 'the hazards of life, social, ethical, spiritual, biological,' she does so with a 'centrally firm sense of his own and other people's reality and identity' (Laing, 1959[1990]: p. 39). Indeed, longitudinal studies show that a 'mutually-responsive orientation' with the caregiver leads to the child's development of empathy, conscience, and cooperation – the development of a prosocial moral self (e.g. Kochanska, 2002; Kochanska et al., 1995). A person raised in a nest-providing, supportive community that provides extensive mentoring for living well in the landscape will have good self-regulation and centre life actions on co-ordinated relations with others (Narvaez, 2013).

Researchers find little sense of ego in small-band hunter-gatherer societies. Aggressive behaviour might emerge during the autonomy surges in toddlerhood or adolescence, but is redirected in a prosocial manner. Skilled companionship care by members of the community provides the appropriate levels of stimulation to maintain adaptive levels of arousal, as in responsive mother-child dyads (Schore, 1991). In this way, species-typical developmental systems foster individuals who largely stay 'on course' as human beings with minor corrections from the community along the way. The slight corrections of teasing rather than coercion keep the individual from becoming arrogant (Lee, 1979). In this way, barring occasional failings, the mature individual behaves in a mostly virtuous manner – inner neurobiological impulses are coordinated with intuitions which are coordinated with explicit understandings that are communally oriented. In a species-typical environment the superego is embodied practical wisdom, sets of associative learnings guided by the mentoring one has received, undergirded by well-functioning self-regulatory neurobiological structures. Practical wisdom allows for living well within the world one perceives with the capacities one has.

Next, we contrast species-typical with species-atypical experience. When the developmental niche or evolved nest is degraded, the species-typical development of the self and of moral virtue is thrown off kilter.

Species-atypical childhoods

What happens when babies do not receive species-typical nurturing? Unfortunately, this is a common occurrence in civilized nations today, where parents often go back to work shortly after birth and send the baby to a child-care centre, or practice 'baby independence' techniques like isolated sleeping and sleep training. At least two things happen physiologically. First, babies experience toxic stress when they are not given what they evolved to need. Not developing within the evolved developmental system leads to physiological distress that for example, increases cortisol levels that melt synapses and creates lifelong stress reactivity (Lupien et al., 2009; Thomas et al., 2007), even bringing about depressive reactions that alter gene expression (Kang et al., 2012) and prevents the self-regulatory systems and networks for prosocial orientations (Schore, 2001, 2003a, 2003b) from growing because the energies toward survival are misdirected under toxic stress. In other words, babies do not receive the appropriate stimulation to grow what is neurobiologically scheduled to grow at that time, much of which is governed by the developing right brain hemisphere that advances more rapidly in the early months and years of life. Human brains are 'plastic,' but not that plastic: children can be left with gaps in various systems undergirding emotional intelligence, physical health, mental health, social and moral capacities, which may not show up immediately but will emerge after further maturation dependent on the earlier, missing, foundations. In a way, development becomes pseudo-development where the caregiving environment not only fails to provide a 'protective shield' for ego development (Khan, 1973), the caregiving environment is misshaping the child's fundamental biological structures. Some gaps are difficult if not impossible to repair later. When needs are thwarted, neurobiological systems will be under- or mis-developed, from vagus nerve, to immune system and stress response. Dysregulation can easily be stimulated by the unfamiliar, as the neurobiological underpinnings of flexible allostasis are impaired, leading to cacostatic response (too much – aggression, or too little – withdrawal) and to long periods of imbalance.

The second general physiological outcome is that foundations for the child's psychology are poorly structured. Inadequate early experience undermines the psychosocial development that is species-typical for human beings. If the child is left to 'cry-it-out' (ignored when distressed and needy), for example, then the child learns that both her body and the world are untrustworthy. She learns to withdraw from living life very fully. She learns procedurally not to rely on such a worrisome world. Anxiety is built into her physiology and becomes part of her personhood. Without companionship care, the infant's trajectory is shifted away from developing full social capacities (Trevarthen, 2005). Unless intensive experience occurs during another sensitive period, the child may remain socially 'naive' or awkward, lacking full capabilities for the social 'dancing' of his culture. These mis-developments deeply influence self-formation.

The psychological impacts are long-lasting. Attachment theory describes the types of attachment a baby builds with the caregiver based on the capacities of the caregiver for responsiveness and social relations (Schore, 2013). When the caregiver is warmly and contingently responsive to the child's needs, the child builds a secure attachment, which represents the development of neurobiological flexibility for social contexts. Both avoidant and anxious attachment styles emerge from experience with an inconsistently responsive caregiver, establishing poor neurobiological structures that are vital for social relations and prevent flexible, egalitarian relational attunement with others in the present moment. Undercare in early life misdirects development into dysregulation, self-centeredness, and social awkwardness, accompanied by aggression and/or depression (Sroufe et al., 2005).

Some caregivers are incapable of mutual, intersubjective recognition and thereby thwart the development of the many-layered micro skills of relational attunement scheduled to develop in the first year (Stern, 2010).

> Rejection of the child's 'gifts,' like any failure to make adequate response, leads to a sense of badness, unlovableness in the self, with melancholia as its culminating expression.
>
> (Fairbairn, 1952: p. 50)

Without recognition as a separate subject, the child will feel negated and move into premature cortical processing, in effect cooperating with the undermining of social and emotional intelligence. Winnicott (1957) identified the false self that can occur with a highly intelligent child. Instead of providing for the child's needs immediately, the caregiver is able to delay their provision because the child learns to dissociate from bodily and psychological needs. The caregiver colludes with the child's capacity to think apart from the body. This act of stepping out of the soma, splits the psyche from the soma to build a false self, an intellectualizer. It might lead to higher achievement later, but at what cost? Intellectualizers are deeply anxious and compensate with achievements in the external world – not always positive ones. The early proto-self is highly insecure. The core self has little confidence or trust. Energy goes into a false self with the life of a mechanized self --- operating in a perceived mechanized world.

Without intervention, a basic sense of unlovableness follows the individual throughout the life course (Balint, 1968). Illusions become an integral part of the self and the self-hardens around self-preservation in order to avoid the pain of re-traumatization (Narvaez, 2014, 2016b). Self-protectionism is apparent in internalizing and externalizing modes which are based on a faulty sense of self. The first self protectionism mode is apparent in the persecutor voice that is internalized, which Daniel Shaw (2014) mimics in reaction to a narcissist caregiver:

> 'No. Do not believe in yourself, do not hope, do not dare. You will only be hurt again.' As the voice becomes more fearful of re-traumatization, it becomes more laden with rejection and hostility, dissociatively identified with and mimicking the traumatizing narcissist caregiver: 'You nothing, you loser! No one could or would ever love you, you're disgusting! Give up!'
>
> (p. 8)

When this mindset trumps other values, it becomes an ethic, an ethic of compliance – abandonment of self and submission to the other (Narvaez, 2014).

The second form of self-preservation is apparent in externalizing, a domination orientation in which the individual aims for and fears the loss of superior power and must insist on the priority of their own subjectivity:

> giving and taking is now based not on good will and gratitude, but on strategic calculations aimed at maintaining dominance, and, at the deepest level, aimed at preventing being destroyed by the other – being the destroyer, not the destroyed.
>
> (Shaw, 2014: p. 6)

This mindset can become a combative ethic – forceful control of others. In both types of early self-protectionism – compliant or combative – intersubjectivity never gets off the ground, collapsing from the failure of mutual recognition as a starting point, and thwarting the otherwise subsequent building of social skills and schemas for living that would follow from experiences of recognition and resonance with others.

Externalizing can also take more intellectual forms, such as dissociated contempt for the needs and vulnerability of self and others, and a reliance on intellect (detached imagination) or an obsessive-fuelled activism (righteous imagination) (Narvaez, 2014, 2016b). Shaw (2014) describes these more intellectual ethics:

> The person maintains 'a manic grandiosity and contempt for others, with a sense of entitlement and self-justification rather than succumbing to a sense of helplessness and despairing of being able to feel recognized, instead develops as an adult into someone who arranges to wield the power to bestow, or not bestow, recognition upon others.'
>
> (p. 8)

This defensive mode maintains a sense of superiority by attending to the inferiority in others.

In short, the morality of a mis-developed self-resides in self-protectionism – forms of self-preservation that are compulsively externalizing, internalizing, or dissociative. Objectively speaking, these orientations typically are not considered ethical because they are self-focused. Yet, subjectively speaking, the individual justifies them as ethical (Gilligan, 1997). Nevertheless, over the course of the 20th century (when the evolved nest deteriorated extensively and social stress skyrocketed), philosophers and others developed rationales for egoism (Shaver, 2015; Weiss, 2012).

Superego as scripted persecutor

When emotion systems and intuitions for the social life have been impaired by under-care (lack of the evolved nest), there is limited self-regulation, a tendency towards impulsivity, where hedonistic or self-oriented 'passions' take over, or else emotions are severely curtailed and the individual prefers a scripted life. In any case, the insecure self harbours a sense of abandonment and badness, which subconsciously flavours interpretation of life experience and propels behaviours to avoid those feelings, demonstrated in neurobiological and social inflexibility ('stiffness' of the mind or 'heart') (Goldberg, 2002). A bracing self results from lack of supportive care (e.g., lack of intersubjectivity, patterns of being left alone in distress, physical isolation) or from later trauma. A bracing, vigilant orientation to social life predominates, though it may be displayed subtly as a lack of openness to unfamiliar ideas or people: self vs. other, human vs. nature, us vs. them – such dualisms emerge from the move to self-protection and a brittle superego develops to go with it.

A brittle superego requires scripts to get along and cannot adequately respond to newness. It is guided by efforts to avoid overwhelming panic. The individual braces the self against the world. The ontologically insecure person is preoccupied with ensuring his survival but it becomes survival as a robopath (Yablonsky, 1972). Already feeling unreal, the insecure person

> may feel more unreal than real; in a literal sense, more dead than alive; precariously differentiated from the rest of the world, so that his identity and autonomy are always in question. . . . He may not possess an over-riding sense of personal consistency or cohesiveness. He may feel more insubstantial than substantial, and unable to assume that the stuff he is made of is genuine, good, valuable. And he may feel his self as partially divorced from his body . . . the ordinary circumstances of living threaten his *low threshold* of security.
>
> (Laing, 1959 [1990]: p. 42)

At least machines are predictable. Scripts work with machines. What a relief.

> If the individual cannot take the realness, aliveness, autonomy, and identity of himself and others for granted, then he has to become absorbed in contriving ways of trying to be real, of keeping himself or others alive, of preserving his identity . . . to prevent himself losing his self.
>
> (Laing, 1959 [1990]: pp. 42–43)

A mechanized, industrialized world of machines seems much safer to one so damaged.

In my view, psychoanalysis has documented the many ways that the biosocial co-construction of a self can go wrong, based on how and when the mis-care occurred. The child whose continuum of relational connection is broken necessarily splits the self for self-protection (which becomes a lifelong compulsion). Though variably formed, the split self is a bracing self. A split self makes virtue untenable and inflates a domineering superego. The domineering superego begins its work in the pre-verbal years when foundations for world-view are established. It comes about from the non-verbal mistreatment of caregivers, later embellished by verbal commands and the emotional and physical distress felt from social communications from adults. The social self is impaired and the individual compensates with a false or pretend self – one that, in terms of morality, follows rules when watched but doesn't feel them 'all the way down' ('know how'). Instead, the child is forced to learn an obedience morality, a set of memorizable rules for social life ('knowing that'). Intellect is separated from and dys-coordinated with dys-regulated emotions and neurobiology. Worse, the individual constantly needs external rules or a script to follow because the sense of broken internal reality does not provide reliable guidance. Morality has no regulated sense of self on which to ground itself. As a result, rules to follow are required to keep the dys-regulated individual in line. Generally, rules are for novices in a domain (Dreyfus & Dreyfus, 1990); the individual with a truncated self remains a social novice throughout life (barring intervention). Rules are needed when intuitive virtue is lacking (or, in the case of a generally well-developed individual, when distress leads to temporary self-protectionism). Individuals with minimal self-regulating capacities require constant effortful control to keep themselves in line to follow rules; not surprisingly, when energy runs out they misbehave, a common occurrence in those from toxically stressful homes (Niehoff, 1999).

This Section has described what happens when under-care predominates. The early mis-care breaks the continuum of relationship, leaving gaps between personal desires and social life, trust of self, trust of others and being in the world. These gaps propel one into a false self, divorced from emotional presence, from being embodied. The dys-regulated body is uncomfortable to occupy, since its functions were not established properly with good care. The body-soma split is part of civilization's undermining of child development and the nurturing that humans require for normal-optimal development. As a result, species-atypical development systems set up lifelong and society-wide problems that must be dealt with through coercion because many individuals have selves that are fragmented, robopathic (Yablonsky, 1972), or empty (Cushman, 1995).

Conclusion

Early experience sets up the moral universe a child will carry with her throughout life, barring later transformation. Species-typical early experience brings about a different moral universe than the species-atypical upbringing. Most children in the last centuries have experienced a species-atypical nest. The shifted baselines for childrearing, away from the evolved nest, contributes to a shift in understanding what is considered to be normal human behaviour and human nature. Superego function has shifted from one of practical wisdom to that of domineering persecutor. Instead of developing with and supporting wise behaviour of an open-hearted relational self, the persecuting superego develops with, and encourages, a self that is braced and self-protective against the world. Behaviours that emerge from a 'protectionist' orientation are win-lose, all or nothing, or zero tolerance, making it difficult to cooperate across perceived divisions (which are everywhere when you are socio-emotionally impaired).

What happens in a society characterized by mis-developed selves? They continue to mis-develop the next generations through under-care and abuse because the adult caregivers are themselves splintered, robopathic, or empty. Denial of needs and punishment continue these patterns and make explicit rules increasingly necessary for governance, as trust, self-control, and social know-how decrease. Sociopathy becomes widespread and integrated into institutional structures and pathways to success, as has apparently occurred in the USA (Derber, 2013). Everyone forgets how to raise a human being to be virtuous from the ground up. They forget what virtue development requires of adults and communities. Adults instead get caught up in relative trivialities – rules for this or that to show loyalty. They lose a connection to the Whole.

The story of civilized superegos contrasts with pre-civilized societies in multiple ways. Our human heritage is one of cooperation and social engagement, which emerge from providing the evolved nest, the species-typical way to raise a child. In SBHG, the self is primarily communal not individual. The self is a river of shifting between non-reflective self-activities and communal levels of being – which include the bio-community (animals, plants, and other earth entities), guided by mostly implicit practical wisdom. Moral virtue notably emerges without coercion in an affectionate community. Moreover, if a person in the SBHG communities moves toward id or ego, the community is there to bring them back to a communally centered self.

Strikingly, a vital part of our species-typical humanity is earth-centered as well, formed in and with a relational embeddedness in the earth community. Other-than-human entities (animals, plants, rivers, mountains) are sensed to be part of one's community. With this in mind, we can re-envision the communal superego's role. In a species-typical environment, caring and responsibility would extend to the bio-community. Practical wisdom would be sustainable and aimed at bio-community flourishing. In the atypical environments that civilization presents, a communal superego is typically lacking, even under the best conditions, keeping a focus of moral concern and responsibility only on human welfare and treating the rest of nature as objects or resources for human well-being. There is little sense of safety in living with Nature, but instead a fear of one's humanity (considered animality) and Nature generally. Thus, un-nestedness (growing up with a degraded nest) fosters also the lack of rootedness in a particular locale on the planet, which can lead easily to the type of ecologically destructive behaviour we see widespread in civilized nations today (Narvaez et al., in press).

Some say that readopting the wise ways of humanity's sustainable past are wishful thinking, or even romantic delusions. I agree with Edmundsen (2015) that people today have become cynical and lowered their standards, their ideals. Our baselines have shifted downward across the lifespan, from expectations for child raising, to expectations for adult behaviour, leading to minimal cultural supports for human flourishing. We are surrounded with media and discourse that tells us 'there is no other way,' that the price of progress is discontented people and a ravaged planet. This view truly is delusional and romantic as it is often accompanied by a belief that humanity will win in the end with its technological creativity. But the long promised 'wonder-world' of technology has brought about a waste world (Berry, 1988).

How do we heal? When things have not gone optimally in childhood, we can take charge of our own healing in adulthood, by revamping our habitual moral orientations and learning to resonate with compassion instead of fear. The persecutory superego can be mitigated through therapy and other more informal means. Transformational ethical therapy occurs when therapists encourage the *re-formation* of life and relationships, rebuilding brain capacities with 'spiritual' practices that foster calming chemicals (e.g., serotonin, oxytocin) and pull the ego away from the single-self to a larger sense of Common Self. Not only do we need to calm down self-protectionist tendencies and regrow our social capacities, we need to expand our imaginations to a heart-mindedness that is ecologically attached (Narvaez, 2014). Interpretations include the learning from adverse experiences. The individual is encouraged to include the old relationships in their world-view, fostering compassion towards victimizers, gratitude for growth and learning opportunities, and forgiveness for transgressions against the self. One signal for these capacities in adults is the ability to free-play reciprocally with others, experiences that also regrow our self-regulation and social capacities (Siegel, 1999). Although we may always harbour woundedness, we can at least ensure proper nurturance of the next generation.

Cultures too can heal. Norway, once violent, is a leading peacemaker in the world (Fry, 2006). Humans have successfully dismantled several moral travesties, such as the Atlantic slave trade. Our societies can shift back to species-typical child raising and to raising human beings who use their potential for caring for the earth instead of destroying it.

Note

1 The feminine gender pronoun will be used throughout instead of masculine or gender-neutral forms.

References

Balint, M. (1968) *The Basic Fault: Therapeutic Aspects of Regression*. London, Tavistock Publications Ltd.
Beebe, B., Lachmann, F. & Jaffe, J. (1997) Mother-infant interaction structures and presymbolic self and object representations. *Psychoanalytic Dialogues*. 7(2), 133–182.
Benjamin, J. (1988) *Bonds of Love*. New York, Pantheon.
Berry, T. (1988) *The Dream of the Earth*. San Francisco, Sierra Club Books.
Cushman, P. (1995). *Constructing the Self, Constructing America*. Reading, Addison-Wesley.
De Mause, L. (1995) *The History of Childhood*. New York, Psychohistory Press.

Derber, C. (2013) *Sociopathic Society*. Boulder, Paradigm Press.
Dreyfus, H.L. & Dreyfus, S.E. (1990) What is moral maturity? A phenomenological account of the development of ethical expertise. In: D. Rasmussen (ed.) *Universalism vs. Communitarianism*.Boston, MIT Press, pp. 237–264.
Edmundsen, M. (2015) *Self and Soul: In Defense of Ideals*. Cambridge, MA, Harvard University Press.
Fairbairn, W.R.D. (1952) *Psychoanalytic Studies of the Personality*. London, Tavistock Publications Ltd.
Fry, D.P. (2006) *The Human Potential for Peace: An Anthropological Challenge to Assumptions About War and Violence*. New York, Oxford University Press.
Gilligan, J. (1997) *Violence: Reflections on a National Epidemic*. New York, Vintage.
Goldberg, E. (2002) T*he Executive Brain: Frontal Lobes and the Civilized Brain*. New York, Oxford University Press.
Gómez-Robles, A., Hopkins, W.D., Schapiro, S.J. & Sherwood, C.C. (2015) Relaxed genetic control of cortical organization in human brains compared with chimpanzees. *PNAS* published ahead of print November 16, 2015, doi:10.1073/pnas.1512646112.
Hewlett, B.S. & Lamb, M.E. (2005) *Hunter-Gatherer Childhoods: Evolutionary, Developmental and Cultural Perspectives*. New Brunswick, NJ, Aldine.
Ingold, T. (2013) Prospect. In: T. Ingold & G. Palsson (eds.) *Biosocial Becomings: Integrating Social and Biological Anthropology*. Cambridge, Cambridge University Press, pp. 1–21.
Kang, H.J., Voleti, B., Hajszan, T., Rajkowska, G., Stockmeier, C., Licznerski, P., . . . Duman, R.S. (2012). Decreased expression of synapse-related genes and loss of synapses in major depressive disorder. *Nature Medicine*. 18(9), 1413–1417. http://doi.org/10.1038/nm.2886
Khan, M. (1973) The concept of cumulative trauma. *The Psychoanalytic Study of the Child*. 18, 286–306.
Kochanska, G. (2002) Mutually responsive orientation between mothers and their young children: a context for the early development of conscience. *Current Directions in Psychological Science*. 11(6), 191–195. doi:10.1111/1467-8721.00198.
Kochanska, G., Aksan, N. & Koenig, A.L. (1995) A longitudinal study of the roots of preschoolers' conscience: committed compliance and emerging internalization. *Child Development*. 66, 1752–1769.
Kupperman, J. (2005) Morality, ethics and wisdom. In: R.J. Sternberg & J. Jordan (eds.) *A Handbook of Wisdom: Psychological Perspectives*. New York, Cambridge University Press, pp. 245–271.
Laing, R.D. (1959 [1990]) *The Divided Self*. London, Penguin Books.
Lanius, R.A., Vermetten, E. & Pain, C. (eds.) (2010) *The Impact of Early Life Trauma on Health and Disease: The Hidden Epidemic*. New York, Cambridge University Press.
Lee, R. B. (1979). *The !Kung San: Men, Women, and Work in a Foraging Community*. Cambridge, Cambridge University Press.
Loewald, H.W. (1979). The waning of the Oedipus Complex. *Journal of the American Psychoanalytic Association*. 27, 751–775.
Lupien, S.J., McEwen, B.S., Gunnar, M.R., & Heim, C. (2009) Effects of stress throughout the lifespan on the brain, behaviour and cognition. *Nature Reviews Neuroscience*. 10(6), 434–445.
Martin, C.L. (1999) *The Way of the Human Being*. New Haven, CT, Yale University Press.

Miller, A. (1983 [1990]) *For Your Own Good: Hidden Cruelty in Child-Rearing and the Roots of Violence*. New York, Noonday Press.

Narvaez, D. (2011) The ethics of neurobiological narratives. *Poetics Today*. 32(1), 81–106.

Narvaez, D. (2013) The 99% – development and socialization within an evolutionary context: growing up to become "A good and useful human being." In: D. Fry (ed.) *War, Peace and Human Nature: The Convergence of Evolutionary and Cultural Views*. New York, Oxford University Press, pp. 643–672.

Narvaez, D. (2014) *Neurobiology and the Development of Human Morality: Evolution, Culture and Wisdom*. New York, W.W. Norton & Company, Inc.

Narvaez, D. (2015) The co-construction of virtue: epigenetics, neurobiology and development. In: N.E. Snow (ed.) *Cultivating Virtue*. New York, Oxford University Press, pp. 251–277.

Narvaez, D. (2016a) Baselines for virtue. In J. Annas, D. Narvaez, & N. Snow (eds.) *Developing the virtues: integrating perspectives*. New York, Oxford University Press, pp. 14–33.

Narvaez, D. (2016b) *Embodied Morality: Protectionism, Engagement and Imagination*. New York, Palgrave Macmillan.

Narvaez, D., Braungart-Rieker, J., Miller, L., Gettler, L. & Hastings, P. (2016) (eds.) *Contexts for Young Child Flourishing: Evolution, Family and Society*. New York, Oxford University Press.

Narvaez, D., Four Arrows, Halton, E., Collier, B., Nozick, R. & Enderle, G. (eds.) (in press) *Indigenous Sustainable Wisdom: First Nation Knowhow for Global Flourishing*. New York, Peter Lang.

Narvaez, D., Panksepp, J., Schore, A. & Gleason, T. (eds.) (2013) *Evolution, Early Experience and Human Development: From Research to Practice and Policy*. New York, Oxford University Press.

Narvaez, D., Valentino, K., McKenna, J., Fuentes, A. & Gray, P. (eds.) (2014) *Ancestral Landscapes in Human Evolution: Culture, Childrearing and Social Wellbeing*. New York, Oxford University Press.

Niehoff, D. (1999) *The Biology of Violence: How Understanding the Brain, Behavior, and Environment can Break the Vicious Circle of Aggression*. New York, Free Press.

Plumwood, V. (2002) *Environmental Culture: The Ecological Crisis of Reason*. London, Routledge.

Reddy, V. (2008) *How Infants Know Minds*. Cambridge, MA, Harvard University Press.

Schore, A.N. (1991) Early superego development: the emergence of shame and narcissistic affect regulation in the practicing period. *Psychoanalysis and Contemporary Thought*. 14, 187–250.

Schore, A.N. (2001) Effects of a secure attachment relationship on right brain development, affect regulation, and infant mental health. *Infant Mental Health Journal*. 22(1–2), 7–66.

Schore, A.N. (2003a) *Affect Dysregulation & Disorders of the Self*. New York, W.W. Norton & Company, Inc.

Schore, A.N. (2003b) *Affect Regulation and the Repair of the Self*. New York, W.W. Norton & Company, Inc.

Schore, A.N. (2013). Bowlby's "Environment of evolutionary adaptedness": recent studies on the interpersonal neurobiology of attachment and emotional development. In D. Narvaez, J. Panksepp, A. Schore & T. Gleason (eds.) *Evolution, Early Experience and*

Human Development: From Research to Practice and Policy. New York, Oxford University Press, pp. 31–67.

Shaver, R. (2015) Egoism. In: E.N. Zalta (ed.) *The Stanford Encyclopedia of Philosophy.* Available at: https://plato.stanford.edu/archives/spr2015/entries/egoism/. [Accessed 17 July 2017].

Shaw, D. (2014) *Traumatic Narcissism: Relational Systems of Subjugation.* New York, Routledge.

Siegel, D.J. (1999) *The Developing Mind: How Relationships and the Brain Interact to Shape Who We Are.* New York, Guilford Press.

Sroufe, L.A., Egeland, B., Carlson, E.A. & Collins, W.A. (2005) *The Development of the Person: The Minnesota Study of Risk and Adaptation from Birth to Adulthood.* New York, Guilford Press.

Stern, D. (2010) *Forms of Vitality: Exploring Dynamic Experience in Psychology, the Arts, Psychotherapy, and Development.* New York, Oxford University Press.

Thomas, R.M., Hotsenpiller, G. & Peterson, D.A. (2007) Acute psychosocial stress reduces cell survival in adult hippocampal neurogenesis without altering proliferation. *The Journal of Neuroscience.* 27(11), 2734–2743.

Trevarthen, C. (1999) Musicality and the intrinsic motive impulse: evidence from human psychobiology and infant communication. *Musicae Scientiae.* Special Issue, 157–213.

Trevarthen, C. (2005) Stepping away from the mirror: pride and shame in adventures of companionship – reflections on the nature and emotional needs of infant intersubjectivity. In: C.S. Carter, L. Ahnert, K.E. Grossmann, S.B., Hrdy, M.E. Lamb, S.W. Porges & N. Sachser (eds.) *Attachment and Bonding: A New Synthesis.* Cambridge, MA, MIT Press, pp. 55–84.

Tronick, E. (1989) Emotions and emotional communication in infants. *American Psychologist.* 44, 112–119.

Watson, J.B. (1928) *Psychological Care of Infant and Child.* New York, W. W. Norton & Company, Inc.

Weiss, G. (2012). *Ayn Rand Nation: The Hidden Struggle for America's Soul.* New York, Palgrave Macmillan.

Winnicott, D.W. (1957) *The Child and the Family.* London, Tavistock Publications Ltd.

Yablonsky, L. (1972) *Robopaths: People as Machines.* New York, Penguin Books.

Author Note

The author recognizes the Virtue, Happiness and the Meaning of Life project funded by The John Templeton Foundation in supporting this work.

Part II

The role of the superego in different states of mind

Chapter 5

'Sorry doesn't make a dead man alive'

The superego behind depressive states of mind

Celia Harding

The train was about to pull into the next station. A group of young people had congregated by the door ready to disembark. Suddenly I heard a gasp and noticed one of the group rush back to her seat. She returned to the door just as the train came to a halt. "Sorry, sorry, sorry . . . my phone . . ." she panted. One companion remarked laconically, "Sorry doesn't make a dead man alive." Overhearing this exchange I recognised in the woman's unnecessary and repetitive apologies someone prone to depression, attempting to forestall a torrent of self-criticism and the shame which could engulf her. She was met by an incarnation of her dreaded superego in her companion's words: an iron fist disguised in the velvet glove of his nonchalantly delivered verdict which gives not one millimetre of margin for error. The smallest mistake is equated with the worst crime. In a flash I recognised in this cameo a characterisation of the superego behind deep-seated depressive states resonant with Freud's (1923) description:

> [Turning to melancholia] we find that the excessively strong super-ego which has obtained a hold upon consciousness rages against the ego with merciless violence, as if it had taken possession of the whole of the sadism available in the person concerned . . . we should say that the destructive component had entrenched itself in the super-ego and turned against the ego.
>
> (p. 53)

Underlying this deadly superego stance towards the self for whatever mistake or failing was committed, in 'weakness, ignorance or own deliberate fault', we meet a bald statement of absolute, certain self-evident truth which precludes the following: question and exploration; discovering proportion and understanding from the context of what happened; a place for doubt and uncertainty; the possibility of forgiveness and/or making amends; the redeeming possibilities of learning from experience. In short, the psychological conditions to mourn the wrong and put things right, are absent (Klein, 1937). The accused ego is trapped in helplessness and despair with, in that moment, apparently nowhere to go except to 'let[s] itself die' (Freud, 1923: p. 58; Sodre, 2005: p. 125).

In this chapter I apply the model of superego functioning proposed in the Introduction to depressive states of mind. I explore the dynamic interactions of aspects of the self-involved in superego activities and a 'back story' of how a depressed internal situation arrives at this lamentable place. I then turn to the psychic work needed for depressed patients to forge a route from depression through mourning and reparation rather than becoming trapped in the dead-end of 'let me die'.[1]

The superego as a moral quartet

The superego utilises resources from the person's entire psychical repertoire, to exercise their moral function: 'the total personality is involved in it; but it is an unconscious process' (Rickman, 1951: p. 322). To illustrate the composition of the superego in 'action' terms (Schafer, 1983) I propose the analogy of a musical quartet: each musician contributing to the music they perform together.[2]

The first contributor to superego music is the ego ideal (see Horne, Chapter 2), the basis for the superego function of regulating our self-esteem through pride and shame (Schore, 1991). Glasser (1996) calls this the 'prescriptive' superego enshrining the goals and ideals we strive towards to become the person we feel we 'should' be. The foundations of the superego established during early infancy (see Hinshelwood, Chapter 1, Narvaez, Chapter 4) develop as young children find their feet and start to explore the world around them. Initially, children experience themselves as extensions of mother assumed to be all-powerful, capable of anything and everything. They return to mother from their forays feeling delighted with their cleverness, assuming her affirmation of their magnificence. When mother's response does not match their expectations they feel shame, distress and depressive reactions (Schore, 1991). With time and repeated experiences of these painful discrepancies between over-estimations of self and mother's (hopefully) more realistic estimations, children begin to realise that they are not so grand and all-powerful, but actually little, weak, dependent on, and separate from, mother. The crucial contingency at this juncture is whether (m)other can understand and help the child to accommodate his shame and disappointments in himself and her and help him discover his realistic capabilities and take pleasure in and confidence from, his realistic efficacy (Novick & Novick, 1991). Without such understanding and help the child is likely to patch-up his self-esteem with omnipotent illusions about himself and what he can be and do. This structures into the psyche a predisposition to collapses of self-worth and depressive episodes, because the person inevitably fails to reach his unattainably high standards and subjects himself to shaming superego music.

The second contributor to superego music includes the social norms and moral values that regulate the expressions of our impulses as we interact with others.[3] Parents instil these social rules as they supervise their child's attempts to get along with others. This is the 'proscriptive' function of the superego which, through 'oughts', 'ought nots' and guilty feelings, regulates and constrains our expressions of impulses and wishes in our internal and external behaviours (Glasser,

1996). Parental frowns and 'no' in response to a child's unfettered expressions of their impulses, alongside the smiles and approvals in response to the child's self-restraint, become internalised and enshrined in his superego music. Again, the crucial contingency for children learning to manage their aggressive feelings is whether or not their parents (representing the social and cultural world) understand and contain their overwhelming frustrated rages consistently and firmly with love (Parsons, 2006, 2009). This helps children learn that their loving feelings can help them contain aggression and frustration (Freud, A. 1949) which lays the basis of benign, protective superego capacities (Schafer, 1960). Without this understanding and loving firmness, children are abandoned to fearing that their aggression endangers their relationships with others, which in turn hinders the developmental task of channelling aggressive energy into life enhancing activities (Parsons, 2006, 2009).

A key developmental stage shaping the way children manage their impulses is toilet mastery (Furman, 1982). Rickman (1951) observes that such learning:

> makes a deep impression on the child and colours his attitude, on the one hand to his body and its functions, and on the other to the relation of friendly cooperation with or hostility to those of whose good regard he so greatly depends.
>
> (p. 320)

Through this learning curve, toddlers experiment with saying 'no'. When parents do not 'take no for an answer', the child's omnipotence and narcissism are affronted, evoking furious tantrums. Abraham (1924) regarded mobilisation of a child's aggressive impulses as inevitable accompaniments of learning to 'let go of' and 'hold onto' urine and faeces. He further suggested that anal 'letting go' may become psychically equivalent to sadistic fantasies of getting rid of (murdering) hateful objects, and holding on to and possessing (controlling) aggressively loved objects.

If toddlers enter this developmental phase *already* primed to resort to omnipotence in the face of helplessness, they bring little confidence of their capacities to have an effective impact on the world. Parents with a strong need to assert their control over their child's body and behaviours, deny them opportunities to develop their own self-controls, sense of agency and realistic efficacy during toilet mastery. Lacking appropriate outlets for accumulating frustration and aggression, the child's experiments with self-assertion may become labelled as aggressive and escalate into battles for control. Such experiences obstruct satisfactions in *realistic* achievements and reinforce the resort to omnipotent expectations (Novick & Novick, 2004). Herein lies a basis for a superego tendency to enforce omnipotent requirements of self-control upon the experiencing ego on an assumption that the individual's impulses are omnipotently powerful. This can predispose people to anxieties about channelling their aggressive impulses into claiming their independent, self-assertive and creative capacities; it also leaves them prone to inhibiting self-expression and to anxieties about social interactions: in short, superego-inducing, anxious and guilty depressive music.

The third contributor to superego music is the repressed aggression accumulated in the unconscious id. As children we fear that expressing aggression will provoke our parents to withdraw their love, just as later – after parental approvals and disapprovals have been internalised in the superego – we fear that it will provoke us to withdraw our superego's esteem. However, restraining and frustrating our impulses and wishes by 'sucking it up' has a price: aggression diverted from the objects who evoked it, is relegated to the unconscious and recycled in self-critical and self-punishing attacks leading to shame for (perceived) failures to reach our ego ideals and guilt for harms (actual or imagined) inflicted on others (Piers & Singer, 1953). The aggression that drives our suspicious self-scrutiny and self-condemnations is disguised as self-righteousness and moral justification. People not helped in childhood to develop realistic knowledge and understanding of their impulses and the measure of them, are unable to integrate them adequately into their sense of self. This leaves them prey to harsh and critical self-evaluations later internalised in and meted out by punitive moral superego inclinations. In such internal circumstances, these individuals become susceptible to melancholic-inducing superego music, leaving them feeling abandoned by and undeserving of the loving, understanding and protective aspects of their superego.

The ego is a fourth contributor to superego music, delegating some of its functions to the superego as a 'specialised ego activity' (Bouchard & Lecours, 2004: p. 885) i.e. for moral duties. Thus, our capacities for self-monitoring, self-observation, self-evaluation and self-regulation of our relationships are conducted through a morally augmented view of reality (Britton, 2003: p. 72). Our realities – of self, others and the world – are morally neutral until we superimpose upon them our social rules and values. Those individuals inclined to depressive reactions and states are likely to observe their internal and external behaviours with a zealously self-critical eye as they monitor their successes and failures to live up to their ideals and moral standards. From their stern and judgemental self-disciplinary stance, they are liable to under-estimate their successes and over-estimate failures, denying credit where due and exaggerating lapses. They tightly limit and regulate expressions of impulses and narcissistic needs and wishes, inhibiting those judged likely to offend or harm another's sensibilities and risk their good-standing with others and themselves. As in the example at the beginning, they accord themselves a negligible margin for error and expect likewise from others. They are tormented by an insistent beat of self-directed disapproval in their mental ears which they anticipate will reach a deafening crescendo at any moment.

Evidently, an individual's superego propensities depend on his ego-strengths and weaknesses. Any fault-lines underlying his ego structure, due to developmental deficits (Yorke et al., 1989), or traumata which overwhelm his processing capacities, are likely to compromise both his protective self-and-other appraisals and his capacity to evaluate his moral observations realistically. The severity of the depression attendant on superego activities will also depend on the developmental level to which the ego regresses (Abraham, 1924; Yorke et al., 1989): individuals subjected to the most discordant, harsh superego tones may lose self-cohesion and/or self-differentiation from others under the weight of their guilt and/or shame. In this event, there is likely to be little or no access to the individual's capacity to observe and reflect upon the helplessness and despair that grips him. Another psychic contingency influencing the severity of the depressive state is the extent to which the person identifies with his lost or disappointing object (Freud, 1917) or, 'ideal state of the self [that was] embodied in the relationship with the object' (Sandler & Joffe, 1965: p. 94).[4]

The superego's melancholic-inducing music

Some people can become gripped by depression after punishing themselves excessively with shame and/or guilt, for falling short of their ideals and/or failing to exercise self-required controls over their impulses. They feel deserted by the loving, protective aspects of their limit-setting and self-containing capacities (Schafer, 1960) and abandoned to the mercy of ruthlessly self-critical superego aspects which mete out harsh, self-punishing 'bad feelings'. In the face of this internal assault they sink into despair. They experience their punitive superego figure as other, not-me, the representative-in-mind of past and present authorities. They rarely recognise their own hidden hand selecting and conducting the loud and violently discordant superego music now penetrating their mind's ears: even in projection they feel that others are blaring 'it' *at or into* them, forcefully torturing them.

The inharmonious, dissonant chords of this superego music induces, in depressed individuals, sadness, heaviness, numbness, apathy, irritability and anger. Self-esteem plummets, as a sense of being hateful and hated consumes them. Depressed people withdraw from active life and relationships, locked into a self-preoccupied inner world, feeling worthless, hopeless and helpless. They feel that physical symptoms, including sleep disturbance, fatigue, lack of appetite, will be bound to augur life-threatening illness. Thoughts follow negative trajectories: the self is an inadequate failure, life is impossible to navigate, full of insurmountable obstacles, the future is hopeless. To an observer these beliefs may bear little relation to reality, but to the depressed person 'as it is now' is self-evidently, as it 'always will be'. In severe depressive states, suicidal thoughts may become increasingly insistent.

The immediate psychical context of a depressed state of mind has a history in the sufferer's childhood experiences: a feeling memory of a long forgotten psychological tragedy which they sustained and have survived the best they could.

The antecedents of depression

A degree of unanimity exists within psychoanalysis that depressive illness and reactions originate in losses of objects or ideal states of well-being and consequently mobilised aggression (Sandler & Joffe, 1965; Hartmann & Loewenstein, 1962; Yorke et al., 1989). Managing the emotional fall-out after sustaining losses hinges on the dilemma of ambivalence (Freud, 1917): rage is a natural and inevitable response to loss whether of a loved object (from death, actual absence, unavailability following the birth of a sibling or illness) or of an ideal state expected of self or other. The object or ideal-state is loved and needed to confer well-being and safety (Sandler & Joffe, 1965). When lost, the person's dilemma is how to express his disappointed rage whilst preserving his loved object or ideal. The person who finds these conflicting feelings unmanageable, unconsciously diverts his hostility from his loved object and consigns it to the unconscious; from there the aggression can be recycled for the moral purpose of keeping hostility in check to protect the loved object or ideal from harm.

This psychical solution to turbulent ambivalent feelings towards disappointing objects is most necessary when children have been raised in unloving, unresponsive, inattentive maturational environments. Such children do not receive, consistently and reliably, the loving, thoughtful, protective but firm help needed to constrain angry feelings. Without loving secure attachments to mother, they lack the emotional resources to rein in their aggression and channel it in ways that will please her and preserve her love. In Anna Freud's (1949) view:

> The pathological factor is found in the realm of erotic, emotional development which has been held up through adverse external or internal conditions, such as absence of love objects, lack of emotional response from the adult environment, breaking of emotional ties as soon as they are formed, deficiency of emotional development for innate reasons. Owing to the defects on the emotional side, the aggressive urges are not brought into fusion and thereby bound and partially neutralized, but remain free and seek expression in life in the form of pure, unadulterated, independent destructiveness.
>
> (p. 41f)

Children lacking secure attachments to (m)other are unlikely to develop strong-enough loving feelings to bind their aggressive impulses. Consequently, they are likely to grow up predisposed to depression and/or to develop defences that keep depression at bay at the cost of restricting development of the buoyant ego-strength needed to face the serial losses which are 'facts of life' (Money-Kyrle, 1971).

Money-Kyrle (1971) condenses the 'facts of life' to three fundamentals. First, the reality that we have needs and depend on others outside ourselves to meet them, encapsulated as 'the recognition of the supreme goodness of the breast'. Second, we must accommodate the parental couple as the source of supreme creativity and our exclusion from their special relationship. This means recognising that we are not the centre of the universe, the source of all creativity. Third, loss is a fact integral to life itself: all good things come to an end, time passes and with it we age and die. The losses we incur, when accepting and accommodating the facts of life, are compounded by attendant losses to our omnipotence and narcissism

(Rusczcynski, 2006). Psychic development and growth depend on the ego-strength to accept, mourn and accommodate the 'facts of life' incrementally and cumulatively over a life-time. However, the ego-strength necessary for this task is unlikely to develop when (m)others have not set consistent limits and boundaries on the child's strong wishes and feelings or helped them manage the narcissistic pains of dependence and neediness, exclusion from parental relationships, and life's other losses. Without those ego-developing conditions narcissistic wounds are left in the wake of losses (Sodre, 2000). The losses sustained in birth, weaning, toilet mastery i.e. graduated separations, are mentally registered by children as evidence of their badness and unworthiness, convictions to be reinforced with future losses. When cognisance of loss is intolerable, psychic development stalls; when loss is resisted development is uneven and sticky: a vulnerability to depressive states is likely.

Losses that cannot be faced are bypassed. Freud (1917) and Abraham (1924) recognised one such bypass: those unable to accept the loss of their loved object identify with its lost and disappointing aspects and instal these as part of their ego. This preserves their loved object as idealised and beyond reproach, whilst rage towards the object's disappointing and betraying aspects is diverted to the superego and converted into self-reproaches. Thus, loss of a loved object transmutes into narcissistic loss and a heightened predisposition to depression (Roth, 2001; Sodre, 2005).

A second emergency solution, for those lacking the ego-strength and supportive attachments to bear the pains of loss, is to patch over the punctures left by encountering the 'facts of life' with illusions of omnipotence. These individuals unconsciously instal omnipotent, unrealistic expectations as central to their ego ideal, experiencing themselves as capable of controlling self, objects and world. When these omnipotent expectations are dashed, they inevitably plunge into depressive despair and rage because they lack the psychic equipment for the hard emotional work of accommodating their losses. Omnipotent defences against loss also have the tragic consequence of magnifying the severity of superego reactions. Self-expectations enshrined in the ego ideal include omnipotent powers to control impulses, needs and passage through the world, and spawn commensurately harsh superego reprisals for failures (Novick & Novick, 2004). The depressive-prone person's superego is primed to regard failures of omnipotent powers and controls as warranting withdrawal of love and approval and deserving of harsh punishment until, in hopeless despair, 'let me die'.

In relation to depression, omnipotent solutions to pains of loss and unleashing of furies may be a resort to manic defences. Freud (1917) and Abraham (1924) regarded mania as the triumphant overcoming of the harsh and torturing superego. Manic defences may take many forms including perverse sado-masochistic 'game playing' of cat and mouse between ego and superego in the mind or enacted between patient and therapist in transference and counter-transference dynamics. These perverse reversals of experienced helplessness and worthlessness into active efforts, dedicated to 'outwitting' the persecuting superego, appear to alleviate depressive despair by conferring a pyrrhic sense of self-worth in victory. Another version of a perverse defence against psychically experiencing painful depression may be to externalise and reproduce a representation of the depressed state of mind in the person's immediate environment: he creates for himself a disordered place of dirt, mess, chaos, clutter, and in extreme, dereliction. This can become a way to actually live his self-loathing, as if to become what he believes himself to be, part of the rubbish with which he surrounds himself.

Manic defences may take less convoluted, more functional forms, such as sustaining busy and active lives, including exercise regimes to safely discharge aggressive impulses into 'healthy' channels, leaving no space for depressive feelings to surface. Another example might be 'workaholics' who submit to 'work expectations' to be available 'twenty-four/seven'. Obsessional defences form another route for the person to convince (as it were) their moral overseer that they are in full charge of their aggressive impulses: e.g. familiar symptoms of obsessional-compulsive-disorders such as hand-washing or repeatedly checking designated sources of danger and insecurity. Control of food intake to anorexic proportions may count as evidence of control over greed; bulimic symptoms, laxatives or colonic irrigation, may represent a mind purged of impure impulses or thoughts. Ruminative thought processes and chronic indecision may represent a person's attempts to safeguard themselves against their fears and wishes to do harm if they act and move.

Omnipotent solutions to depressive states of mind appear to give reassurance of the 'safe disposal' of worrying aggressive feelings and a bypass around depression. But omnipotent illusions and magical thinking contain the seeds of their own destruction, liable to fray or break under the pressure of stresses, traumatic experiences and/or illness, which cannot be brought under conscious controls.

A patient who kept feelings of helplessness and worthlessness at bay by 'making things happen', driven by her slave driver superego propensities, developed incapacitating pain in her back and legs which could grind her to a halt at any time. She came face to face with limitations she could not overcome by will. Initially she refused 'to be beaten' but, when she was forced to concede 'defeat', she castigated herself for being weak and useless, convinced that her friends would spurn her for having limitations and needs that had to be accommodated.

At this point, lacking the ego-strength to face the nodal points behind the warded-off depression and to mourn their losses, the person is liable to take refuge in melancholic withdrawal from their objects and the world. Although painful and restrictive, it feels familiar and secure: a psychic equivalent to an ex-prisoner's unconscious motives to re-offend and engineer a return to the containment of prison, where, under lock and key, he can feel safer with self and others.

How then may we envisage more effective and robust remedies for the depressive-prone person predisposed to capitulate to their superego harsh, discordant, melancholic-inducing music or escape into omnipotent, manic solutions?

A therapeutic route out of depression

Abraham (1924) describes a recurring dream reported by one of his depressed patients:

> I was standing in front of my parents' house, where I was born. A line of carts came up the street. The street was otherwise quite still and deserted. Each waggon had two horses in front of it. A driver walked beside the horses and beat them with his whip. The cart had tall sides so that I could not see what was inside. There was something mysterious about it. Underneath it there hung a man, tied up and dragged along by a rope. There was a rope round his neck, and he could only manage to draw a little breath with great difficulty and at long intervals. The sight of this man who could neither go on living nor die affected me very much. Then I saw to my horror that two more carts followed the first one and each presented the same terrible spectacle.
>
> (p. 466)

This dream portrays an intense and entrenched melancholic state of mind and depicts the internal dynamics pertaining between different parts of the self, highlighting the brutal superego 'in charge'. Abraham comments: 'It was evident that the dreamer was represented in at least three different figures: as the onlooker, as the horse and as the bound man' (p. 466), whereas the horse-beating driver is identified with father. This illustrates for me the tendency for a depressed person to experience his tyrannical superego activities as coming from a 'not-me' figure in his mind, an authority with whom he complies or defies, but is unable and ineligible to question. The patient is apparently unconscious of his own authorship of and subscription to his moral judgements – that his hand wields the whip that drives him, and ties the rope which binds him. This coincides with my experience of working with patients in entrenched depressed states of mind. Even one less gripped by depressive reactions, who may speak of "beating myself up", feels at the mercy of their flagellating self, unable to actively engage it in genuine debate.

A patient suddenly found himself profoundly depressed and unable to speak about it. I said eventually that it was as if he had awoken in a nuclear wasteland. It was some time before he was ready to recognise and explore the fury which drove him to push the nuclear button.

Unlike omnipotent remedies or 'the final solution', a therapeutic route from deep-seated depressed states means long-term painstaking work for both therapist and patient, involving attention on three inter-related and mutually enhancing fronts. First, therapists attend to strengthening the ego through providing within the therapeutic relationship aspects of the maturational environment that were deficient or absent in the patient's early relationships.[5] Second, therapists embody a consistent auxiliary benign, protective and thoughtful superego figure, available for patients to internalise in order to moderate their severe and harsher superego tendencies

(Strachey, 1934; Schafer, 1960). Third, therapists facilitate a new collaborative relationship between the patient's ego and superego aspects, to address the subservience of the vulnerable ego in thrall to their tyrannical moral inclinations (Britton, 2003; Reddish, 2014). Patients need help to develop 'mind[s] of their own' (Caper, 1999) with which to re-evaluate their moral views in the light of their present realities and circumstances.

In sum, focusing on these three areas follows Freud's aim for psychoanalysis:

> to strengthen the ego, to make it independent of the super-ego, to widen its field of perception and enlarge its organisation, so that it can appropriate fresh portions of the id. Where id was, there ego shall be.
>
> (Freud, 1932: p. 80)

Britton (2003) and Reddish (2014) have elaborated this endeavour by theorising the process of forging a more independent relationship between ego and superego.

Essential to this task is the 'action language' proposed by Schafer (1983), to convey, with immediacy, the patient's agency in the workings of their own mind. Using 'action language' – as in the previous example – to explore ego, id and superego activities, is important to guard against the dangers of reifying parts of the mind when using these shorthand referents (Harding, Introduction). Use of 'action language' addresses the patient as 'a unitary person' with agency:

> [who is] pursuing incompatible and contradictory courses of action or wishing to do so, experiencing distress in this regard, and attempting to carry out renunciations or develop compromises or highly synthesised solutions of the dilemmas both created and confronted.
>
> (Schafer, 1983: p. 142)

Understanding patients as unified beings, as their own agent, contrasts with a patient's defensive efforts to disclaim agency of himself: '[excluding] certain actions from the concept of oneself and others as active responsible beings' (Schafer, 1983: p. 143).

Action language conveys to patients their agency over themselves: their impulses, self-punishing actions and defensive self-preserving measures. It is the patient who advocates (or refuses) and upholds his standards and expectations and who falls short of, or reaches, them, who resents binding himself to his contradictory values and priorities and who feels ashamed or proud of, and/or guilty about himself.

The ego-strengthening potential of the therapeutic relationship

By providing a reliable relationship over time, therapists offer their patients a secure containing object with whom to access their impulses, feelings and fantasies, particularly in relation to their therapist. With growing trust in the therapist's responsive attention and understanding patients gain more confidence about allowing feelings and impulses to surface for exploration which are liable to set their moral alarm-bells ringing (Strachey, 1934). As patients begin to integrate more of themselves into their experiencing ego, they gradually develop their capacities to differentiate self from other, internal from external, part from whole and past from present.

Depression-prone patients find their aggressive impulses particularly troubling, regarding these as endangering their relationships: feeling bad – as in unhappy – equates with moral badness; they believe their aggressivity makes them in essence morally bad and wrong; they doubt the strength of their love and concern to contain their aggressive and destructive impulses. Such assumptions leave patients apprehensive about exploring the measure of their destructive impulses, fearful of mobilising overwhelming guilt and shame that could plunge them into despair, worthlessness and helplessness. They may be unaware that their aggression is often a self-preservative reaction to the fear of losing something or someone considered essential for well-being and psychological safety.[6] The therapist's understanding and interpretation of anxieties behind a patient's aggressive reactions becomes key to the ego-strengthening task. Under the influence of omnipotent superego assumptions, and under-developed ego capacities, patients are likely to equate temporary with permanent losses. When all aggressive inclinations, minor or serious, equate with murderous violence, patients need their therapist's help to differentiate between grades and shades of feeling and loss. Such patients are also liable to over-estimate their impact on, and influence over, others and the harm they have done and could do. To avoid (self-) reproach they may restrict their self-expressions to doing and being 'right' within the narrow-minded terms of their severely self-critical estimations. Therapists can offer alternative 'multiple perspectives' (Phillips, 2015) from which to evaluate and observe themselves and can introduce the possibility of allowing for realistic uncertainties and doubts when considering issues from different angles rather than playing-safe by doing the (assumed) 'right thing'.

The strengthening of a benign and protective superego

Patients predisposed to depressive states and reactions are liable to approach their therapist with caution, anticipating that her moral evaluations of him will echo his own severe and hasty self-judgements: assuming the worst of him and summarily writing him off. Patients need to test their assumptions many times and in many ways. The therapist's consistent offer of benign, understanding, protective and firm evaluative experiences is essential to provide depressed patients with opportunities to internalise a different moral regulator with which to moderate their ruthlessly harsh superego inclinations. Through processes that Strachey (1934) describes, the patient begins to feel safe-enough to risk introducing his more troubling wishes and impulses into the relationship under the therapist's oversight as a thoughtful, realistic and accepting auxiliary superego. When patients discover that their therapist receives their shameful and guilty impulses and experiences with equanimity, respect and thoughtful understanding, they may integrate these into their sense of self. However, for the protective and beloved superego (Schafer, 1960) to gain resilience, the patient needs to experience his self-critical and self-punishing tendencies, and his shame and guilt, in his therapist. This means that the therapist's benign superego functions will inevitably, and necessarily, lapse. The patient will be unconsciously alert for any hint of the therapist's irritation with and criticism of him, any suggestion that she unjustly denied him credit where due, any exaggeration of his misdeeds and failures, and any adoption of a moral high-ground towards him and judgement of him from that lofty position. In such events, patients are liable to retaliate by turning their punishing critical sights on the therapist, alerting her to her unconscious attack that was disguised as a therapeutic intervention. These occasions provide the therapeutic couple with opportunities to explore what happened between them; for the therapist to own her part in the exchanges, make sense of them, and offer these understandings to the patient in ways that demonstrate that their relationship can survive spats and failures. Such lapses and restorative work can serve to strengthen the benign protective superego function both within the relationship and in the patient's mind.

Claiming agency over the superego

For many reasons, depressed patients disclaim their self-directed moralising and experience it as 'other', a not-me presence in the shadows of their minds. The superego originates from the young child's social and cultural worlds of his relationships with others and this reinforces a sense that his values are instilled and enforced from outside. Then there is his unconscious knowledge that his criticisms of self and others are driven and infused by his recycled aggression, which is uncomfortable to admit. In addition, news delivered by superego faculties is often unwelcome, generates conflicts with impulses and wishes and causes him troublesome management difficulties. Before the patient is able to reclaim his superego activities as his own, he needs help to recognise and become more conscious of his moral doings as part of him. Only then might he be able to work towards developing a different relationship between his conflicting wishes and feelings. Bouchard and Lecours (2004) outline the course that this developmental trajectory may take. It begins when the therapist attunes to signs of an as yet unrecognised aspect of self at work in the patient's mind, perhaps dimly sensed by him as a threatening figure or presence in the background.

> *One patient represented this awareness in the presence of a hostile and critical student who submitted an excoriating complaint about him to his manager.*
>
> *Another patient envisaged this 'vicious' presence as like a cancer eating away his insides and though it felt like an invasive something that he was absorbing, he also knew that it was his own doing to himself.*

The therapist is alerted to this threatening presence by signs of deflation in her patient's mood as if precipitated by some unconscious inhibiting and prohibiting force. This may herald the culmination of a 'back-story' involving the patient's wish to accommodate some new aspect of self or experience in his mind, but he had unconsciously snuffed-out this expansionary hope. Feeling deflated the patient retreated to the familiar safety of depressed hopelessness and helplessness.

> *A patient dared to let himself plan and look forward to a holiday but, in anticipation of a disappointment and things going wrong, missed his flight, gave up and went home. He later understood that he had extinguished his own excitement to be on the safe side.*

As the therapist draws the patient's attention to the presence of this hostile, threatening but shadowy aspect of himself, the patient may start to give it a shape and form (see examples above). This helps him to become more conscious of this unknown part of himself, and more attuned to registering such deflating interventions. His moral values come into sharper focus, the values to which he subscribes and with which he – on automatic – regulates his impulses and self-esteem. He discovers his values are frequently contradictory and conflicting and notices discrepancies between values he inherited and those he adopted because they make sense to him. He may recognise feeling certain freedoms and constraints when he applies his values in particular circumstances. He may realise that his choices are often unconsciously determined by his fears and wishes about the impulses behind his intentions.

Patients use their moral values to safeguard themselves from crossing lines that they fear could risk their good-standing with self and others. When patients start to attend to this process, they have opportunities to re-examine their values, set them aside and think through how and why they are applying them from a more realistic standpoint than their usual, automatic, morally infused assumptions. This process may equip patients to re-evaluate their own judgements about what they think is 'right' or 'wrong' in the particular circumstances. In shorthand, we are considering here the ego claiming and exercising a position of independence from the superego.

> *A patient spoke of his moral dilemma: his elderly aunt gave him money to buy himself a present in advance of his graduation ceremony. After he graduated she sent him a cheque with a congratulations card. The patient, who helped his aunt a great deal, wondered whether he should bank the cheque on the grounds that he had earned it, or tear it up on the grounds that she was muddled. Thinking it through he realised that there was a him who had felt hard done-by throughout his life and who was unconsciously seeing this as an opportunity to compensate, rather than work through, past deprivations. Having worked out what this situation meant to him he could then refer to his values and do what felt right to him.*

Conclusion

Patients enabled to claim their agency over their impulses, self-punitive tendencies and anxiety-driven defences, may become less prone to succumb to depressive states of mind. Under the modifying auspices of a more firmly established 'beloved and protective' superego, the patient's healthy ego capacities are supported. When the patient needs to re-activate his omnipotent, murderous superego propensities he is more equipped to draw on his more protective, realistic, proportionate, compassionate, forgiving and reparative resources to recover and learn from his experiences. Having forged a more independent and collaborative relationship with his moral quartet the patient can use this aspect of himself as a resource rather than as a cacophony of deafening sound to blast him into submission. He is now more equipped to mourn his losses and disappointments, to find ways of repairing damages done and sustained, and get on with living rather than dying.

Acknowledgements: I am indebted to Marianne Parsons and David Riley for their insights and guidance without which I could not have written this chapter; also, to my patients whose experiences of depression inform this chapter.

Notes

1 In this chapter I do not address the valuable distinctions between mourning and melancholia as these have been amply and extensively explored since Freud's seminal paper (1917) recently re-visited and re-envisioned by Leader (2008). Instead I have concentrated on addressing the developmental achievements which are necessary before mourning and reparation become possible.
2 For clarity of distinction I usually use a female referent generically to denote the therapist and a male referent to denote patient (or child).
3 References to impulse restraint include expressions of sexuality and aggression, but in the context of this chapter I focus on the latter.
4 I borrow from Sandler and Joffe (1965) their distinction between depressive reactions and depressive states to convey differentiation between entrenched depressive states and more transitory depressive reactions.
5 Schore (2012) provides evidence that a psychotherapist's exquisite attunement to dissociated aspects of self, particularly crippling shame, can be reflected in new neural pathways in the patient's brain that translate psychically into substantial ego-strengthening developments.
6 Aggressive reactions often defend the ego against fundamental anxieties in the face of psychical dangers (Freud, 1926): of losing the object necessary for physical and psychological survival; of surviving birth/changes and separations; of physical or psychical castration when effective potency feels threatened; of fear of losing the parents' love, transferred in adulthood to fear of losing the superego's approval. Schafer (1983) adds to these dangers: 'loss of self-cohesion and loss of differentiation of self from the object' (p. 32f). As Garland observes, 'these anxieties have a crucial feature in common: they consist of the separation from or the loss of, anything that is felt to be essential to life, including life itself' (Garland, 2002: p. 16).

References

Abraham, K. (1924) *A Short Study of the Development of the Libido, Viewed in the Light of Mental Disorders: Selected Papers on Psychoanalysis.* Maresfield Reprints, London, Karnac Books, 1979.

Bouchard, M. & Lecours, S. (2004) Analysing forms of superego functioning as mentalizations. *The International Journal of Psychoanalysis.* 85, 879–896.
Britton, R. (2003) *Sex, Death and the Superego.* London, Karnac Books.
Caper, R. (1999) *A Mind of One's Own.* London, Routledge.
Freud, A. (1949) Aggression in relation to emotional development; normal and pathological. *The Psychoanalytic Study of the Child.* 3, 37–42.
Freud, S. (1917) Mourning and melancholia. In: *The Standard Edition.* Volume XIV. London, Hogarth Press.
Freud, S. (1923) The ego and the id. In: *The Standard Edition.* Volume XIX, London, Hogarth Press.
Freud, S. (1926) Inhibitions, symptoms and anxiety. In: *The Standard Edition.* Volume XX. London, Hogarth Press.
Freud, S. (1932) New introductory lectures. In: *The Standard Edition.* Volume XXII. London, Hogarth Press.
Furman, E. (1982) Mothers have to be there to be left. *The Psychoanalytic Study of the Child.* 37, 15–28.
Garland, C. (2002) *Understanding Trauma.* 2nd Edition. London, Karnac Books.
Glasser, M. (1996) Aggression and sadism in the perversions. In: I. Rosen (ed.) *Sexual Deviation.* 3rd Edition. Oxford, Oxford University Press.
Hartmann, H. & Loewenstein, M.D. (1962) Notes on the superego. *Psychoanalytic Study of the Child.* 17, 42–81.
Klein, M. (1937) Love, guilt and reparation. In: *Love, Guilt and Reparation and Other Works 1921–1945.* London, Virago Press, 1988.
Leader, D. (2008) *The New Black.* London, Penguin Books.
Money-Kyrle, R. (1971) The aim of psychoanalysis. *International Journal of Psychoanalysis.* 52, 103–106.
Novick, J. & Novick, K.K. (1991) Some comments on masochism and the delusion of omnipotence from a developmental perspective. *Journal of the American Psychoanalytic Association.* 39, 307–331.
Novick, J. & Novick, K.K. (2004) The superego and the two-system model. *Psychoanalytic Inquiry.* 24, 232–256.
Parsons, M. (2006) From biting teeth to biting wit: the normative development of aggression. In: C. Harding (ed.) *Aggression and Destructiveness.* London, Routledge.
Parsons, M. (2009) The roots of violence: theory and implications for technique with children and adolescents. In: M. Lanyado & A. Horne (eds.) *The Handbook of Child and Adolescent Psychotherapy.* London, Routledge.
Phillips, A. (2015) Against self-criticism. *The London Review of Books.* 5 March, 13–16.
Piers, G. & Singer, M.B. (1953) *Shame and Guilt: A Psychoanalytic and Cultural Study.* Republished 2015, Mansfield Connecticut, Martino Publishing.
Reddish, E. (2014) *The Petrified Ego. A New Theory of Conscience.* London, Karnac Books.
Rickman, J. (1951) The development of the moral function. In: P. King (ed.) *No Ordinary Analyst.* London, Karnac Books.
Roth, P. (2001) *The Superego (Ideas in Psychoanalysis).* Cambridge, Icon Books Ltd.
Rusczcynski, S. (2006) The problem of certain psychic realities: aggression and violence as perverse solutions. In: C. Harding (ed.) *Aggression and Destructiveness.* East Sussex, Brunner-Routledge.
Sandler, J. & Joffe, W.G. (1965) Notes on childhood depression. *The International Journal of Psychoanalysis.* 46, 88–96.

Schafer, R. (1960) The loving and beloved superego in Freud's structural theory. *The Psychoanalytic Study of the Child*. 15, 163–188.

Schafer, R. (1983) *The Analytic Attitude*. London, Hogarth Press.

Schore, A.N. (1991) Early superego development: the emergence of shame and narcissistic affect regulation in the practising period. *Psychoanalysis and Contemporary Thought*. 14, 187–250.

Schore, A.N. (2012) *The Science of the Art of Psychotherapy*. New York, W.W. Norton & Company, Inc.

Sodre, I. (2005) The wound, the bow and the shadow of the object: notes of Freud's 'Mourning and Melancholia'. In: R. Perelberg (ed.) *Freud: A Modern Reader*. London, Whurr Publishers.

Sodre, I. (2000) Non vixit. A ghost story. In: I. Sodre (ed.) *Imaginary Existences*, Sussex, Routledge, 2015.

Strachey, J. (1934) The nature of the therapeutic action of psychoanalysis. *International Journal of Psychoanalysis*. 50, 275–291, 1989.

Yorke, E.C., Wiseberg, S. & Freeman, T. (1989) Developmental disharmonies and manic-depressive depressions. In: *Development and Psychopathology*. London, Yale University Press, pp. 184–207.

Chapter 6

Superegos in patients with problems of perversion

Heather Wood

Introduction

It would be a mistake to think that people who commit sexual acts that are deemed criminal or compulsive are somehow lacking a superego. What we discover when working therapeutically with such patients is that they often have a ferocious superego, and then act in defiance of this apparently merciless judge. While thus subjected to harsh internal condemnation, they also often evoke society's disapproval and sometimes the disapproval of the therapist as well. Superego functioning turns out to be central to the dynamics of, and the response to, these problems.

The classical notion of the superego is that it derives from the resolution of the Oedipus Complex (Freud, 1923); in internalising the taboo on incest, the child lays the foundation for the development of a moral code. According to this model, the birth of the superego occurs relatively late in child development (age four or five) and the superego will have relatively stable characteristics, shaped by the experience of the Oedipal stage. However, if the Oedipus Complex has been only partially resolved, the individual's moral sense may be less 'formed', or, in some individuals, lacking altogether.

This classical notion of the superego has been criticised elsewhere (see for example Reddish, 2014). Therapeutic work with patients whose problems may be regarded as 'perversions' underlines the need for a more flexible and differentiated model of superego functioning. This chapter explores a model that recognises:

i) the range of superego manifestations in any one individual, and the shifting, fluid quality of superego functioning;
ii) the distinction between a 'harsh' superego and one infused with libidinal excitement that might be thought of as 'sadistic' or 'perverse';
iii) the range of superego transference and countertransference configurations that may be enacted between patient and therapist; and,
iv) the foundations of a harsh or perverse superego in early infantile development, and the value of addressing the profound depression associated with failures of early experience if the ferocity of the superego is to be modified.

Before elaborating this model it is important to delineate the characteristics of 'perversions' as the term is used here. A contemporary psychoanalytic notion of perversions encompasses three elements. First, the use of sexualisation as a defence, not just against castration anxieties in men as Freud (1927) described, but also, in men and women, against the primitive anxieties aroused by intimacy.[1] Second, rather than a benign integration of libido and destructiveness where the loving impulses modify and mitigate the potentially destructive force, a fusion of sexualisation and aggression that adds excitement and pleasure to the enactment of destructiveness. Through sexualisation, the destructiveness is not modified but given extra charge. This is a view initially associated with Glover (1933) and implicit in subsequent theories of perversion. Third, a marked degree of compulsion and repetition in the enactment of the chosen behaviour(s). Sexual experimentation casually undertaken, or unusual sexual behaviours that are not experienced as compulsive, would not warrant being described as perverse. Perverse behaviours tend to have a quality of concreteness, where the person feels compelled to repeat the behaviour in pursuit of some unconscious aim which is never satisfied, even when there is physical sexual fulfilment.

Drawing on Segal's (1957) notion of the difference between symbols and symbolic equations, it is possible to see perverse behaviour functioning as a symbolic equation, in which something is urgently sought – such as a the approving smile of a woman to whom a man has exposed his genitals. We may surmise that at an unconscious level the woman's smile stands for the loving and approving maternal gaze for the child's body, sexuality, or productions. But because there is no conscious awareness of this longing, there can be no mourning when it is not satisfied, and consequently no development of mature symbols (see Wood, 2013). Even if the woman to whom he has exposed himself smiles, it will never be the mother's smile. The behaviour cannot be given up because it appears to promise fulfilment of deeply held unconscious desires, yet there is neither real satisfaction nor development.

Within this definition it is not the behaviour, per se, which is perverse, though there may be certain behaviours, such as compulsive exhibitionism, which typically demonstrate all of these characteristics. What is distinctive about perversions is the repetitive use of sexualisation as a defence against largely unconscious anxieties or aggression.

Not one but many superegos

In individuals who present with these types of compulsive sexual behaviours we do not observe a single superego with consistent characteristics, ('the' superego); instead we see marked variations in superego functioning. While at times there may be something resembling a superego that has internalised cultural and familial laws and rules, at other times there is evidence of an extremely harsh and persecutory superego. In patients in whom sexualisation is pervasive and who present with compulsive sexual behaviours, there is often a third type of superego, one charged with excitement, hell-bent on destruction, deception, corruption, or seduction.

> Mr A came for therapy after serving a prison sentence for the sexual abuse of a boy. The boy had been pre-pubertal at the time of the abuse. Neither the boy, nor Mr A, told anyone what had happened for several years. The boy eventually told a member of his family, who reported the allegation. When challenged, Mr A immediately confessed, pleaded guilty in court, and was convicted. He told himself that he had confessed to ensure that the now teenage boy was not required to give evidence in court; this might be seen as a manifestation of a superego that could feel concern to protect the boy from any further harm. It may be that he also confessed to assuage his conscious and unconscious guilt, feeling that he deserved punishment, administered by the legal system, for his assault on the boy. Again, this might be seen as a manifestation of a 'mature' superego. But Mr A was also convinced that his confession was the culmination of a highly masochistic act, an act which not only harmed the boy but destroyed his own life, his reputation, and many of his close relationships; in this respect, his ego may have been subservient to a sadistic superego driven to see him suffer. A policeman involved with the case said to him that by confessing he had convicted himself, and he ruminated about what would have happened if he had not done so. Later in therapy, when talking about the culture of secrecy in his family and the need to maintain appearances, he admitted that, had his parents still been alive at the time of the allegation, he probably would have denied the charge.

In Mr A there seemed to be several superegos, or several superego manifestations, operating at different points in this process: one superego founded in something like depressive-position functioning, capable of guilt and concern for the boy; one, respecting a legal and mature moral code in which a criminal and abusive act should be punished; one wondering whether he could have got away with lying and denial; one sadistically wanting to destroy himself and his life; and another, imagining protecting the 'law of the father' – in his family, not a conventional Oedipal morality, but a culture of secrecy and a tacit injunction to conceal any problems and maintain an impressive facade. This suggests that the superego is not a static entity and the product of a consistent process of development, but that there will be parallel strands in development, some leading to a capacity for 'mature' superego functioning, alongside others characterised by much more primitive levels of functioning, and still others bearing the imprint of the individual's unique familial and cultural experience. This may be conceptualised as there being many possible superegos which hold sway over the psyche at different times, or, alternatively, that the superego 'function' can take many guises.

While Freud's first topographical model of the mind is deemed a 'spatial' model, differentiating the conscious from the pre-conscious and unconscious, the second model, the 'structural' model, distinguishes between 'agencies' within the psyche, the id, ego, and superego (see Tonnesmann, 2005). Implicit in contemporary Kleinian thinking about the superego is what might be seen as a third model. Theorists such as Riesenberg-Malcom (1999) and Britton (2003) think not in terms of 'the superego' as a static entity with more or less fixed characteristics in one individual, but in terms of space to be occupied by a dominant internal object, so that different internal objects might function as 'a superego' at different times. Britton (2003) refers to this variously as a space and a structure:

> *all* internal objects *might* operate as the superego and . . . there is a great deal of difference *when* they do if they are hostile and tyrannical. . . . I see the position of the superego as a place to be occupied; indeed, I see it, as Freud did, as an inherent structure.
>
> (p. 74, his emphasis)

When working with the fluid mental functioning and shifting identifications of patients presenting with perversions, this thinking provides a conceptualisation of superego functioning which is more useful than a notion of a static superego. It leads us to ask, not 'What is the nature of the superego?', but 'What is the quality of superego functioning at this point in time?' This is pertinent not only when considering the dynamics of a particular patient such as Mr A, but also when we consider the topic of perversions. This is a subject that can evoke the thoughtful response of a benign superego, perhaps founded in the depressive position, which considers the harm that might be done to the individual and their psyche by their mode of functioning, and the gains as well as the costs of their behaviour. Alternatively it can evoke a response which is much more resonant of a harsh superego, splitting 'normal' from 'abnormal', 'acceptable' from 'deviant', and condemning the behaviour or the individual.

The operation of a superego

What does a superego do? O'Shaughnessy's (1999) notion that it is a 'super-ego' is useful: it operates over and above the ego. We typically use the term 'superego' to refer to two functions: on the one hand, observing, commenting, and passing judgement on the functioning of the ego, and on the other, providing structure and guidance. Britton (2003) proposes that the ego learns from experience whereas the superego operates on the basis of principle. This may be the principle of what would broadly be regarded within a cultural group as a moral stance, but as recent theorists point out, the 'principle' might be one of destroying links (O'Shaughnessy, 1999) or of simulation or deception (Glasser, 1986). If we think in object-relations terms and assume there is always a relation to an object, then a third function of the internal superego object would be to observe and comment on the relation of the self to the object; in the therapeutic situation, the relation to the therapist or analyst. This becomes of particular significance when perverse dynamics prevail and the other is to be feared or controlled. This differs from an 'observing ego' in that it is not concerned with evidence (as Britton describes) but with asserting a principle – in the case of a perverse or persecutory superego, the principle of attacking dependency, vulnerability, and genuine 'intercourse' with another (see Joseph, 1997).

Taking O'Shaughnessy's (1999) distinction between a normal and an abnormal superego, one might think that under 'normal' conditions a superego functions either like a benign autocracy, in which the superego observes and guides ego functioning, but in a tolerant, forgiving way, or it functions like a democracy, in which the multiple voices of different internal objects are heard. Under the sway of an abnormal superego, there is tyranny, domination, and persecution. Amongst Kleinian writers, there are persuasive accounts of this type of tyrannical superego, born out of the persecution of the paranoid-schizoid position (Klein, 1958) or the dissociations of early experience (O'Shaughnessy, 1999). Klein views the ferocity of the persecutory superego as deriving from the death instinct.

In work with perverse patients, the notion of an abnormal superego seems insufficient, because what we observe is not simply a pure culture of something 'deathly' and destructive, but something attacking and destructive *fused with* gratification, excitement, and pleasure. It is this characteristic which specifically distinguishes what might be called a 'perverse superego'.

> *When in the grip of something hell-bent on destruction, Mr B described it as 'the fucker in the driving seat'. When the fucker was in the driving seat his ego and I were relegated to helpless passengers as destructiveness took the wheel of the car – and this was not just any car, but a high performance car turbo-charged with libidinal pleasure. But it would be a mistake to think he was only the victim of this, as he was at times also strongly identified with this powerful internal object. In this state of mind he would describe charming his way into the upper echelons of organizations he was involved with, and let me know that, once there, he was thoroughly enjoying metaphorically 'sitting at high table', out of my reach.*

How does it happen that what might have been a persecutory superego becomes sexualised and so sadistic or perverse? Glasser (1978), in his paper on the superego in exhibitionism, refers to the ego forming a sadomasochistic relation to the superego but does not specify how this occurs. Writing about sexualisation more generally, Coen (1981) notes that 'libidinalization' and 'sexualization' are used by many authors without clarification of the processes involved. Certain themes recur in the literature that might account for a reliance on sexualisation as a mode of defence: an over-stimulating or overtly sexualised relation between mother and son (e.g. Glasser, 1978); libidinalisation of the body or premature development of sexual behaviours to compensate for deficiencies in maternal care (e.g. Greenacre, 1970); the particular facility of sexualisation to defend against excessive aggression (e.g. Coen, 1981); and the use of sexualisation to confer an illusion of omnipotent and pleasurable control (Coen, 1981). Constitutional differences in the level of libido may also play a role. Clinical work with the patients described here suggests that there are many routes to a reliance on sexualisation as the predominant mode of defence. But whatever the aetiology of a perverse superego, it seems that, through the injection of sexualised excitement, the experience of being a helpless victim in relation to a punitive superego can be transformed into an exciting internal battle characterised by defiance, provocation, and pleasure in inflicting and bearing suffering.

Once the superego has acquired this quality of excitement fused with destruction, sadomasochistic relations prevail. These may be between a sadistic superego and a masochistic ego. Alternatively, the individual may be in identification with the sadistic superego and relating to an external object in the position of the helpless, suffering victim. In another variant, the perverse or harsh superego object may be projected on to the therapist. Therapeutic change will be more likely when the individual can recognise both the experience of being in identification with this object and the experience of being the victim of it. Therapeutically, it can be helpful to point out to the patient how, when he feels himself to be most identified with it (and hence feeling excited and invulnerable) there is another part of him that is simultaneously the victim of this excited cruelty and being made to suffer.

Reflecting on patients who might be deemed to have perversions, what is striking is the variety of superego configurations in evidence. All have an extremely harsh, destructive/self-destructive streak which is evident at times, but the extent to which pleasure in cruelty, defiance, transgression, and deception prevails is variable. Different configurations are described here to demonstrate a range of possibilities, rather than to propose narrow consistencies.

Variants of the perverse superego – malignant scrutiny, bogus morality, and exciting secrecy

Mr C came to therapy in his thirties after receiving a conviction for looking at indecent images of children on the internet. Over the course of several years in treatment, it became clear that this was driven more by a masochistic relationship to persecutory internal objects than by a paedophilic sexual interest (see Wood, 2014). There were two salient images of a sadistic superego in his treatment: one, frequently referred to in his therapy by variations on the theme of 'malicious scrutiny', projected onto the criminal justice system and myself; and the other, a more denigrated, unthinking, vigilante-style morality, captured by his use of the phrase 'white van man'. For him there was great excitement in provoking these internal and sometimes projected objects. Creating an exciting internal battle filled an intolerably depressed, empty space, sometimes evoked by the image of a desert. While waiting to go back to court to challenge an order imposed on him, he filled the anxious space with fantasies of close police scrutiny:

PATIENT: *What are they up to? I imagine myself being followed. I went for a run on Saturday and lay in the sun in the grass in the park. A man came and sat*

> down nearby me with two dogs and a phone, very noisy. And I thought, 'Is he police?' Another time, in a different park, five or six men came towards me, one on a bike with an earpiece. And he obviously heard something and said 'Oh OK', and veered off. I phoned the [police sexual offending team] and said 'What's going on?' and the man said, 'I haven't got the money to keep you under surveillance. It must have been something else'. I don't have it when I am at my parents' house. But I assume in parks around here, they have people who have a list of who is on their books and I'm one of them.
> [LATER IN THE SESSION] THERAPIST: *This month of waiting to hear about the court case feels very empty, and you could fill it by this sense of being locked in a battle with the police*
> PATIENT: *It is very empty. When waiting for the court case I phoned the [suicide helpline] who said, 'Well you know what you looked at'.*

This feeling that he is being watched is not just straightforwardly paranoid, it becomes exciting for him to feel that, far from being forgotten or unseen, there is a team of police officers watching him – the scrutiny is malicious and suspicious, but at least he is the centre of attention. He reveals that the emptiness of waiting and feeling forgotten leaves him feeling suicidal, hence his phone call to the helpline, but unfortunately there he does not encounter an understanding object but another harsh superego that reprimands him for his crime.

He would describe how creating this excited, sadomasochistic internal fight was a response to feeling condemned by a harsh, judgemental internal authority. From his material it was possible to reconstruct a sequence of psychic events, in which an experience of terrible emptiness and desolation invoked a harsh, condemnatory superego. Feeling crushed and negated, he would sexualise this internal battle, so that the superego object now became cruel and sadistic, and he provocative, defiant, and excited. In this state, what were fundamentally self-defeating, masochistic acts gave an illusion of potency and vitality. It was as though both depression and ordinary sexual urges represented a longing for connectedness that evoked a powerful 'anti-libidinal' response from a destructive internal object. By engaging with this object in an excited, sadomasochistic way he found a kind of connectedness, but one born of disconnection (as O'Shaughnessy (1999) describes) rather than the connectedness and satisfaction of object relatedness.[2] In this state he finds an ersatz potency, rather than a potency founded in a secure sense of self and a trust in the relatedness between self and other.

In the following material he describes how his guilt about ordinary lust, presumably engendered by a harsh superego which prohibits ordinary sexuality, becomes transformed into a sadomasochistic game in which he takes control by making himself into someone 'vile'. Yet underpinning this is emptiness and loss:

> PATIENT: *It was like a game. I had Grand Theft Auto on my phone. You are basically learning to be a drug dealer. It was like that joining these sites. Like a game. I'd signed up to a forum. The police said, 'You would have no reason to be on*

this forum unless you had a sexual interest in children'. But it wasn't like joining the Masons where you would think really hard about whether you really wanted to do this. All you had to do was give an email address and a password.

I'd always felt so guilty about lust. About having lustful thoughts. Even towards people of my own age. Even from when I was a teenager . . . I felt if I even had feelings of my own – it was like a motor that was going to take me in a particular direction – and that wasn't allowed. I always felt that what I was doing was vile. I was making myself into someone vile. On some sites you had to give an age and I'd give it as 40 or 50, and for a password I'd put 'pervert'.

. . . . I felt I was doing it because of a sense of loss. I felt it here [in his stomach]. That I could never put the clock back and have those childhood years.

Later in his treatment, there was evidence of a more corrupt superego, which was alternately idealised, denigrated, and defied:

I'm preoccupied with the [tabloid newspaper with a reputation for salacious stories] – I can't stop thinking about it. I was thinking about it before all of this happened. I held them up as an arbiter of standards. Before I was offending, their 'name and shame' campaign was going on. I see them as upholding something. They believe the worst thing anyone can do is harm or exploit children. And because I feel I'm disgusting, I recreate that relationship . . . so I do the very thing they think is the worst.
THERAPIST: *You say you feel you are disgusting*
PATIENT: *It's how I've felt all my life. [Talks about wetting himself at school in assembly and being treated with disgust when at school]*

In my mind, white van man, who has these values, if he feels that harming or exploiting children is the worst thing anyone can do – I look up to that – but also feel an urge to challenge it. And I feel fear . . . and excitement. Getting caught up in that makes me feel vital – and potent. . . . If I don't, I feel very blank and empty. As if I don't exist . . . in the past, if everything was going along smoothly – just vanilla – I'd feel very uneasy and unnerved.

In a subsequent session, he told me that the tabloid newspaper was now the subject of criminal investigations:

PATIENT: *There's something about this incredibly powerful group of people who are corrupt, and they are just driven by money. It's how I've always felt, that there was this malicious regime. It's like my fascination with [the Orwell novel] 1984. And where there is this malicious regime that I feel I must defy . . . I feel I'm in the wrong . . . but I feel alive, excited.*

On one level he knows that the tabloid press is not an arbiter of moral standards; his contempt is implicit in his choice of the phrase 'white van man', often used to describe the stereotype of an unthinking skilled labourer. Yet he pretends to idealise them, imagines them disapproving of him, and then feels compelled to act in a way that is provocative and defiant. Implicit in this is the triumph he feels when the representatives of bogus morality or the corrupt superego condemn and judge him, and in so doing, expose their stupidity.

Mr C mostly felt himself to be the victim of these variants of harsh or perverse superego. In other people, such as Mr D, one sees a much clearer identification with the cruel or bogus morality. This perverse superego may triumph over a tame, mundane, 'moral' superego and what might be seen as a boring ethical stance in the external world and in the therapist.

> *Mr D was charged for a second time with internet offences. Believing his solicitor to have acted improperly in showing him some of the images for which he was being charged, he sacked his solicitor and decided to represent himself in court. He did not just acquaint himself with the law, but told me that he had stolen a law book from his local library which he believed to be worth several hundreds of pounds, and took it with him to court so that he could quote chapter and verse to the judge. With his stolen book, and his appropriated legal knowledge, he imagined himself triumphing over the judge, who, by implication, would be too stupid to realise the theft.*

Mr D thus appropriates the legal book which gives him the bogus morality, the 'law' obtained by corrupt means, by which he may triumph over the apparent arbiter of moral standards, the judge in court, and thereby render him ridiculous.

The excitement of perversions is often bound up with secrecy and deception. The 'thrill' of transgression is often of seeing what can be got away with without being detected, by a partner, or, in the case of illegal acts, by representatives of the law. As in the game of 'playing chicken', people run closer and closer to danger in order to test where the limits are, almost seeming to provoke detection. For some people it is as though they are also seeing what they can get away with without wakening a sleeping superego. The harsh superego then becomes the thing that is prodded, provoked, teased, and then evaded. In one session Mr C described people getting caught up on the periphery of a riot and then attracting relatively punitive sentences, and how he felt that something similar had happened to him.

PATIENT: *When you are doing something like that – it's like a game. There's ambiguity about where the boundaries are. It seems as though there is no-one watching. You put a toe over the line and see if anything happens and then run back. The next time you go a bit further. If when you went on the internet and typed in a dodgy search term and the minute you did that a message came up from the police that what you are doing might be illegal – it would be much clearer. But it doesn't. The sites I looked at . . . specifically looked as though it was legal . . . and you might know that what you were doing was **morally** wrong, but it was not clear if it was illegal.*

To return to Mr A, he had grown up in a family where any problems were to be kept secret and swept aside as one moved on. When he was sexually abused as a boy, he relished this 'secret' relationship, and found pleasure in keeping his silence when the abuser was arrested and imprisoned. As a teenager he enjoyed knowing that he knew more about sex than all his peers, despising them for their ignorance. Secrets were power. As our work was nearing the end, he told me that 'secrecy was my milk'. I suggested to him that in fact it had been his 'diet Coke', that is, without nutritional value, which he acknowledged. To believe that secrecy was 'milk' is a perversion of feeding, involving the idealisation and libidinalisation of the **avoidance** of human connectedness and contact. In our work together, the first regret he was able to acknowledge about the abuse that he had experienced as a boy was that it distanced him from his peers and the normal, if sometimes embarrassing process of sexual discovery and experimentation that is an important part of growing up. This marked the beginning of him recognising the importance of ordinary connectedness in preference to manic secrecy.

Transference and countertransference

Forms of sexual acting-out that might be considered perverse typically evoke strong reactions in others, of shock, disgust, and sometimes condemnation. People who commit sexual assaults are frequently described in the tabloid press as 'vile', 'monstrous', and 'evil'. While psychotherapists and psychoanalysts would be unlikely to react so vehemently, there is no doubt that the disclosure of extreme or harmful sexual behaviours can evoke marked countertransference responses. Specific forms of perversion may be accompanied by distinctive transference and countertransference patterns, such as exhibitionism and voyeurism as described by Ogden (1997), and doubt engendered by paedophilia and the sexual abuse of children, as described by Campbell (2014). Ogden (1997) proposes that 'the analysis of perversion necessarily involves the analysis of the perverse transference-countertransference as it unfolds in the analytic relationship' (p. 67). Indeed, it can be argued that until the perversion itself comes into the consulting room in some form, it is difficult to work directly with it.

Focusing here on aspects of the countertransference specifically associated with superego functioning, the therapist or analyst will inevitably be invited both to assume the role of harsh superego, judging and condemning the individual and their behaviour, and to turn a blind eye and collude with corruption. The patient may also imagine that the therapist's judgement will be avoided if he or she can be made to feel sexually excited and titillated by the material. The challenge therapeutically is to find a stance that is not without morality but that seeks to understand, to name, and if necessary to impose boundaries, while not being drawn into collusion, mutual excitement, criticism, or rejection.

While the invitation to react as a harsh or judgemental superego will always be present to some degree, probably more challenging is the pressure to become caught up in a sadomasochistic superego enactment. It has frequently happened to me that what had seemed like a 'neutral' interpretation, often about some aspect of reality, such as boundaries, or ending, or absences, is taken by the patient as a cruel and sadistic attack, justifying a reciprocal attack on me as a cruel, bad therapist out to hurt/reject/punish my patient. It is often hard to withstand this provocation, and the urge to retaliate in a punitive way can be strong. The 'fight' obscures, and maybe is meant to obscure, how painful it can be for the patient to face the reality of loss or the limits to omnipotence.

Patients with problems of this kind often feel intense self-disgust, and the therapist may be invited to be disgusted either by the material the patients bring or by their physical presentation in the room, sometimes unwashed and odorous, or wiping mucous away on a sleeve. Chasseguet-Smirgel (1985) emphasises the regression in perversions from phallic functioning to an anal universe in which there is a denial of difference between genders and generations, and indeed between developmental stages, so that anality substitutes for genitality. Some patients convey an acute sense of being 'shitty' and disgusting, often defended against by a sexualised excitement about faeces or anality.

Where there is an internal dynamic of a humiliated self and a mocking superego, the therapist may be invited to mock or ridicule the patient, or be subjected to overt or covert mocking for their helplessness or ineffectual work. At times the therapist is left to carry the projected 'mature' superego while mocked and ridiculed by an excited, omnipotent, perverse superego.

In some patients presenting with compulsive sexual behaviours, their vulnerability is all too evident alongside their capacity for cruelty and triumph. This enables the therapist to keep in mind both the 'perpetrator' and the 'victim' within the patient, the cruel part of them as well as the part that suffers. More challenging is when the patient seems wholly identified with the cruel or perverse superego and any vulnerability is projected, often into the therapist. Meeting force with force, through exclusively interpreting the destructiveness in play, risks perpetuating the sadomasochistic dynamic. In this regard, Glasser's (1979) theory of the core complex provides an invaluable foundation for interpretation: in his view sadomasochism is a defence against the terrors evoked by intimacy. This underpins a style of interpretation which both recognises the excited destructiveness *and* the underlying anxiety, and is less likely to be experienced by the patient as reactive or retaliatory.

Change

How does change occur in people with these superego configurations? A contributory factor may be the therapist or analyst repeatedly pointing out the ferocity of the internal object or the excitement and illusion of strength associated with the internal sadomasochistic fight. But enduring change probably requires an increased ability to tolerate the depression or the emptiness of failed early relationships which seem to underpin the resort to sexualisation and sadomasochism, similar to the 'dissociations' of early life that O'Shaughnessy (1999) sees as underpinning the development of an abnormal superego. If the depression and failures of early experience can be known, and the splitting and persecutory objects of the paranoid-schizoid position reduced, there will be less need to fill the empty space with an exciting sadomasochistic internal or external battle. O'Shaughnessy (1999) suggests that the analyst's ability to function with a 'normal' superego, 'a normal superego, but one with an analytic attitude' (p. 869), enables the patient to 'escape the clutches' of an abnormal superego and connect with an object with normal superego aspects. In her words,

> This means not giving verdicts (guilty, not guilty, etc) or pronouncing sentence (on probation, condemned to. . . . etc) on the patient, but recognising things for what they are in the ethical domain.
>
> (p. 869)

This is highly relevant to clinical work with patients who, as a result of their sexual behaviours, may have experienced social and sometimes legal condemnation, and sometimes have experienced the force of media hostility and disdain. The patient will expect to encounter a condemnatory superego in the therapist or analyst, and while this is counterproductive if enacted, neither is it helpful to feign an absence of any moral stance. The challenge for the therapist will be to maintain a connection with a superego that acknowledges when harm is done and the unconscious drivers and external consequences of actions, without judging, condemning, or implicitly passing sentence on the patient.

What is striking in patients who have experienced long-term psychotherapy is that, when they start to notice that change has occurred, they make reference to changes in their conscience or their morality. Mr A told me that he had decided to list the things that he had gained from therapy. He reflected on his feelings towards the boy he had abused, and his troubled relationships to women, and the fact that he now knew that there were some things in life that could not be put right. Of significance in terms of the superego, he told me he was now more honest, less secretive, and that his feelings and experience connected up more. He also told me that his conscience was 'real' now, and that it had not been before. But while the changes he noticed could be thought of as indicators of a more 'normal' superego, this 'list' was the culmination of therapeutic work that was for him a gruelling exploration of depression and guilt. He had recognised the shallowness of his relationship with his mother, consisting of mutual admiration, and he described the profound disturbance for him of witnessing the last days of her life when she was reduced to a pathetic figure and he could no longer see an inflated version of himself reflected in her gaze. He had faced profound disillusionment about the abuse he experienced as a boy, which he had always prized as a special 'love' relationship. But most painful for him was the realisation that he had abused a boy whom he loved, but when he was abusing him the boy was, in himself, of no significance at all. The abuse was an enactment of Mr A's own internal drama. The realisation that the boy had been a narcissistic object for him, and that he had 'used' him in this unconscious way as well as abusing him sexually, was a source of acute pain and guilt.

For Mr C, signs that a shift from perverse or abnormal superego to a more normal superego was occurring were evident just before a Christmas break:

PATIENT: *I think coming here means there's someone monitoring my brain – not in a malicious way, and I'm anxious that without that people will misunderstand me and I won't be able to defend myself.*
THERAPIST: *As if my keeping an eye on you keeps you safe, and without that, you fear you'll be vulnerable to being defined by others and feeling misunderstood.*
PATIENT: *I think that's right . . . [He links this to the experience of being left by his mother as a child in a frightening situation]. Here, it is like doing lengths in a swimming pool. In the breaks, I'm out in the ocean and there are sharks.*

I used the phrase 'keeping an eye on you' to contrast this with the malicious scrutiny frequently attributed to me and others in the past. This is a benign oversight that holds him, but without it he is at risk of being misunderstood, triggering a cycle of grievance and retaliation. The holding is precarious; when I'm away (and presumably when his mother left him), he is once again in the frightening waters of his own rage about being left, swimming with the 'sharks' of his persecutory internal objects, which are both potentially dangerous and excitingly powerful.

Conclusion

The classical notion of the superego has limited value when working with patients with problems of perversion, and perhaps more generally. Just as we would not talk about 'the internal object' so we cannot expect to find consistency in the characteristics of superego 'objects'. These will be idiosyncratic, fluid, and fluctuating within any one individual. Working with patients presenting with problems of perversion, it is more useful to think, what are the characteristics of the object that is observing, commenting, directing the ego and its relation to external objects at any one time, and how does the ego relate and respond to that object? And what does this configuration defend against?

Where there is sexualisation there will be gratification, and identifying where this is located will be important because this will be part of the resistance to any therapeutic efforts. When there is an excited, sadistic superego, this will confer an illusion of power and strength that, understandably, the patient may be reluctant to relinquish. The nature of the superego is often known in the countertransference, as we are invited to join with a harsh superego in condemning the patient or to join with a perverse superego in mocking the patient, or, alternatively, siding with the patient in ridiculing 'boring' conventional morality. Or we may be subject to the full force of a cruel superego as we are chastised for our lame attempts to help the patient, or our 'naive' belief that we might be of some value, or our unprofessional inability to contain our own reactions to provocation. Engendering an illusion of exciting strength in the face of emptiness and depression is part of what drives this cruel or perverse superego; bearing the underlying experience of desolation is likely to be a necessary part of any therapeutic work. For the therapist or analyst, bearing provocation without retaliation is often central to the task.

Notes

1 This is exemplified by Glasser's notion of the core complex (1979), in which feelings of desire for the object evoke a terror of being taken over by the object with consequent loss of self, and so evoke intense feelings of aggression towards the object of desire. However, to enact those feelings threatens to destroy the very object of desire, while withdrawal risks abandonment, isolation, and depression. Glasser's view is that, the solution to this dilemma found by people who go on to develop a perversion, is to sexualise the aggression so that the object is treated sadistically, but is not destroyed. Sexualisation then defends against the aggression and anxiety aroused by the prospect of intimate engagement.
2 Greenacre (1970) also describes how, where there has been severe deprivation or mistreatment in infancy, the mounting frustration and aggression can lead to 'premature sadomasochistic erotization' sometimes associated with premature genital stimulation as early as the second year of life, paving the way for subsequent disturbances such as adult perversions 'or character deformations with ego and superego defects'.

References

Britton, R. (2003) *Sex, Death and the Superego: Experiences in Psychoanalysis*. London, Karnac Books.
Campbell, D. (2014) Doubt in the analysis of the paedophile. *International Journal of Psychoanalysis*, 95(5), 1011–1020.
Chasseguet-Smirgel, J. (1985) *Creativity and Perversion*. London, Free Association Books.
Coen, S.J. (1981) Sexualization as a predominant mode of defense. *Journal of the American Psychoanalytic Association*. 29, 893–921.
Freud, S. (1923) The ego and the id. In: *The Standard Edition*. Volume XIX. London, Hogarth Press.
Freud, S. (1927) Fetishism. In: *The Standard Edition*. Volume XXI. London, Hogarth Press.
Glasser, M. (1978) The role of the superego in exhibitionism. *International Journal of Psychoanalytic Psychotherapy*. 7, 333–351.
Glasser, M. (1979) Some aspects of the role of aggression in the perversions. In: I. Rosen (ed.) *Sexual Deviation*. 2nd edition. Oxford, Oxford University Press.
Glasser, M. (1986) Identification and its vicissitudes as observed in perversions. *International Journal of Psychoanalysis*. 67, 9–17.
Glover, E. (1933) The relation of perversion formation to the development of the reality sense. *International Journal of Psycho-Analysis*. 14, 486–504.
Greenacre, P. (1970) The transitional object and the fetish with special reference to the role of illusion. *International Journal of Psychoanalysis*. 51, 447–457.
Joseph, B. (1997) 'Where there is no vision': from sexualisation to sexuality. In: D. Bell (ed.) *Reason and Passion: A Celebration of the Work of Hanna Segal*. London, Karnac Books, Tavistock Clinic Series.

Klein, M. (1958) On the development of mental functioning. In: M. Klein (ed.) *Envy and Gratitude and Other Works 1946–1963*. London, Hogarth Press, pp. 236–246.

Ogden, T. (1997) The perverse subject of analysis. In: T. Ogden (ed.) *Reverie and Interpretation*. Lanham, MD, Jason Aronson.

O'Shaughnessy, E. (1999) Relating to the superego. *International Journal of Psychoanalysis*. 80(5), 861–870.

Reddish, E. (2014) *The Petrified Ego: A New Theory of Conscience*. London, Karnac Books.

Riesenberg-Malcom, R. (1999) The constitution and operation of the superego. In: R. Riesenberg-Malcom (ed.) *On Bearing Unbearable States of Mind*. Hove, E.Sussex, Routledge, New Library of Psychoanalysis.

Segal, H. (1957) Notes on symbol formation. *International Journal of Psychoanalysis*. 38, 391–397. Reprinted in: E. Bott Spillius (ed) (1988) *Melanie Klein Today: Volume 1: Mainly Theory*. London, Routledge, New Library of Psychoanalysis.

Tonnesmann, M. (2005) Towards the structural model of the mind. In: R.J. Perelberg (ed.) *Freud: A Modern Reader*. London, Whurr Publishers.

Wood, H. (2013) The nature of the addiction in 'sex addiction' and paraphilias. In: M. Bower, R. Hale & H. Wood (eds.) *Addictive States of Mind*. London, Karnac Books.

Wood, H. (2014) Internet offenders from a sense of guilt. In: A. Lemma & L. Caparotta (eds.) *Psychoanalysis in the Technoculture Era*. Hove, E.Sussex, Routledge.

Chapter 7

About the analyst and patient

The superego in borderline states of mind

Jack Nathan

Introduction

I will use the term 'the borderline state of mind' to explore its impact on the functioning of both practitioner and patient. The term 'patient' references 'one who suffers', a psychic state that both participants have to navigate within the psychoanalytic paradigm. This is particularly the case when working with patients formally diagnosed with 'borderline personality disorder' (USA) or 'emotionally unstable personality disorder' (Europe). There is a contradiction at the heart of our work with this patient group: their struggles, sometimes literally of life and death, are essentially those of the 'normal neurotic'. It is the 'volume' laid bare, through verbal and non-verbal violent behaviour, usually in the form of self-harm, that marks out the borderline patient's psychopathology. The superego is at the heart of these struggles. Thus, in offering psychoanalytic treatment, we essentially agree to take on the dysfunctional workings of our own superego, as well as that of our patients.

We enter dangerous psychic territory by agreeing to participate in a therapeutic crucible which sanctions the emergence of the patient's already deeply unstable, 'archaic superego' (Strachey, 1934). As practitioners we must not underestimate what it means for us when patients 'get under our skin' (Carpy, 1989). Driven by unconscious forces within, practitioners can find themselves ending therapy because the patient constantly undermines the therapist, when that is at the core of what brought them into therapy in the first place. We have what is, in essence, an ethical responsibility in this regard as the analytic journey we offer specifically invites the patient to enter such regressed, destructive and self-destructive aspects of their personality.

For the therapist this means participating in a

> repetitive enactment using a part of his ego which is capable of accompanying the patient in his regressive transference immersion while at the same time remaining an observer of the double regression: his own and that of the patient.
>
> (Andrade, 2005: p. 683)

The analyst does not accompany the patient solely from a position of 'cool observer' but lays themselves psychically open to the patient's projective provocations that will unavoidably excite disturbing reactions. I believe that analytic work with severe borderline patients requires such emotional engagement. We have to allow ourselves to be aroused by the patient's projective provocations. Such psychic engagement literally incarnates the borderline patient's most disturbed and disturbing relationship dynamic. Working with this patient group we are drawn in to a primitively terrifying world, chillingly evoked by the psychic catastrophe Bion (1962) terms, 'nameless dread'. In this narrative the borderline state of mind is 'too' alive, wild, and in a state of uncontained fragmentation, floating in mid-air. For the practitioner, this inevitably means engaging with what I call the 'elemental superego': a superego, ever present in the borderline patient, but one shared by us all. And, as with patients, it is made up of our own, unworked through pathological organisation, immersed in a scripted language and driven by forces that are punitive, destructive, anti-life and above all, marked out by sadomasochism. The borderline patient forces us to confront the regressive forces that substantiate our own elemental superego, co-produced, alongside the patient's, during the course of therapy.

The elemental superego is a force that stands in marked contrast to the benign superego that 'demands' a psychic complexity that includes owning the forces of hatred, as well as love, in us all. Within such parameters the benign superego supports the ego to develop and grow. In summary, if the elemental superego is 'ego-destructive' (Bion, 1959), then the benign superego is ego facilitative.

The maternal object's making of a whole subject

Bion (1962) contrasts the borderline state of chaotic 'identity diffusion' (Kernberg, 1975) with 'normal development': a state of being that is fundamentally shaped by 'maternal reverie'. In optimal circumstances, the maternal object makes available her receptivity to the infant's life-threatening projections containing, detoxifying and returning them to the infant in a modified form: the unbearable is made bearable. There are two outcomes for the infant. The first is existential: the infant re-introjects an externally containing mother 'saving the infant's life'. The message sent out (projected) by the infant has been received, and through introjective identification, the maternal object makes sense of and contains that which is then re-stored (re-introjected) by the infant. What is re-stored now includes the message that the infant has been experientially taken in by the maternal object, a 'thinking breast'-in-reverie, complementing their projective phantasies. This function enables the 'mother' 'to feel the infant in her, and to give shape and words to the infant's experience' (Vaslamatzis, 1999: p. 433). Such transactions constitute a complex set of dynamics: by introjecting her infant's overwhelming experience, mother lends her own infantile self to her infant. By offering a psychoanalytic treatment that facilitates the patient's 'regressive transference immersion'

(Andrade, 2005) we, too, make our vulnerable infantile selves available as the instrument by which we attune to the patient's experience. But in the maternal object, who is the 'she' that is making available this most vulnerable aspect of her psyche? I believe it is the benign superego, what Money-Kyrle (1956) has called the 'predominantly friendly and helpful' superego. It is through the agency of this benign superego that symmetry of meaning is created and experientially understood by both infant and 'mother'.

A second outcome, derived through cumulative experiences of containment, is the infant's concurrent re-introjection of the 'container-contained' relationship, that the infant can gradually lodge within their developing psychic organisation as a good object, existentially experienced internally. In this developmental process, Bion highlights that healthy psychic development depends on cognitive functioning i.e. K (Knowledge), where experiences can be thought about and understood. From birth the infant is assailed by a terrifying chaos of inchoate proto-thoughts that Bion (1962) refers to as 'thoughts without a thinker'. The capacity to stand back, reflect and thereby have thoughts that give shape, meaning and relief to the nascent psyche, requires an 'apparatus for thinking' (Bion, 1962). Development of this 'apparatus' can only happen through another mind, through the container role of maternal reverie. The infant then re-introjects a 'mother' capable of containing both the infant's fears and, in vivo, establishes internally a projective identification-containing-object, with which the infant can identify and build up a good internal object, the benign superego.

The maternal object's making of a fragmented subject

What happens when the infant is not brought into an optimally developmental environment? Bion (1962) argues the infant

> has an inborn disposition corresponding to an expectation of a breast, . . . (such that) When the pre-conception is brought into contact with a realisation that approximates to it, the mental outcome is a conception.
> (p. 306)

His model can be summarised thus:

(Infant) Pre-conception + (Maternal) Realisation = Conception (Healthy Development)

This earliest form of 'conception' is the template for all future life-enhancing relationships. It is this relationship template that is 'absent', or severely compromised in borderline patients, such that the greater the 'absence', the greater the psychic deficit.

When confronted by the 'projective identification-rejecting-object' (Bion, 1962), 'a wilfully misunderstanding object', the infant meets a 'mother' with her own unresolved infantile pathology, where the elemental superego reigns supreme. The baby faces a 'maternal' object now, not only intolerant of her own infantile needs, but also the needs of her 'demanding' baby. Being brought up in an environment saturated by the punitive superego, massively compromises the infant's capacity to tolerate frustration. For Bion (1962) the capacity for tolerating frustration 'enables the psyche to develop *thought* as a means by which the frustration that is tolerated is itself made more tolerable' (p. 307, my emphasis). Where this is not the case, consequences follow.

Going beyond 'realistic' projective identification (Bion, 1962) that can be used as an instrument for the communication of disturbance, the infant turns away and/ or is unable to tolerate frustration, using instead 'excessive' projective identification to evacuate overwhelming disturbance. There is in effect, 'breakdown of interplay through projective identification between the (infant's) rudimentary consciousness and maternal reverie' (Bion, 1962: p. 309). Instead of Pre-conception + Realisation = Conception (manifested as thought), the infant acts to eliminate psychic content. Bion (1962) concludes that what should be a thought becomes a bad object, 'fit only for evacuation'. 'The end result is that all thoughts are treated as if they were indistinguishable from bad internal objects' (p. 307). The apparatus for thinking thoughts is now replaced by an apparatus for ridding the psyche of bad internal objects.

Consequently there is little capacity to contain and thereby modify frustration. The immature ego is left contending with mother's rejection of their projections, having to take in the 'mother's' own pathological projections embedded in her response. The infant then identifies with this complex re-introjected object relationship mimicking the object's own evacuations, similarly experienced as a bad internal object. We see this 'double dose' pathology in our borderline patients, traumatically combining both profound infantile vulnerability with the 'mother's' own unmetabolised psychic disturbance. Confronted by a 'projective identification-rejecting object' the infantile psychic experience becomes: 'I am a "demanding" baby, I am therefore "bad"', undermining their capacity to develop beyond an elemental superego that is both 'deservedly' self-destructive as well as punishing of the 'projective identification-rejecting object', now 'seen' in every object, including the analyst. It is the force of these primitive dynamics that characterises the borderline patient's terminally punitive, life-rejecting superego, one that makes psychic change arduous and long in coming, if at all. By contrast, 'the projective identification-containing object' represents a benign authority figure able to countenance the infant's (patient's) experience prior to their own, which in this way facilitates the evolution of an internalised benign superego.

In the absence of a developing apparatus for thought, a patient apparently contemplating their next self-harming action, is actually engaging in circular action, compulsively ruminating rather than thinking thoughts that can be reflected upon. Thinking has a linear quality, requiring painful step-by-step activity with different possible outcomes. Ruminative actions bypass thinking. Circular ruminations that constitute the core self-harming cycle can be stated thus:

I am Bad (severely persecuting superego) therefore I self-harm (punishment). I self-harm therefore I am Bad (severely persecuting superego)

Introducing thinking to such a patient can in itself be profoundly disturbing. One patient, Paula, found any utterance that did not accord with hers, as further evidence that I did not understand her. I was meeting her elemental superego, saturated in a savage determination to get me to 'stop that fucking thinking' (Britton, 1989), instead projecting her own savagery to communicate how intolerable her own elemental superego, now made manifest in me, was for her. I was being given an experience in the counter-transference of a ferocious superego, determined to deny me an existence, which is precisely what Paula felt I was doing to her. In these circumstances her psychic apparatus functioned only to rid itself of the bad external object I now came to represent. My thoughts were violent intrusions, denying her very existence. When this failed she had to literally deny my existence by storming out.

The patient's elemental superego in the transference

I now explore what the practitioner faces when dealing with the borderline patient's elemental superego through the way my patient Tom 'suffers' his borderline state of mind.

A bright middle-aged man, his childhood marked by an absent father and a physically violent mother who went out at night with different men, leaving him from the age of five to look after his younger brother. He was petrified of her guttural roar that he often re-produced in sessions to convey the full intensity of his experience. Tom, himself, became full of fury, excoriating me in his rage, for suggesting in a letter to his GP that, as a child, men in cinemas had sexually abused him. I had no understanding of him: 'paedophiles had saved me. Only they showed me any love!'

Having survived this and other onslaughts, Tom developed a more 'idealised' relationship, which I unconsciously assumed meant a greater depth of understanding and trust. This assumption proved erroneous, when Tom asked me to let him recharge his phone during one session. On reflection, I realised his was a courtesy request conveying no doubt that I may refuse, revealing me as a 'lassoed' (Symington, 1986) object in his mind – more controlled than idealised. At the time I only felt frustration, aware that this casual expectation reflected something of his tendency to seek solutions from others to resolve his problems – on this occasion excitedly telling me of a job offer that he could miss if his phone was not charged. I was also aware that he was prone to explode when he met with any kind of refusal 'outside'. This occasion was no exception. In this context, and this probably contributed to my counter-transference frustration, he clearly saw me as his 'mate'. Initially, he countered my refusal by repeating the urgency of his request. I let him know I understood that he was upset by my refusal and was feeling rejected by me, but I stood by my view that it was an inappropriate request. His response now turned to rage: 'I ask you a simple question, and you turn on me'. Tom was now in a tormented state, deaf to my continuing efforts to attune with him. Having failed to give him any sense that I was attempting to articulate what a patient once called, his 'hurtnanger', I appealed to his more cognitive self, explaining that we were in a therapy relationship and that if we were friends I would have readily agreed to his request: a big mistake. Tom now shouted that I was effectively telling him I did not want to be his friend because I saw him as 'a piece of shit'. He left the session enraged, wanting to end therapy.

What are we to make of this scene? First, whilst I remained an idealised, or lasso-controlled object he had had no conscious anxiety, that I might say 'no'. My refusal traumatically emptied Tom of this experience, replaced instead with the all-too-common experience of, yet again, pre-conception not being met by a 'maternal' realisation. Like Paula, from a position of being the hated, repulsed subject (child, patient), Tom gave 'voice' to his hatred of me for rejecting him. His elemental superego, full of 'justified' fury made so much sense to him that any attempt to clarify my position was met with further verbal violence. For my part, I was, as he had been in childhood, left 'silenced' at the receiving end of a 'projective identification-rejecting object', now denying my existence – what in Transference Focused Psychotherapy (TFP) represents a relationship dyad (Yeomans et al., 2014) which in this case, forms a 'reverse transference' where I was now the tormented subject. Second, his reaction prompted a counter-transference response, driven by my frustration. I was claiming separateness against Tom's wish that I collude with his narcissistic internal object world made manifest in the external object relationship in therapy. Third, what the 'affect storm' (Yeomans et al., 2005) made palpable, was Tom's 'identity diffusion' (Kernberg, 1975), where relationships are experienced in intensely black and white terms, maintained by dissociating one state of mind from the other. When these rigidly compartmentalised states of mind break down, the patient is catapulted into an intra-psychic world of terrifying affective collapse and inter-psychic turmoil.

Finally, Tom highlights the therapist's vulnerability when working with 'explosive' borderline patients, tempted to unconsciously collude with the patient's destructive narcissism (Kernberg et al., 1989). Brenman-Pick (1985) encapsulates the problem we face when she states:

> The analyst, like the patient, desires to eliminate discomfort as well as to communicate and share experience; ordinary human reactions. In part, the patient seeks an enacting response, and in part, the analyst has an impulse to enact.
>
> (p. 158)

To avoid becoming Bion's (1962) 'projective identification-rejecting-object', we need to be conscious of these kinds of dangers. It is to these I now turn.

The analyst's elemental superego in the counter-transference

Like the good-enough mother who engages emotionally with her own infantile self as well as her baby's, immersion in the regressive transference requires the good-enough practitioner to do likewise, knowing that the borderline's thin-skinned, easily aroused and intensely experienced affect, will inevitably, and without exception, get 'under the skin'. Carpy (1989) describes a patient who sees she is 'inducing' powerful feelings: 'it allows her to observe him attempting to deal with these feelings' (p. 292). In his view the patient's projections must be absorbed without gross acting out. Nevertheless, 'it is inevitable that if the projections are fully experienced, then the countertransference will be acted out to some partial degree' (p. 289). Such enactment can be expressed in the therapist's tone but at a deeper level still, the very 'act' of interpretation can be an enactment: an exploitation of what the analyst experiences as a valid interpretation that masks the hostility of a punitive superego often suffused with impotent rage.

By being in therapy the patient in effect insists that through an emotionally charged identification, the analyst accompanies them on their journey into their most primitive 'regressive transference immersions'. With the higher functioning patient, as Money-Kyrle (1956) contends, the analyst can function 'without becoming emotionally involved' in the patient's conflicts thereby preserving the therapist's containing function. However, this is never possible when working with borderline patients: the therapist is inevitably exposed to their own never-fully resolved psychopathology. The patient is confronted by a practitioner whose own regressive tendencies exposes them to the dangers of an unworked-through internal object relationship. For borderline patients this usually means the emergence of the most primitive object relations: a sado-masochistic relationship where the relationship dyad constellates the role pairing of sadist and victim. "The transference/counter-transference enactments emerge either as a sadistic counter-transference re-enactment (see Joseph, 1982) or, a 'reverse transference' where the analyst is positioned to enact the patient's masochistic experience (Nathan, 2018: p. 62). It is the therapist who now has to work through the disruption of their 'normal' state of being. As Money-Kyrle (1956) points out, such disturbance is commensurate with the severity of the therapist's own superego.

> [A]nalysis is also a form of work required of us by this inner figure . . . If our superego is predominantly friendly and helpful, we can tolerate our own limitations without undue distress, and, being undisturbed, will be the more likely soon to regain contact with the patient. But if it is severe, we may become conscious of a sense of failure as the expression of an unconscious

persecutory or depressive guilt. Or, as a defence against such feelings, we may blame the patient.

(p. 361)

The work of recovering our self-analytic ego functions requires us to recognise that we are being driven by unconscious psychic forces that are being enacted.

How does this pathological dynamic come about? Strachey (1934) identifies one element when he describes the patient as someone who is, 'all the time on the brink of turning the real external object (the analyst) into the archaic one' (p. 146). In such circumstances the analyst is in danger of succumbing to the patient's projective provocations and becoming that superego figure. This entails taking up not only the patient's 'relationship script', but the therapist's equivalent, internalised 'script', drawn from their own history now painfully reconstituted in the present. We are thereby drawn into our own paranoid-schizoid world, not just the patient's.

In terms of the transference/counter-transference dynamics, instead of being available to the patient as 'a projective-identification-containing-object', we fall prey to the patient's pre-existing 'scripted trap', fulfilling their relationship template as a 'projective identification-rejecting-object'. Brenman-Pick (1985) observes that projection is not just a matter of attributing an evacuated aspect of the patient's self to the analyst, but a demonstration of the patient's uncanny capacity to pinpoint their projective attacks on vulnerabilities within the practitioner. Carpy (1989) describes a patient who had developed a 'lifelong, and perfectly honed, ability to get under people's skins' (p. 292). According to Pick (2015) this happens because we are never really 'cured' of our early problems. This coupled with the borderline patient's capacity to evoke our most primitive responses, means it is vital to own these experiences, through our self-analysis and supervision, in order to maintain what I term, benign authority, something I will elaborate later. For Carpy (1989) this meant reflecting on his own regressive counter-transference immersion experienced as an impotent rage at being dismissed as useless by his patient. Recognising this as a projection of her feelings, he nevertheless goes on to own his experience concluding that 'I myself must be significantly susceptible to such feelings on my own account for such a successfully massive "transfer" of them to have taken place' (p. 290).

Here we see an analyst's own elemental superego activated and engaging with his primitive self. As Andrade (2005) shows, we are consciously using ourselves as an 'instrument of research' (Heimann, 1950) by encouraging an enactment of the patient's pathological organisation to develop within the human laboratory of the consulting room. We become both emotional collaborator and reflective practitioner – a participant-observer to our own, as well as the patient's, regression. We thereby also make available our not-entirely worked-through pathological selves. In so doing, we actively offer ourselves as 'the other' in a unique two-person psychodrama that encompasses both the patient's and the analyst's 'regressive transference immersion'. The patient's psychic conflict is now 'mapped' onto our own psychic organisation, generating a psychic conflict within us. It is not the analyst's regression per se that makes the practitioner vulnerable, but those aspects of the never-fully resolved ego, id or superego conflicts that are triggered. Sedlak (2016) suggests that the development of the 'normal' superego,

> does not mean that the pathological superego ceases to exist; it continues to be a potential regressive possibility at times of stress, particularly in reaction to narcissistic injury and frustration.
>
> (p. 1507)

Feldman (2009) contends that in these circumstances the analyst has to,

> be able to tolerate such experiences, and, where possible, to recover his analytic functions by re-establishing contact with his own internal objects; objects that have doubts, but are not filled with doubts.
>
> (p. 230)

The work required of the analyst is about a shift, once more, from the regressed elemental superego to the life-long maturing of the benign superego. The analyst can only help the patient to evolve a more benign superego after undertaking this internal work of re-establishing their own benign superego.

Before looking at the way benign authority links to the evolutionary gestation of a benign superego, I will briefly elaborate the Kleinian view of the superego.

The Kleinian superego and its implications for the analyst and patient

As Sedlak (2016) recently re-emphasised:

> [Klein] greatly amplified the role of love in the formation of the superego. . . . She considered that the creation of the good object was in the first instance dependent on the infant's love which was projected into the breast and created the sense of a good breast. Thereafter, if the caretaker was capable of providing good enough care, love was able to balance hate and destructiveness.
>
> (p. 1504)

Klein (1958) transformed the view of the superego by introducing its bi-focal quality: its 'protective' as well as its 'threatening' qualities, 'bound up' with the good internal object striving for life, mirrored in the loving good-enough mother, whilst also bound to death instinctual forces, where the mother is perceived as a frustrating figure arousing enormous persecutory anxiety. Through the process of integrating both loving and hating forces, the infant establishes a superego that is:

> in close relation with the ego and shares different aspects of the same good object. This makes it possible for the ego to integrate and accept the superego to a greater or less extent.
>
> (p. 241)

In its severe and punitive form, made explicit in self-harming patients, the elemental superego is constantly being constructed around a drive that seems to have a life of its own, endlessly perpetuating the self-harming cycle. The work with severe borderline pathology requires nothing less than a re-structuring of the pathological organisation. For Kernberg the key therapeutic task comprises movement from 'identity diffusion' (Kernberg et al., 2008), mirroring the development of a mind rigidly addicted to the paranoid-schizoid position, to depressive position functioning. Interpretation is therefore geared to promoting identity integration whereby the patient can tolerate experiencing:

> appropriate depressive affects, reflecting the capacity for acknowledging one's own aggression that had previously been projected or experienced as dysphoric affect, with concern, guilt, and the wish to repair good relationships damaged in fantasy or reality, becoming dominant.
>
> (p. 605)

To achieve this outcome requires an emotional engagement that inevitably and profoundly challenges the analytic practitioner, because we have to emotionally and intellectually understand that the borderline patient is inexorably driven by dyadic relationship templates where the elemental superego reigns supreme, and that these intra-psychic dynamics will inevitably get played, inter-psychically, in therapy. In that sense, it is more accurate to say that we deal with patients suffering from borderline interpersonality disorder. In practice this means responding to the relentless evacuation of the internal bad object that attacks any linking and indeed thought itself, as well as projective provocations geared at 'toppling' the practitioner from being able to function analytically. It is in response to having to deal with such a treacherous inter-psychic environment, that the idea of operating from a position of benign authority has been developed.

Benign authority: a working definition

Building on the original work of Mclean and Nathan (2007), I define benign authority as: the practitioner's capacity to respond to the dialectical tension that arises from attuning to the patient's emotional experience, whilst also setting limits to their behaviour. This formulation is geared to support the analytic practitioner's attention to counter-transference dynamics aroused by the borderline patient. It operates at two levels: the core and developmental levels. For the purposes of this chapter I focus on the core level that has a direct bearing on the way in which the elemental superego manifests in both patient and analyst.

At this core level benign authority manifests in the practitioner as a dialectical tension in the intercourse between 'maternal' affective attunement and 'paternal' limit setting. Adopting an analytic stance from a position of benign authority makes no attempt to achieve analytic perfection: in benign authority terms that would constitute an enactment predicated on idealisation of the analyst. Rather, holding the dialectical tension hinges on the practitioner closely monitoring their responses for unthought about, non-reflective 'maternal' masochism or 'paternal' sadism. For example, my irritation with Tom's casual request was given voice through my appeal to his more cognitive, ego-functioning self, which Tom understood more as an equally casual rejection of him by a 'projective identification-rejecting-object' (Bion, 1962). In his case, an important shift in Tom's psychic organisation emerged as he came to recognise that his relentless and intensifying rage at my attempts to attune to his pain, became understood by him as an expression of his hostile rejection of me, culminating in his literally storming out. He could 'see' his own aggression, in the past projected onto others, had emanated from his sense of victimhood, 'justifying' his giving full vent to his elemental superego. Equally important was 'the emotional work' (Hinshelwood, 1985) that I had to go through, acknowledging that I too had acted out my own irritation.

Benign authority and its relationship to the superego

When operating optimally, the therapist manages the dynamic tension between an intense empathic identification with the patient's experience whilst maintaining appropriate boundaries through limit setting. Money-Kyrle (1956) captures this optimal state when he speaks of:

> the phase in which the patient is the representative of a former immature or ill part of himself, including his damaged objects, which he can now understand and therefore treat by interpretation.
>
> (p. 361)

In this clinical environment, arousal of the analyst's own superego represents something the analyst recognises and has worked through. By contrast, with borderline patients, practitioners are confronted by challenges that disrupt their professional equilibrium. In one case a patient insisted that this was his space to be listened to without interruption. This was rationalised by the patient as his need to be heard because he was 'not ready' for any interpretations about this behaviour. However, it became clear, the therapist had already been 'toppled' from her role as a functioning practitioner: in benign authority terms, a collapse of her 'paternal' limit-setting function, left instead in a state of masochistic impotence. Ideas about appropriate 'paternal' limit setting, of time or availability, become redundant in cases involving suicidal threats when the practitioner is drawn into a symbiotic relationship, most often linked to their own pathology, as their conviction grows that only they can save the patient's life.

In its 'sadistic' form, the analytic response can acquire a more rigidly defensive quality. This may be masked by interpretations that denote a range of reactive responses including fear, dismissal and retaliation that reflect a need to regain control: a case of the practitioner's elemental superego given voice under the cover of an analytic 'interpretation'. Hinshelwood (1985) has explored the patient's disturbing impact on the practitioner's psychic equilibrium which gives rise to, 'the patient's defensive analyst'. He focuses on the way the patient 'interprets interpretations' to work out the impact that her disturbed (and disturbing) mind is having on the analyst's mind. This is most profoundly tested when the analyst finds himself struggling to attune to a patient's intra-psychic experience, especially when it is at odds with external reality. He instances a patient who clings to her belief that he is 'mistaken'. Though Hinshelwood's (1985) interpretations are 'correct', the patient understands that:

> In a sophisticated way she was actually describing the defences she believed my mind was using to avoid contact with her despair – an intellectual clinging to my theory against the floods of her feelings; and a narcissistic concern with my own products (theories).
>
> (p. 34)

He advises that to re-instate 'the projective identification-containing-object' requires emotional work from the analyst to recognise that he is being perceived as an 'analyst who has made a mistake'. And if the analyst is hesitant or resistant to recognise it, he does indeed make a mistake that confirms his patient's view of him (p. 30).

The patient 'knows' that attunement to their affective experience is absent as the analyst defensively tries to re-instate his own equilibrium. Two alternative clinical outcomes lie ahead: the patient's 'transference need' to re-experience their failing object re-enforces their sense of justified grievance and victimhood, a pathological organisation that helps to maintain the destructive psychic equilibrium (Hinshelwood, 1985). The other makes therapeutic use of such (re-) enactments requiring the 'emotional work' by the analyst confronting their own limitations and mistakes. Through this work the 'toppled' practitioner can reinstate their analytic position and, 'start to make interpretations about the patient's fear that his analyst's mind is under threat' (Hinshelwood, 1985: p. 40).

I will now turn to a clinical example from supervisory work with an experienced psychotherapist who became caught up in such a re-enactment and how benign authority helped support the supervisee regain her analytic equilibrium.

Eliciting the analyst's elemental superego in the counter-transference

The supervisee, 'Lydia', brought a patient with whom she had worked for some years. The therapist had begun to see a pattern, finding herself caught up in affect storms taking the form of arousing the patient's, as well as her own, intense rage, most often when she thought she was attuning to the patient's enormous pain. In the sequence presented, the patient describes herself as living 'a solo life', hiding her feelings from her 'absent', highly critical father and stepmother, emotionally regulating her experiences by self-harming from the age of six. The patient repeats her longing to have had parents who noticed her scars. They didn't, resorting to self-harm as the only 'object' relationship she could ultimately trust (Nathan,

2018). Whilst acknowledging her experience, Lydia points out that she was noticing her patient's pain.

The patient comes to the following session 'more defended', describing in great detail just how absent her parents were. Lydia finds herself, once again, feeling furious, and comments on the discrepancy between the measured way the patient is verbally communicating, whilst non-verbally communicating her rage at having had to live a solo life. What is striking is that at this moment Lydia is exactly mirroring her patient's verbal and non-verbal forms of communication, verbally measured and yet, as the patient 'understands', communicating her non-verbalised rage. The patient picks up on this after Lydia asks 'where do these feelings go?' as she goes on to accuse Lydia of being 'unapproachable'. Whilst acknowledging this may be the case, Lydia persists, now asking whether she has any interest in her responses. The patient explodes and says, 'what's the point?' Lydia is bemused, accused by the patient of 'squashing' her, just as she was by her parents. A 'transference need' (Hinshelwood, 1985) had been met – all objects let the patient down. She had successfully positioned Lydia as a highly critical bad object/stepmother, recreating the internalised relationship template shaped by a persecutor-victim constellation in which the distinctive and habitual affect is of being persecuted by the object, on this occasion, by her therapist.

Lydia is left, once again, defeated by the toxicity of the patient's experience. What began to emerge in supervision was the sense that this sequence of sessions reactivated Lydia's own pathological organisation leaving her deprived of her usually available observing 'triangular space', encapsulated by Britton (1989) as:

> a capacity for seeing ourselves in interaction with others and for entertaining another point of view whilst retaining our own, for reflecting on ourselves whilst being ourselves.
>
> (p. 87)

The patient actualised, in the here and now of her sessions, a dominant and disturbing relationship template that had Lydia in its grip, given expression by the patient's dismissive rage when Lydia was trying hard to 'meet' her patient. As in childhood, this triggered Lydia's own ancient-but-current rage. She attempts to mask her own psychic dis-equilibrium by trying to get her patient to listen to an interpretation. Here we see the part in us all that continues to nurture an unresolved wound. At such points our capacity to hold a simultaneous 'third position', that includes being attuned to the patient, whilst containing our own 'idiosyncratic' counter-transference reactions (Nathan, 2010), is replaced by our punitive, and seemingly justified, elemental superego.

Re-establishing her analytic equilibrium required painful 'emotional work' piecing together a picture of her own upbringing, where her attempts to gain her parents' approval invariably failed, leaving Lydia powerless and enraged. She also recognised that the scenario with her patient replicated the affect storms that were played out with her sister: 'I got caught up with my own and the client's superego', adding, 'that in certain circumstances with particularly aggressive and passive patients (who I work hard to help) they can indeed trigger my powerless rage'. We also came to see that however 'correct' her understanding, it was part of a continuing inner narrative, driven by her need to be heard. In this way Lydia was once more re-enacting the patient's 'transference need', affectively abandoning her patient, who was left unheard and attacked.

With this kind of understanding Lydia was able to 'return' to her patient, no longer a toppled, non-containing object, but one now able to reclaim her analytic stance. She was also more emotionally able to meet her patient's anxieties by affectively attuning into the patient's internal world where her experience had a profound and intimate logic. This included Lydia's understanding that her patient's hostility was a survival mechanism: what Glasser (1998) terms, 'self-preservative violence', which he defines as a 'fundamental, immediate and substantial response triggered by any threat to the self with the aim of negating this source of danger' (p. 889). As Lydia put it, "the defensive nature of my patient's behaviour is very important for her because in her mind she has realised that she is not going to get the care that she needs. Therefore 'she heads for the hills', a mechanism that is positive for her. This is important to understand when my patient withdraws (when it feels so easily 'not positive' for the work)"

We also came to recognise that by so doing, her patient also wants to punish Lydia, as she did her step-mum, for not attuning to her experience. From this perspective Lydia could see that by re-enacting her transference need, the patient was also 'sharing a great deal' of her tortured inner world. Finally, Lydia was able to track back to her own experience of hurt and rage about not being heard, an instance of an idiosyncratic counter-transference, reflective of her past, whilst simultaneously reflecting the patient's experience. Lydia concluded: 'I am now internally clear, and no longer triggered by my patient's "resistance", as I truly understand it was the best chance of survival in a non-attuned and emotional neglectful and persecutory world. That leaves us able to study her inner world without the escalation and cluttering from mine!'

Discussion

The work with borderline patients asks an enormous amount of practitioners because it requires them to re-engage with unresolved aspects of their own pathological organisation, reflected through the prism of the elemental superego. Within the psychoanalytic paradigm organised around benign authority, the psychotherapeutic task is one of maintaining the dialectical tension between 'maternal' affective attunement and 'paternal' limit setting. As I have shown in this chapter when benign authority breaks down, which it inevitably does with borderline patients, we are driven by a usually 'unseen', punitive superego. To re-establish benign authority, neither captured by masochistic collusion nor sadistic retaliation, requires 'emotional work'. The 'work' of re-engaging the benign superego is painful as we are compelled to deal with our own 'ego-destructive superego' (Bion, 1962). It is a force that represents the antithesis of our avowed intention, and something borderline patients are habituated to. Referencing Klein, Britton (2003) argues that the 'ego-destructive superego' (Bion, 1962) can only be mitigated by introjecting 'a loving mother and father'. In benign authority this takes the form of holding the tension between the receptive 'maternal' object able to absorb, reflect upon and give back to the patient something of their experience articulated in words, whilst simultaneously setting limits to behaviour that, 'paradoxically, communicates a benign "action" that can liberate the patient from a life that is profoundly self-destructive' (Nathan, 2018: p. 62). In this way, as Loewald (1960) puts it, "the analyst makes himself available for the development of a new 'object relationship' between the patient and the analyst" (pp. 224–5).

Having recognised her own difficulties, Lydia was able to evolve from a psychic position that gave voice to her own punitive, elemental superego, to one where she was able to re-make an emotional contact with her benign superego, that could tolerate a level of psychic violence perpetrated against her by the patient and re-find her 'third position' enabling her to re-function as a psychotherapist. This restored her to her patient as a practitioner less 'cluttered' by her own difficulties, once more present and able to facilitate her patient's 'ego-enhancing superego'.

References

Andrade, V.M. (2005) Affect and the therapeutic action of psychoanalysis. *International Journal Psychoanalysis*. 86, 677–697.

Bion, W.R. (1959) Attacks on linking. *International Journal of Psychoanalysis*. 40, 308–315.

Bion, W.R. (1962) The psycho-analytic study of thinking. *International Journal of Psychoanalysis*. 43, 306–310.

Brenman Pick, I. (1985) Working through in the countertransference. *International Journal of Psychoanalysis*. 66, 157–166.

Britton, R. (1989) The missing link: parental sexuality in the Oedipus complex. In: J. Steiner (ed.) *The Oedipus Complex Today: Clinical Implications*. London, Karnac Books.

Britton, R. (2003) *Sex, Death, and the Superego*. London: Karnac Books.

Carpy, D.V. (1989) Tolerating the counter transference: a mutative process. *International Journal of Psychoanalysis*. 70, 287–294.

Feldman, M. (2009) *Doubt, Conviction and the Analytic Process: Selected Papers of Michael Feldman. Filled with Doubt*. London, Routledge.

Glasser, M. (1998) On violence: a preliminary communication. *International Journal of Psychoanalysis*. 79, 887–902.

Heimann, P. (1950) On counter-transference. *International Journal of Psychoanalysis*. 31, 81–84.

Hinshelwood, R. (1985) The patient's defensive analyst. *British Journal of Psychotherapy*. 2(1), 30–41.

Joseph, B. (1982) Addiction to near-death. *International Journal of Psychoanalysis*. 63, 449–456.

Kernberg, O.F. (1975) *Borderline Conditions and Pathological Narcissism*. New York, Jason Aronson.

Kernberg, O.F., Selzer, M.A., Koenigsberg, H.W. et al. (1989) *Psychodynamic Psychotherapy of Borderline Patients*. New York, Basic Books.

Kernberg, O.F., Yeomans, F.E., Clarkin, J.F. & Levy, K.N. (2008) Transference focused psychotherapy: overview and update. *International Journal of Psychoanalysis*. 89, 601–620.

Klein, M. (1958) On the development of mental functioning. In: *Envy and Gratitude and Other Works 1946–1963*. 236–46, London, Hogarth Press.

Loewald, H.W. (1960). On the therapeutic action of psychoanalysis. In: *Papers on Psychoanalysis*. New Haven, CT, Yale Univeristy Press, 1980, pp. 221–256.

Mclean, D. & Nathan, J. (2007) Treatment of personality disorder: limit setting and the use of benign authority. *British Journal of Psychotherapy*. 23(2), 231–246.

Money-Kyrle, R.E. (1956) Normal counter-transference and some of its deviations. *International Journal of Psychoanalysis*. 37, 360–366.

Nathan, J. (2010) The place of psychoanalytic theory and research. In: M. Webber & J. Nathan (eds.) *Reflective Practice in Mental Health: Advanced Psychosocial Practice with Children, Adolescents and Adults*. London, Jessica Kingsley.

Nathan, J. (2018) The use of benign authority with severe borderline patients: a psychoanalytic paradigm. *British Journal of Psychotherapy.* 34(1), 61–77.

Pick, I.B. (2015) Irma Brenman-Pick on 'Working through in the Countertransference'. *International Journal of Psychoanalysis*. PEP/UCL Top Authors Project, 1(1), 1.

Sedlak, V. (2016) The psychoanalyst's normal and pathological superegos. *International Journal of Psychoanalysis*. 97, 1499–1520.

Strachey, J. (1934) The nature of the therapeutic action of psychoanalysis. *International Journal of Psychoanalysis*. 15, 127–159.

Symington, N. (1986) *The Analytic Experience: Lectures from the Tavistock*. London, Free Association Books.

Vaslamatzis, G. (1999) On the therapist's reverie and containing function. *Psychoanalytic Quarterly*. 68(3), 431–440.

Yeomans, F. E., Clarkin, J.F. & Kernberg, O.F. (2005) *A Primer of Transference-Focused Psychotherapy for the Borderline Patient*. New York, Jason Aronson.

Yeomans, F. E., Clarkin, J.F. & Kernberg, O.F. (2014) *Transference-Focused Psychotherapy for Borderline Personality Disorder: A Clinical Guide*. Washington, American Psychiatric Association.

Chapter 8

The role of the superego in psychopathic states of mind and personality

Celia Taylor

From moral insanity to psychopathy: a brief history of the modern concept

The German physician Koch (1889) introduced the term 'psychopath': he described the disorder as an 'inferiority' resulting, he believed, from a congenital defect of the brain. Hallucinations and delusions were absent, while severe disturbance and unprincipled behaviour featured prominently. The physician JC Prichard (1837) termed the condition 'moral insanity', at a time when 'moral' could refer to emotions rather than ethics. In these men, he observed:

> The active principles of the mind are strongly perverted or depraved; the power of self-government is lost or greatly impaired; and the individual is found to be incapable of . . . conducting himself with decency and propriety in the business of life.
>
> (p. 15)

Finney (1840), a Presbyterian minister, was also shocked by the apparent coexistence of normality with sheer malevolence:

> The man retains his intellectual powers unimpaired, but he sets his heart fully to evil. He refuses to yield to the demands of his conscience. He practically discards the obligations of moral responsibility. He has the powers of free moral agency, but persistently abuses them.
>
> (p. 2)

'Moral insanity' became a recognised diagnosis in the United States and Europe until the end of the nineteenth century, when Koch's term 'psychopath' replaced it as agreement spread that the condition was primarily innate. Freud (1928) attributed a binary nature to criminals with a psychopathic nature:

> Two traits are essential in a criminal: boundless egoism, and a strong destructive urge. Common to both of these, and a necessary condition for

their expression, is absence of love and lack of an emotional appreciation of (human) objects.

(p. 178)

Thirteen years later, Cleckley (1941), a psychiatrist, vividly portrayed psychopathy in his famous book, 'The Mask of Sanity'. Building upon the importance Freud stressed, of the coexistence of pathological narcissism and cruel aggression (Meloy & Shiva, 2007), Cleckley suggested that the psychopath presents as a normal, principled and even charming character, hiding beneath this façade his profoundly destructive intentions and utter lack of humane feeling. He initially appears engaging and kind. Only later does one discover his lack of empathy, affection or guilt; that callous lies underpin a capacity for parasitic exploitation, that he deflects personal responsibility for blatant misdeeds. Cleckley called the empty, shell-like quality of the psychopath's speech and behaviour, 'semantic dementia': it is as though these individuals say and do the right thing, without authenticity. Greenacre (1945) describes a further, common but perplexing trait:

> Characteristically, [these individuals] appear to live in the moment, with great intensity, acting without plan and seemingly without concern for the consequences. Indeed, the lack of practical appreciation of time, and the inability to learn from experience, stands out as cardinal symptoms.
>
> (p. 495)

Among other distinctive features she cites poor tolerance of pain, and polymorphous sexual perversions.

At the beginning of the twenty-first century, patients could be sectioned under the 1983 UK Mental Health Act category of Psychopathic Disorder, defined as:

> A persistent disorder or disability of mind (whether or not including significant impairment of intelligence), which results in abnormally aggressive or seriously irresponsible conduct on the part of the person concerned.
>
> (Legislation.gov.uk, 2015)

Although the term 'Psychopathic Disorder' was removed by a 2007 legislative amendment, the concept was given modern relevance through psychologist Hare's revised Psychopathy Checklist (PCL-R; Hare, 1991). This, now widely used psychological assessment tool, rates a person's behaviours and personality traits by a semi-structured interview, combined with a file review of collateral information. Hare drew on many of Cleckley's earlier observations, as well as his own experiences of working with male offenders. In an approach resonant with Freud's, the tool delineates two distinct facets of psychopathy: interpersonal-affective traits and indicators of antisocial behaviour (although this structure continues to be debated).

Factor 1

Glibness/superficial charm
Grandiose sense of self-worth
Need for stimulation/proneness to boredom
Pathological lying
Cunning/manipulative
Lack of remorse or guilt
Shallow affect [i.e. superficial experience and expression of emotions]
Callous/lack of empathy

Factor 2

Parasitic lifestyle
Poor behavioural controls
Promiscuous sexual behaviour
Early behaviour problems
Lack of realistic long-term goals
Impulsivity
Irresponsibility
Failure to accept responsibility for own actions
Many short-term marital relationships
Juvenile delinquency
Revocation of conditional release
Criminal versatility

Figure 8.1 Hare Psychopathy Checklist (PCL-R) factors 1 and 2 (Hare, 2003: p. 79)

Hare, R.D. (2003). *The Hare Psychopathy Checklist – Revised (PCL-R)*, 2nd Edition, p. 79. New York: Multi-Health Systems Technical Manuals.

The checklist has been criticised as merely reflecting many clinicians' strong, negative counter-transference reactions to these individuals, amounting to intense dislike, even hatred (Searles, 1979). Symington (1980) reminds us that the psychopath 'stirs our own primitive sadism', resulting in either condemnation or, more dangerously, collusion. However, high PCL-R scores are statistically associated with increased risk of violent offending (Hare et al., 2000). Furthermore, the clinician might be wise to recognise, at some level, the true nature of his patient: 'The central motivation of the psychopath is to dominate his objects' (Meloy & Reavis, 2007: p. 180). These authors illustrate how practitioners can experience strong, atavistic responses in the presence of a psychopath – 'my skin was crawling'; 'I was frozen with fear' – that warn of danger. As Van den Berg and Oei (2009) put it, 'members of this group seem to function socially as if they were hunters and other people were (literally) "fair game"' (p. 16).

> Therapeutic nihilism/condemnation
> Illusory treatment alliance
> Fear of assault or harm (sadistic control)
> Denial and deception (disbelief)
> Helplessness and guilt
> Devaluation and loss of professional identity
> Hatred and the wish to destroy
> Assumption of psychological maturity

Figure 8.2 Common countertransference reactions to the psychopathic patient (Meloy & Reavis, 2007: p. 186)

Meloy, J. R. & Reavis, J. A. (2007) Dangerous cases: when treatment is not an option. In: B. Van Luyn, S. Akhtar & W. J. Livesley (Eds.) *Severe Personality Disorders*. Cambridge, University Press, 181–195.

As well as developing the PCL-R, Hare wrote a book about various manifestations of the psychopath in society – from the white-collar conman to the serial killer – which he named, 'Without Conscience: The Disturbing World of the Psychopaths Among Us' (Hare, 1993). This title reminds us that a most disquieting feature of these individuals is their complete lack of guilt, remorse or self-reflective authority exercising moral judgement – in other words, a superego.

Is the psychopath born and made?

Modern studies show that normal children begin to behave altruistically very early in life. For example, one-year-olds can comfort those in distress and help adults with tasks (Svetlova et al., 2010). Schmidt and Sommerville (2011) showed that babies who were sensitive to the fair distribution of food were also more likely to share a toy. This raises a question about what has gone wrong in those destined to become psychopaths? Is the condition inherited or acquired? Is there more than one form of it?

Since modern brain scanning techniques were introduced, the brains of psychopathic individuals show quite specific abnormalities, largely in the prefrontal-temporo-limbic circuit – regions involved, among others, in emotional and learning processes (e.g. Weber et al., 2008). Similar findings were reported by Gregory et al. (2012), who note the association of these areas of the brain with a poor response to fear and distress, and a lack of self-conscious emotions such as guilt or embarrassment, as well as mentalising. While such studies cannot tell us the origin of these abnormalities, there is growing evidence of causal factors on both sides of the nature/nurture divide. For example, recent research in children has shown that 'callous, unemotional traits', like limited empathy and shallow affect, are strongly heritable (Jones et al., 2009). Many such children also experience related difficulties, with peer relationships, social interaction and hyperactivity. On the other hand, environmental factors have also been found significant to the development of psychopathy. Thus Porter (1996) found that severely abused children could learn to 'turn off' their emotions as a way of coping. Psychopaths' callous and unfeeling behaviour might be understood, therefore, as emotional adaptation to severe parental maltreatment (Skeem et al., 2007). The impact of such experiences on psychic and neuronal development will be considered further below.

As with other complex conditions – such as schizophrenia – the debate is moving towards concluding that both genes and environment play an aetiological role. A meta-review of fifteen twin studies estimated the relative contribution of each as being approximately equal (Evertsson & Meehan, 2012). Someone who inherits a genetic vulnerability, therefore, might not exhibit full-blown psychopathy unless exposed to significant environmental adversity. In fact, early lack of maternal care, abuse and resulting disturbances of attachment have been linked not only been to callous-unemotional traits and aggressiveness (Kimonis et al., 2013), but also to damage in the same regions of the brain shown to be abnormal in psychopaths (Narvaez, 2014). It is important to bear in mind, however, the evidence that psychopathy is not a uniform condition and that subtypes exist (e.g. Murphy & Vess, 2003).

The psychopath's early development

The psychopath's indifference to the suffering he inflicts on others has been understood psychodynamically as due to faulty superego development. Freud (1930) contended that children develop a conscience in response to aggressive wishes towards their parents for exerting authority over them. Rather than act on these aggressive wishes and risk losing a parents' love, children identify with and internalise a capacity to control their aggression in a process that results in the superego or conscience. Klein (1933) described young children's experiences of their parents as 'internalized wild beasts and monsters', bearing little resemblance to how they are in reality. This evokes enormous anxieties in the infant, generating corresponding aggressive impulses, which, via projection, he displaces outwards. In Klein's view, when this early superego is not modified as the child develops, he will develop severely antisocial and criminal tendencies. Bowlby (1944) recognised this phenomenon from studying juvenile thieves who exhibited a form of 'affectionless psychopathy'.

Greenacre (1945) described how the child psychopath is often raised by a remote and stern father who tends to occupy a position of public trust and authority – such as a judge or police officer – whilst mother is overly permissive and attached to her son as an extension of herself. The child's difficulty in identifying with the distant, fierce father, in conjunction with his prolonged emotional enslavement to the mother, thwarts his growth into a separate, distinct individual. Furthermore, he is invariably 'on show' and any imperfections are denied, concealed or explained away. He is thus defrauded of reality testing experiences, learning that what *seems* to be is more valued than what *is*, thus amplifying his own narcissistic fantasies of omnipotence.

Anthropologist Eli Sagan (1988) argued that our moral sense originates in the maternal relationship and the child's identification with the mother/nurturer from which develop our capacities for pity, kindness and compassion, i.e. the bedrock of conscience. The corollary is that a pathological mother–infant bond can be highly detrimental to this process. Winnicott (1960) too described an overly narcissistic mother's contribution to a pathological developmental trajectory: her affection is contingent on his compliance, impeding the normal process of individuation and leaving him unable to differentiate himself from her imposed, self-gratifying perception of him.

Much more recently, Fonagy and Bateman (2008) describe how disturbances of attachment can lead to a failure to 'mentalize', to develop a reflective function about the minds of others. Insecure early attachments in particular undermine and distort the mentalising capacity. An individual whose care in infancy was highly deficient will grow up to view the social world as dangerous, and develop a moral mind-set in which self-protection overrides any empathy or altruism. Acting from self-interest, he will be prepared to exploit, shame and deceive others with impunity (Narvaez, 2014). As Van den Berg and Oei (2009) point out, to survive, which is what people with very unsafe attachments have to do, the obvious 'choice' is to enter into instrumental relations whose goal is the acquiring of power (p. 15).

Some have challenged the notion that psychopaths do not possess the theory of mind required for empathy – for example, Dolan and Fullam (2004) found that some can indeed take a victim's perspective, but use it to exploit, rather than care for, the vulnerable other: they display contempt for neediness in others, deriving gratification from exerting power and mastery over people in distress (Adshead et al., 2013). Esperger and Bereczkei (2012) note that those employing 'Machiavellian' strategies successfully use their 'empathic' understanding of others, to determine exactly how to mislead, exploit and hurt them most successfully. Van den Berg and Oei (2009) have argued that psychopathic personalities without experience of secure attachments regard others only as objects or opponents they have to deal with for the sake of survival, with no requirement for reciprocity.

Others have challenged the notion that psychopaths lack a superego. Clinical observation suggests that some serious criminals are wedded to a 'moral hierarchy' of different types of crime or matters of loyalty. Thus, within prison cultures, murderers are accorded high respect, while child sex offenders are frequently sought out for stabbings with home-made 'shanks'. A particularly harsh superego can develop in the context of the withholding and judgemental maternal bond that many psychopaths have experienced. Rather than be crippled by anxiety and self-condemnation, this superego is disavowed and externalised, driving the psychopath to exercise a ruthless and merciless control over others (Parsons, 2009). As has already been mentioned, individual psychopaths differ in the degree to which they lack theory of mind or a superego.

Anna Freud (1936) described a defence she called 'identification with the aggressor': these children, rather than perpetually being preyed upon, grow up to wield the terror against others – sometimes their own children – as adults. Ferenczi (1988) also describes the psychic impact of childhood maltreatment by a parent: the victim introjects the terror, identifies himself with it thus remaining a victim throughout his life by repetition compulsion. Meloy and Shiva (2007) referred to this identification in the psychopath as 'a predator part-object': his entire, idealised sense of self is built around the control and subjugation of his objects, denigrating and dismissing them thus, maintaining the architecture of his being. This damage is likely to begin during infancy, 'the psychopath has suffered a loss while mother and infant were still a unit' (Symington, 1980: p. 294).

Gilligan (1996) worked for many years with very violent men as Director for Mental Health of the Massachusetts prison system. Like other psychiatrists, he found these violent men to have been repeatedly shamed whilst growing up, through suffering unthinkable severe neglect, abuse and humiliation:

> They have seen their closest relatives – their fathers and mothers and sisters and brothers – murdered in front of their eyes, often by other family members. As children, these men were shot, axed, scalded, beaten, strangled, tortured, drugged, starved, suffocated, set on fire, thrown out of windows, raped, or prostituted by mothers who were their 'pimps'; their bones have been broken, and they have been locked in closets or attics for extended periods.
>
> (p. 45)

Schore (1998) has described how shame originates in the normal toddler's occasional experiences of mother's disappointment in him, which act as an early, necessary regulator of narcissism in social relationships. Shame can become crippling, however, when the child is subject to unceasing rejection, ridicule or fear (Herman, 2012): over time, it solidifies into an entrenched sense of self-loathing (Fonagy et al., 2003). The psychopath has, however, successfully disavowed these intensely painful emotions along with the vulnerability they bring, resulting in what Gilligan (1996) has called the 'death of the self' – a loss of any capacity to feel love, guilt or remorse, reflected by the cruelty they inflict on their victims. This resonates with Shengold's concept of 'soul murder': the destruction of 'a child's capacity for joy and inhibiting the power to care and to love' (1989, p. 114). Gilligan argues that any perceived threat to the masculinity of such men – any sign of being disrespected or 'dissed' – is experienced as a matter of life and death; a violent response is not just warranted, it is required.

Circling back to the impact of chronic childhood maltreatment on the brain: long-term, severe stress leads to excessively high cortisol levels, which damages structures such as the hippocampus and amygdala (King, 2016). Eventually, the complex feedback system that normally suppresses excess production of cortisol is over-ridden, and the capacity to discriminate between threat levels fades away. Eventually, everything seems dangerous, resulting in a constant state of fear, or nothing does, resulting in depression and burnout. Teicher and Samson (2016) have established that maltreatment at various early developmental stages is associated with damage to regions of the brain that transmit both the physiological feelings, and the emotions, that identify terror. Teicher (2002) concludes, ' "maltreatment is a chisel that shapes a brain" to contend with strife, but at the cost of deep, enduring wounds' (p. 13).

The psychopathic superego in action

Examples of individuals exhibiting the severest forms of superego pathology are mostly encountered within prisons and forensic mental health units too dangerous and destructive to function within normal society. Even whilst securely detained, some will damage the institutions, staff and other residents.

Betrayal and vengeance

Gregory,[1] was subjected during childhood to erratic and cruel treatment by his mentally ill mother – for example, made to eat from a dog's bowl in the garden and abandoning him whilst out, leaving him lost and alone. She committed suicide when Gregory was fifteen years old. Subsequently he became involved in increasingly violent robberies and burglaries, and eventually imprisoned. Shortly before release from open prison, he was allowed to visit his father. Instead, he broke into a lone woman's house, tied her up and stole her car. Gregory then drove to a friend's house, demanded cash and battered the man to death when he could not, or would not, oblige. Astonishingly, he was convicted of Manslaughter on the grounds of diminished responsibility and disposed to a maximum secure hospital rather than returned to custody. There, he turned against a fellow inpatient, throwing two jugs of boiling water over the man whilst he sat watching television, burning him so severely he required skin grafts. Gregory explained that his victim deserved it for acting as the 'ward bully', whilst he had taken a principled stand for the sake of his more vulnerable peers.

Back in prison, there was no sense of Gregory taking responsibility, or acknowledging the immorality of his exploitative and terrifying crimes. He illustrates the psychopath's near complete failure to internalise any values; his indifference to his victims echoes of the way Gregory's mother treated him. In the 'ward bully' he encountered an external representation of his own identification with the predatory stranger. After these events, Gregory adopted the role of victim – which, of course, he was, as a child – who suffered from similar mental health problems like his mother. He consolidated his belief in the righteousness of his actions: he was a martyr, now paying an unfair price for protecting others; failed by the professionals, who were too selfish to give him the sympathy and care he so clearly deserved; making distressed appeals on this basis to new staff, who could be susceptible to the lure of being the 'rescuer'. He thus inverted the truth of the situation, by passing on the guilt to them: Gregory showed little sign of a capacity to form attachments to staff attempting to treat him beyond evincing feelings of guilt and failure.

Sadism

Michael was the youngest child of a disciplinarian father and affectionate mother. From an early age he responded to her attempts to impose reasonable boundaries with rage and repudiation. Feeling excluded from the favoured place he believed his sister occupied, he developed a smouldering resentment towards her and towards women in general. By the time he reached puberty, he had attacked and stabbed two female strangers, and been hospitalised for psychiatric treatment. After his discharge, Michael attempted unsuccessfully to form sexual relationships with women, but experienced the final moment of ejaculation as profoundly threatening, and learned to withhold it. He came across an online account of the capture and arrest of a notorious Belgian sadistic murderer; the story included pictures of his bound, dead victims. Michael concluded that bondage was 'the solution' to his problems: whilst living an outwardly 'normal' life, he honed a technique of stalking unsuspecting victims before tricking, capturing and tying them up and torturing them over lengthy periods. He described killing one of them when he became convinced that she was 'still in charge of the situation,' when in reality she was helpless.

Michael represents many aspects of Glasser's (1996) 'core complex' anxieties experienced by violent individuals in intimate relationships. His hatred of his victim, and inability to tolerate her seeming to be 'in charge', was the spur for him to exert the ultimate control by taking her life. He appeared to be – in some senses was – a kind and unassuming gentleman, capable of showing respect and interest. Indeed, this was the person one met in one's clinical role, necessitating a surprising mental effort to keep his offences in mind. This, no doubt, was the man his unsuspecting victim met and trusted. Once she was captured and under his control, Michael could vent all his anger and hatred through a prolonged act of repeated rape and torture. Schurman-Kauflin (2005) suggests that these individuals are masters of deception, living otherwise ordinary, even charitable lives: Jimmy Saville, for example, raised millions of pounds for various charities. Michael hotly denied being a psychopath, citing, correctly, his capacity for close emotional affinity with his targets. He was not able to recognise that using this to control his targets was his substitute for a real intimacy – one that would threaten his psychic survival. When finally arrested, his lack of any attempt to defend or justify his behaviour, or even express anger at being caught, was striking: he was simply indifferent to social opprobrium. He had no capacity to see himself as others did, or to comprehend their abhorrence of his cruelty.

Exploitation

Adam's parents were violent towards each other and towards him from a young age. This, Adam said, affected his whole life: 'I became panicky and paranoid, and hit people for no reason'. He escaped to his uncle's house, but was sexually abused there. At school Adam fought 'with bullies', and defied his teachers.

Adam's father tried to strangle his mother; Adam saw her being resuscitated by an ambulance crew before admission to intensive care. Father was convicted of attempted murder serving eight years in prison. Adam recalled his remorse: 'he was a good man deep down inside'. Adam said afterwards 'I lost my own soul and totally shut off from people'. He started taking drugs and was convicted of a string of vicious burglaries, typically of pubs with rough landlords who challenged his ability to prevail in a violent situation.

In prison Adam formed a relationship with a female teacher in the prison's Education Department. An older woman, she was despondent about being in a childless, unhappy marriage. Over time, she yielded to his influence, agreeing to smuggle in drugs, a mobile phone and pornography. When the relationship was discovered, she was sacked and reported, effectively ruining her chances of re-employment. Adam, indifferent and blasé, boasted of her 'usefulness' to him, including the money he made by selling the contraband. Some years later, Adam was sent to an open prison and allowed rehabilitative home visits. But instead of spending time with his mother, he met with a young female prison officer for illicit sex. He eventually absconded with her, and when caught was returned to closed prison conditions. The young prison officer was convicted and sent to prison herself – an intensely shaming end to her career.

It is clinically recognised that some victims of abuse harbour the most rage towards the one who failed to protect them. Unconsciously, Adam despised his mother's victimhood; even when given chances to visit her, he spurned the contact for sexual gratification. Identifying with the aggressor, his father, he grew up not only to brutalise other men through violence, but also to seduce women by convincing them he was a deeply regretful, reformed character. Contemptuous of their neediness, he derived a sense of triumph from misleading and exploiting them. They were objects he used for his own ends, for whom he felt no pity. As Symington (1980) suggests, 'the needs of survival do not allow [the psychopath] to attack his primary love object – the mother' (p. 293). Rage and revenge will therefore be displaced onto others, compounded both by the psychopath's capacity to mask his true feelings (Porter et al., 2011), and by his denial of the reality of his victim as a whole object with her own wishes and feelings. Adam's self-diagnosis was correct: he had lost his own soul.

Psychopathy and punishment

It is a fundamental moral principle that people should respect the rights of others to property, physical integrity and life itself. Adshead (1996) refers to a quote from an early Chinese philosopher, illustrating how most abide by this principle, because they 'have a mind which cannot bear to see the suffering of others' (p. 279). For centuries, societal responses to our worst criminals have been retributive via the deprivation of life and/or of liberty. Sentencing guidelines for UK judges advise taking into account expressions of remorse as a mitigating factor. However, as I have shown, psychopaths consciously experience no regret or inhibitions about replaying their misdeeds. Psychopaths seem to be incapable of showing authentic remorse, since they care nothing for the distress of others, indeed may actively take pleasure in it, while empathic concern and pity are foreign to them. It has been argued that these deficits negate criminal responsibility, because psychopaths cannot form 'other-regarding' moral beliefs or affective capacity (Adshead, 1996), and thereby lack what is required to be a 'responsible agent' (Fields, 1996) and might more justly be considered criminally insane.

The logical conclusion of such arguments – that psychopaths should be exempt from punishment – is something that wider society would baulk at. Modern insights into the way psychopaths' brains function imply that while 'justice served' is important, especially for victims and their families, it teaches these people no useful lessons. Using functional MRI scanning of brain activity, Gregory et al. (2015) found that psychopaths do not change their behaviour when positive consequences shift to negative or from reward to punishment. In fact, they showed *increased* activity in certain parts of the brain, indicating that they process punishment differently: put simply, psychopaths do not comprehend or learn from sanctions. As clinicians can attest, most psychopaths have been repeatedly punished from an early age, with no discernible benefit.

Psychopathy and treatment

Since most psychopathic offenders will one day be released, it behoves us also to consider how we can prevent recidivism. Rehabilitation is an important second limb of the criminal justice system in most modern societies, but are psychopaths treatable? Given the extreme damage, suffering and distress caused by this small group of people, the search for successful remedies has been the Holy Grail of research and clinical endeavour in the field.

Attempts to treat a condition in which a façade of principled charm conceals profoundly destructive intentions risk not just failure but fanning the flames of the psychopath's fire. A study by Rice et al. (1992), examining the efficacy of a maximum secure therapeutic community, concluded that treatment made psychopaths *worse*. The authors speculated that improving psychopaths' perspective-taking skills, finessing emotional intelligence and social interchanges simply increased their capacity to manipulate and exploit others. The validity of this study has been questioned (Porter et al., 2009). Other studies are more optimistic that cognitive-behavioural therapy can ameliorate some undesirable behaviour, like overt anger and substance misuse, and to some extent reduce recidivism (e.g. Olver, 2016).

Treatment is usually confined to secure institutional settings. Many clinicians hesitate before attempting the task, because the generally corrupting influence of antisocial patients within therapeutic facilities is well recognised:

> The decision to hospitalise . . . usually leads to regret. His disruptive behaviour may grossly interfere with the treatment of other patients and may bring all therapeutic programmes to a grinding halt. These patients will steal from,

sexually exploit and assault other patients; they will also lie to and ridicule staff members, smuggle drugs and alcohol into the unit, ridicule the treatment philosophy and corrupt staff members into dishonest and unethical behaviours. Some will systematically destroy any therapeutic relationship other patients have developed with the treatment staff.

(Gabbard, 2000: p. 500)

Müller-Isberner and Hodgins (2000) similarly found psychopaths to be highly troublesome in treatment units, preferring to undermine others' progress rather than straightforwardly refusing to comply. As a consequence, they are likely to be screened out, to drop out or to be expelled (Caldwell et al., 2006).

Undertaking individual or outpatient treatment is likewise fraught with difficulty and dire warnings: 'When psychopathy enters the consulting room, for the psychotherapist or psychoanalyst it is a sign of danger' (Meloy & Reavis, 2007). Mental health professionals tend to be interested in the welfare of their patients, highly sympathetic to their difficulties and committed to their recovery. The psychopaths' talent for intuiting what is wanted of them, and – if it suits their own ends – providing it subverts the clinicians efforts. Unwary therapists can easily believe they have created a working relationship that is, in reality, fake. Meloy (1988) has called this phenomenon 'malignant pseudo-identification': another form of trickery, from which psychopaths gain a sense of scornful conquest. Experienced professionals within the criminal justice system are not immune: one study showed that psychopathic offenders are twice as likely to be granted conditional release (Porter et al., 2009), despite it being known that their risk of serious reoffending is high.

There is little evidence that psychopaths can benefit from conventional psychodynamic psychotherapy (Kernberg, 1998). Nevertheless, a few intrepid clinicians – largely forensic psychotherapists working in secure institutions – do make the attempt with a select few, either individually or in groups (Cox, 1998). Much guidance exists as to how to approach this onerous task safely and with the best hope of achieving improvements. Kernberg (1998) particularly writes about the therapist's problematic counter-transference experiences during treatment, saying it is important to find a potentially likeable, authentic and human aspect to the patient: 'When such a core of object relation investment can be found, it assures a capacity for authentic dependency and the establishment of a therapeutic relationship' (p. 381). Meloy and Yakeley (2007) also advise extremely careful assessment of risk and personality characteristics amongst other features of each case. Those likely to be less amenable to therapy include individuals without capacities for anxiety or attachment, because they will relate to the therapist solely on the basis of power (Meloy, 1988). As we have seen, highly narcissistic patients will employ aggressive devaluation to buttress their grandiosity against emotional wounds (Meloy & Yakeley, 2007), which can be acted upon to a fatal degree.

In conclusion, the wise clinician will make an informed selection of a less extremely disturbed individual, and bear in mind the physical, psychological and legal pitfalls that can arise during treatment. Above all, self-reflection and honesty in appraising progress – or lack of it – are required qualities in the therapist, as they will be lacking in his or her patient.

Note

1 Vignettes are anonymised composites from the author's clinical practice.

References

Adshead, G. (1996) Commentary on 'Psychopathy, Other-Regarding Moral Beliefs, and Responsibility'. *Philosophy, Psychiatry, & Psychology.* 3(4), 279–281.

Adshead, G., Moore, E., Humphrey, M., Wilson, C. & Tapp, J. (2013) The role of mentalizing in the management of violence. *Advances in Psychiatric Treatment.* 19(1), 67–76.

Bowlby, J. (1944) Forty-four juvenile thieves: their characters and home-life. *The International Journal of Psychoanalysis.* 25, 19–52.

Caldwell, M., Skeem, J., Salekin, R. & Van Rybroek, G. (2006) Treatment response of adolescent offenders with psychopathy features: a 2-year follow-up. *Criminal Justice and Behavior.* 33(5), 571–596.

Cleckley, H.M. (1941) *The Mask of Sanity: An Attempt to Reinterpret the So-called Psychopathic Personality.* St. Louis, The C.V. Mosby Company.

Cox, M. (1998) A group-analytic approach to psychopaths: 'The ring of truth'. In: *Psychopathy: Antisocial, Criminal, and Violent Behavior.* New York, Guilford Press, pp. 393–406.

Dolan, M. & Fullam, R. (2004) Theory of mind and mentalizing ability in antisocial personality disorders with and without psychopathy. *Psychological Medicine.* 34(6), 1093–1102.

Esperger, Z. & Bereczkei, T. (2012) Machiavellianism and spontaneous mentalization: one step ahead of others. *European Journal of Personality.* 26(6), 580–587.

Evertsson, H. & Meehan, A. (2012) *Genetic and Environmental Influences on Psychopathic Personality Traits: A Meta-Analytic Review.* Örebro, Örebro University.

Ferenczi, S. (1988) Confusion of tongues between adults and the child: the language of tenderness and of passion. *Contemporary Psychoanalysis.* 24(2), 196–206.

Fields, L. (1996) Psychopathy, other-regarding moral beliefs, and responsibility. *Philosophy, Psychiatry, & Psychology.* 3(4), 261–277.

Finney, C.G. (1840) *Views of Sanctification.* Cleveland, James Steele.

Fonagy, P. & Bateman, A. (2008) The development of borderline personality disorder – a mentalizing model. *Journal of Personality Disorders.* 22(1), 4–21.

Fonagy, P., Target, M., Gergely, G., Allen, J.G. & Bateman, A.W. (2003) The developmental roots of borderline personality disorder in early attachment relationships: a theory and some evidence. *Psychoanalytic Inquiry.* 23(3), 412–459.

Freud, A. (1936) Identification with the aggressor. In: *The Ego and the Mechanisms of Defence.* London, Hogarth Press, pp. 117–131.

Freud, S. (1928). Dostoevsky and parricide. In: *Standard Edition of the Complete Psychological Works of Sigmund Freud.* Volume XXI, London, Hogarth Press.

Freud, S. (1930) *Civilization and Its Discontents.* New York, W.W. Norton & Company, Inc., 1962.

Gabbard, G.O. (2000) *Psychodynamic Psychiatry in Clinical Practice*. Washington, American Psychiatric Publications.

Gilligan, J. (1996) *Violence: Our Deadly Epidemic and Its Causes*. New York, GP Putnam.

Glasser, M. (1996) Aggression and sadism in the perversions. In: I. Rosen (ed.) *Sexual Deviation*. 3rd edition. New York, Oxford University Press, pp. 279–299.

Greenacre, P. (1945) Conscience in the psychopath. *American Journal of Orthopsychiatry*. 15(3), 495–509.

Gregory, S., Blair, R.J., Simmons, A., Kumari, V., Hodgins, S. & Blackwood, N. (2015) Punishment and psychopathy: a case-control functional MRI investigation of reinforcement learning in violent antisocial personality disordered men. *The Lancet Psychiatry*. 2(2), 153–160.

Gregory, S., Simmons, A., Kumari, V., Howard, M., Hodgins, S. & Blackwood, N. (2012) The antisocial brain: psychopathy matters: a structural MRI investigation of antisocial male violent offenders. *Archives of General Psychiatry*. 69(9), 962–972.

Hare, R.D. (1991) *The Psychopathy Checklist: Revised Manual*. Toronto, Ontario, Canada, Multi-Health Systems.

Hare, R.D. (1993) *Without Conscience: The Disturbing World of the Psychopaths Among Us*. New York, Guilford Press.

Hare, R.D. (2003) *The Hare Psychopathy Checklist – Revised (PCL-R)*. 2nd edition. New York, Multi-Health Systems Technical Manuals, p. 79.

Hare, R.D., Clark, D., Grann, M. & Thornton, D. (2000) Psychopathy and the predictive validity of the PCL-R: an international perspective. *Behavioral Sciences & the Law*. 18(5), 623–645.

Herman, J.L. (2012) Shattered shame states and their repair. In: K. White & J. Yellin (eds.) *Shattered States: Disorganised Attachment and Its Repair*. London, Karnac Books.

Jones, A.P., Laurens, K.R., Herba, C.M., Barker, G.J. & Viding, E. (2009) Amygdala hypoactivity to fearful faces in boys with conduct problems and callous-unemotional traits. *American Journal of Psychiatry*. 166(1), 95–102.

Kernberg, O.F. (1998) The psychotherapeutic management of psychopathic, narcissistic, and paranoid transferences. In: T. Millon, E. Simonsen, R.D. Davis & M. Birket-Smith (eds.) *Psychopathy: Antisocial, Criminal, and Violent Behavior*. New York, Guilford Press, pp. 372–392.

Kimonis, E.R., Cross, B., Howard, A. & Donoghue, K. (2013) Maternal care, maltreatment and callous-unemotional traits among urban male juvenile offenders. *Journal of Youth and Adolescence*. 42(2), 165–177.

King, A. (2016) Neurobiology: rise of resilience. *Nature*. 531(7592), S18.

Klein, M. (1933) The early development of conscience in the child. In: *Love, Guilt and Reparation: And Other Works 1921–1945 (The Writings of Melanie Klein, Volume 1)*. New York, Simon and Schuster, pp. 248–257.

Koch, J.L.A. (1889) *Kurzgefaßter Leitfaden der Psychiatrie. Mit Rücksichtnahme auf die Bedürfnisse der Studirenden, der practischen Aerzte und der Gerichtsärzte*. 2nd edition. Ravensburg, Dom.

Legislation.gov.uk. (2015). *Mental Health Act 1983*. [online] Available at: www.legislation.gov.uk/ukpga/1983/20/contents [Accessed 27 January 2018].

Meloy, J.R. (1988) *The Psychopathic Mind: Origins, Dynamics, and Treatment*. Northvale, NJ, Jason Aronson.

Meloy, J.R. & Reavis, J.A. (2007) Dangerous cases: when treatment is not an option. In: B. Van Luyn, S. Akhtar & W.J. Livesley (eds.) *Severe Personality Disorders*. Cambridge, Cambridge University Press, pp. 181–195.

Meloy, J.R. & Shiva, A. (2007) A psychoanalytic view of the psychopath. In: A. Felthous & H. Sass (eds). *The International Handbook of Psychopathic Disorders and the Law*. Hoboken, Wiley Blackwell, pp. 335–346.

Meloy, J.R. & Yakeley, J. (2007) Antisocial personality disorder. In: G.O. Gabbard (ed.) *Gabbard's Treatments of Psychiatric Disorders*. Washington, American Psychiatric Publications, pp. 1015–1034.

Muller-Isberner, R. & Hodgins, S. (2000) Evidence-based treatment for mentally disordered offenders. In: S. Hodgins (ed.) *Violence, Crime and Mentally Disordered Offenders: Concepts and Methods for Effective Treatment and Prevention*. Toronto, John Wiley & Sons, Ltd., pp. 7–38.

Murphy, C. & Vess, J. (2003) Subtypes of psychopathy: proposed differences between narcissistic, borderline, sadistic, and antisocial psychopaths. *Psychiatric Quarterly*. 74(1), 11–29.

Narvaez, D. (2014) *Neurobiology and the Development of Human Morality: Evolution, Culture, and Wisdom*. New York, W.W. Norton & Company, Inc.

Olver, M.E. (2016) Treatment of psychopathic offenders: evidence, issues, and controversies. *Journal of Community Safety and Well-Being*. 1(3), 75–82.

Parsons, M. (2009) The roots of violence: theory and implications for technique with children and adolescents. In: M. Lanyado & A. Horne (eds.) *The Handbook of Child and Adolescent Psychotherapy: Psychoanalytic Approaches*. 2nd edition. London, Routledge, pp. 361–380.

Porter, S. (1996) Without conscience or without active conscience? The etiology of psychopathy revisited. *Aggression and Violent Behavior*. 1(2), 179–189.

Porter, S., ten Brinke, L., Baker, A. & Wallace, B. (2011) Would I lie to you? 'Leakage' in deceptive facial expressions relates to psychopathy and emotional intelligence. *Personality and Individual Differences*. 51(2), 133–137.

Porter, S., ten Brinke, L. & Wilson, K. (2009) Crime profiles and conditional release performance of psychopathic and non-psychopathic sexual offenders. *Legal and Criminological Psychology*. 14(1), 109–118.

Prichard, J.C. (1837) *A Treatise on Insanity: And Other Disorders Affecting the Mind*. Philadelphia, Haswell, Barrington and Haswell.

Rice, M.E., Harris, G.T. & Cormier, C.A. (1992) An evaluation of a maximum security therapeutic community for psychopaths and other mentally disordered offenders. *Law and Human Behavior*. 16(4), 399–412.

Sagan, E. (1988) *Freud, Women and Morality: The Psychology of Good and Evil*. New York, Basic Books.

Searles, H.F. (1979) *Countertransference and Related Subjects: Selected Papers*. Madison, International Universities Press, Inc.

Schmidt, M.F. & Sommerville, J.A. (2011) Fairness expectations and altruistic sharing in 15-month-old human infants. *PloS One* 6(10), 23223.

Schore, A.N. (1998). Early shame experiences and infant brain development. In: P. Gilbert & B. Andrews (eds.) *Series in Affective Science. Shame, Interpersonal Behavior, Psychopathology, and Culture*. New York, Oxford University Press pp. 57–77.

Schurman-Kauflin, D. (2005) *Vulture: Profiling Sadistic Serial Killers*. Irvin, Universal Publishers.

Shengold, L. (1989) *Soul Murder: The Effects of Childhood Abuse and Deprivation*. New Haven, CTT, Yale University Press.

Skeem, J., Johansson, P., Andershed, H., Kerr, M. & Louden, J.E. (2007) Two subtypes of psychopathic violent offenders that parallel primary and secondary variants. *Journal of Abnormal Psychology.* 116, 395–409.

Svetlova, M., Nichols, S.R. & Brownell, C.A. (2010) Toddlers' prosocial behavior: from instrumental to empathic to altruistic helping. *Child Development.* 81(6), 1814–1827.

Symington, N. (1980) The response aroused by the psychopath. *International Review of Psychoanalysis.* 7, 291–298.

Teicher, M.H. (2002) Scars that won't heal: the neurobiology of child abuse. *Scientific American.* 286(3), 68–75.

Teicher, M.H. & Samson, J.A. (2016) Annual research review: enduring neurobiological effects of childhood abuse and neglect. *Journal of Child Psychology and Psychiatry.* 57(3), 241–266.

Van den Berg, A. & Oei, K. (2009) Attachment and psychopathy in forensic patients. *Mental Health Review Journal.* 14(3), 40–51.

Weber, S., Habel, U., Amunts, K. & Schneider, F. (2008) Structural brain abnormalities in psychopaths – a review. *Behavioral Sciences & the Law.* 26(1), 7–28.

Winnicott, D.W. (1960) The theory of the parent-infant relationship. *International Journal of Psychoanalysis.* 41, 585–595.

Chapter 9

Fundamentalism and the superego

Lesley Murdin

Introduction

In this chapter I will set out a psychoanalytic understanding of the role of the superego in fundamentalism. 'Fundamentalism' has become a familiar signifier in our times. Away from the drama of the news stories on terrorism, we can recognise a mind-set in the consulting room in either or both of the therapist and patient couple. Because of the nature of this mental position I will argue that there is a theoretical and technical question for the therapist who needs to understand the role of the superego. Even though fundamentalism is an essentially defensive position it often appears as an attack driven by a cruel and demanding superego. In the fundamentalist mind-set, the fear of the sexual and aggressive impulses may be so great that the superego's demands for cruel and aggressive attacks on the perceived enemy are accepted by the ego. Since the attack on the Twin Towers in New York in 2001, the phenomena of fundamentalism have been discussed in analytic circles as well as in the world at large, but to understand the processes we need to look at the particular nature of the superego that oversees action in the mind of the individual.

One of the difficulties of writing about fundamentalism arises from the multiplicity of definitions available. There are dictionary definitions, common sense definitions and most importantly for this purpose are psychoanalytic definitions. Dictionary definitions emphasise strict adherence to a set of beliefs which are often religious or acquire a religious force. The term 'fundamentalism' originates from a set of books published in the early twentieth century called *The Fundamentals*, resisting the influence of modernism by advocating a return to the founding beliefs of Protestantism (Summers, 2006: p. 329). These definitions often emphasise rigidity and hostility to any challenge. Hostility is aroused in part by fear of those who might not share the same conviction. Like an animal in the territory of strangers, a person in this position may, with violence, turn against those who are not members of the circle of believers.

Current definitions of fundamentalism in common circulation night be applied to religious convictions maintained in spite of conflicting evidence or rational argument. David Black (1993), writing about the nature of religion, points out that its objects are neither wholly internal nor part of shared reality in the usual sense although they do have a shared social existence:

> Because the objects created by religious traditions are shared with other believers and have imported asserted characteristics which differentiate them from similar objects in other religions and even from similar objects in heretical or sectarian schools, they are not, or should not be available for omnipotent individual manipulation.
>
> (p. 622)

Why then should some people seek to force everyone to submit to 'omnipotent manipulations'?

The engine of fundamentalism

If we agree that fundamentalist mind-sets are often connected to sadistic aggression, the psychodynamic enquiry must ask where this connection originated and how it can be understood. Ruth Stein (2006) contextualises the fundamentalist movements of the twenty-first century within the paternalistic world-view which underpins monotheistic religions suggesting that these provide a fertile ground for what she calls 'a violent homo-erotic self-abnegating father-son relationship'. This leads to a 'violent fundamentalism' as a 'degeneration of the exalted paternal inner object into a murderously persecutory one' (p. 2).

This statement is powerful but very concentrated and will receive careful consideration in the rest of this chapter. Essentially, the argument is that an infant has desires and needs which are not acceptable to his parents or important adults. He develops a superego which prohibits carrying out these wishes and inflicts guilt for wishing for what is forbidden. Punishment is then inflicted on others who manifest the kind of behaviour that is wished or imagined. The rest of this chapter will seek to apply this understanding to the individual as well as to the social phenomenon of fundamentalism.

Contemporary fundamentalism is often associated in popular culture with violence and sadism. Jessica Benjamin (2002), writing soon after the attack on the Twin Towers in New York, considered the importance of guilt and self-righteousness and the way in which the two interact. This is an important element of the fundamentalism in the consulting room. Every therapist experiences guilt at some point for what is done badly or not done at all and what we do with this guilt is vital both for our own health and for the sake of the patient. Benjamin usefully confronts the liberal tendency to split as the response to fundamentalist attacks. Because we are all dealing with fear of weakness and ultimately death, we are all subject to the wish to evacuate feelings of weakness and fear and to experience instead self-righteousness and moralism. She emphasises how much danger lies in the inevitable consulting room split. 'I sit in my therapist's chair and you are the patient'. Here is the point at which the therapist must face her own fears and her own wish to eliminate guilt. The superego can speak in terms of tolerance and benevolence to the Other but it is still allowing a split and prohibiting feeling that we are all in this together.

The power of the guilt and anxiety experienced in each of us, is such that we may develop rigid defensive structures in the mind to protect the psyche from the inner attacks of the superego. Ruth Stein (2006) uses the metaphor of a carapace to describe the sense of a hard, rigid shell surrounding the terrified, persecuted ego which has survived from childhood. If we take her central image of the vertical structuring of the psyche, we have an all-powerful god, superior to a man who is superior to unbelievers and to all women. The believer knows that his god/father is right and wishes to make his superego persecute others, not him, as punishment for his forbidden wishes. We also have the myth of the father whose superego tells him to sacrifice the son. This of course took on terrible reality for those who lived through the two great wars of the twentieth century. If this image represents a psychic reality, there would be no surprise if the son were filled with homo-erotic hatred simultaneously with love for the powerful father as Stein (quoted above) suggests.

Novels such as *The Reluctant Fundamentalist* by Mohsin Hamid (2007), *A Song for Issey Bradley* by Carys Bray (2015) and *Jack* by Ariel Hammon (2017) demonstrate the power of the fundamentalist position to terrify and overpower the Other. Mohsin Hamid (2007) writes of the experience of a young Pakistani Muslim man in the United States and his disillusionment with western societies feeling disrespected and unrecognised as a man who can love a woman. This leads to a profound sense of narcissistic injury, which the American man whom he is addressing in a café in Lahore does not seem to grasp. What the American shows is fear reflecting one of the countertransference feelings provoked in the therapist in relation to a fundamentalist mind-set. Hamid's narrator is unfailingly polite but he raises the pitch of ominous threat until we are left uncertain at the end whether the American is to be shot or whether he is getting out a weapon with which to shoot the waiter. For both characters at this point the superego might enjoin killing the other. Both wish to project their respective shame and guilt as may therapist and patient in the transference and countertransference. Clearly we see the importance of the superego in therapeutic work as the agency responsible for guilt. The individual, who is seeking to free himself from his guilt and fear, wishes to be sure that others feel the terror that he most profoundly wishes to remove from his mind.

The child in such a position is concerned with a feared authority who must be obeyed in order to avoid punishment and disapproval. Situations where revenge is sought because of a sense of not being sufficiently respected indicate a superego at this early stage where what matters is an authority that can approve or disapprove. Since all children have experiences of disapproval from parental figures, we might expect a harsh superego until it has been mitigated by the knowledge of being loved. This assumption now seems obvious but is only generally accepted because of Freud's insights. In his collection of essays published in 1913, *Totem and Taboo*, he set out his provocative views on human experience. Freud did not intend his work to be seen as only mythogenic because he wished to derive a psychological theory from it. He based his ideas on studies of Australian aborigines, although he also cites many other tribes which were at the time labelled as 'primitive'. He says that he wrote this work primarily to demonstrate the importance of taboos and the way in which such groups manage to restrict their impulses and desires. In other words, he was interested in the way in which they managed to inhibit the free practice of sexuality, especially when it constituted incest and parricidal and murderous impulses towards rivals.

The myth that Freud proposes is the foundation of the Oedipus complex. The brothers in one totem or related group desire the mother, or the sister or a woman who is forbidden to them. The authority who forbids the free expression of these desires is the Father. He may or may not be the genital father of any given person but he is felt to be the authority prohibiting gratification. The brothers then agree to remove the Father and they get together and kill him. This is the crime of which every child is guilty whether the authority is a father or someone else and whether a crime is actually committed in some way or is only wished. Freud himself pointed out very explicitly that for all neurotics, wishes that were only imagined and wishes that were put into practice and enacted can be treated by the superego as the same. Unconscious guilt can be activated by a wish:

> We do not find deeds, but only impulses and feelings which sought evil but which were restrained from carrying it out. Only psychic realities and not actual ones are at the basis of the neurotics' sense of guilt. It is characteristic of the neurosis to put a psychic reality above an actual one and to react as seriously to thoughts as the normal person reacts only towards realities.
> (Freud, 1913 [1934]: p. 3)

Freud here is describing the difficulty of working with the precursor of the next stage where the brothers seek a new authority that will be strong enough to prevent a crime from being committed. This is where the young man is in danger of seeking the authority of the fundamentalist cult leader who will provide clear and demanding statements about what must be done or not done and will allow no arguments. This leader must be in possession of absolute power and must use the most severe punishments for those who do not follow his rules. The therapist may try to convey to a patient that the guilt from which he suffers is related to a wish and not to a deed as most people wish to kill someone, but do not act on that wish. Nevertheless, the power of the wish is strong and leaves a stain which is difficult to remove.

Fundamentalism as defence against fear

Freud's description of the brothers' fear of the father is helpful but circumvents the even more primitive picture of the infant's fear of separation from the mother. Frank Summers (2006) discusses this in terms of the fundamentalist use of splitting: good from bad, believers from unbelievers, right from wrong. He argues that this is a defence against the infant's fear of the loss of safe maternal holding. This fear implies a need to hold on very strongly to certainties which in the case of religious fundamentalism in particular requires total adherence to the text. James Strachey (1934) refers to a 'primitive superego' as a way to characterise the cruel and vicious character of the authority which is internalised in the child's mind and forms the basis of the child's internal moral authority (p. 276). This superego may not reflect accurately the actual parents whom the child experienced but may be informed by and infused with the return of his own projected hatred and demands of himself.

Other attempts to characterise the fundamentalist position in relation to a primitive superego highlight the terrifying helplessness behind the often violent aggression expressed in fundamentalist mind-sets and actions. Because inducing terror in others is a way of trying to evacuate the terror of powerlessness it often arises from humiliation. John Alderdice (2005), writing mainly about the violence in Northern Ireland, advocated seeking a psychoanalytic understanding of the reasons why ordinary citizens would become terrorists. He does not focus on religion, or devotion to a particular text, but instead on power, respect and the sense of an injury committed in the past which must be avenged.

> The set of thoughts and feelings that has impressed me as most significant in generating violence has to do with experiences of disrespect and humiliation. All of us have an almost insatiable desire to be treated with respect. Where individuals and communities are despised and humiliated a bitter sense of injustice is stored up and an almost unquenchable desire develops for vengeance and the righting of the wrong. . . . The sense that the very existence of a community and all that it holds dear has been threatened provokes deep fears and creates a capacity for responses at least as violent as those which it has experienced.
> (p. 583)

If we take this to contribute to a psychoanalytic understanding of the fundamentalist's motivation, we find ourselves in familiar psychoanalytic territory.

Of course, each person develops a unique set of moral imperatives. In the consulting room we encounter a series of phenomena which are troublesome both to the patient himself and to those around him. The chief characteristics of this mind-set might be described as:

- Guilt and anxiety leading to the wish for a powerful authority;
- Debate about the meaning of the words of this authority but not about its validity;
- Enjoyment arising almost solely from violent, often sadistic punishment of those who infringe the rules of the authority;
- A strong sense of group cohesion with dehumanisation of those outside the group;
- Paranoid schizoid functioning (in Kleinian terms).

Developmental conditions

Ronald Britton (2006), as a Panel member considering the impact of difficulties caused to infants by parental sexuality during the years when the Oedipus complex is at its height, hypothesises that a frightened and anxious child might develop a sadistic and cruel superego which attacks the self as well as the Other and makes thinking feel dangerous. This arises from despair because the child sees no possibility of allowing the parents to come together while safely maintaining the position of observer:

> a destructive superego is a symptom of psychotic functioning and is the outcome of the breakdown in the capacity to think. Where there is no psychic intercourse between two minds, containment fails and alpha elements cannot be generated. It is these elements that give thinking a resonance that makes it personally meaningful. When alpha elements are available and used, there is a proper repression in place that keeps a flowing unconscious dimension separated, but underpinning waking life. When this process breaks down, a person can no longer think, in the sense that the unconscious phantasy life, which accompanies experience and gives it an inner sense, no longer functions. This brings symbol formation to an end. It is out of this wreckage that a malignant superego steps out.
>
> (p. 290)

Britton is pointing here to the consequences for the young child when its feelings and phantasies about parental sexuality are not contained and made manageable. Those disturbing aspects of parental sexuality can then interfere with symbol formation and through that, with thinking. This failure to develop a capacity to think supports the development of a malignant superego which urges cruel and sadistic behaviour towards others to eliminate guilt and shame through action and because there is no possibility of distinguishing the present object from the primitive persecutor by thinking.

The superego reacts to thoughts of crimes of passion and the earliest desire of the child. For the older child or adult, the superego is formed from projections, the residues in fact of many relationships to parents, siblings, teachers and authorities of all sorts. This is the superego that Freud called the heir to the Oedipus complex. It is formed through fear at that point when the child longs for the opposite sex parent's total attention and love but is prevented by love and fear of the other parent whose vengeance might be expected. The little boy fears castration and this keeps him inclined to obey his internalised authorities. The little girl is of course more difficult to theorise in this way and may perhaps be more disposed to continue to seek her goal of acquiring phallic power through devotion to the external figure of a man.

Classical views of the superego help us to understand the fundamentalist position. Idealisation of the authority to which the fundamentalist submits and subscribes is also a feature of the fundamentalist mind-set. The superego can be thought of as incorporating reintrojected projections, bringing together the fear of a cruel authority with the love and admiration for an ideal. This aspect of fundamentalism can be seen in the phenomenon of cult leaders of all sorts. 'The Peoples' Temple' cult of Jonestown, Guyana, was led by Jim Jones in 1978. Nearly 1,000 of his adherents were willing to follow him to mass suicide. An important element in his charisma seems to have been his personal conviction of his own power and truth. Jim Jones himself demonstrates the rigidity of the person who takes up a position which may in itself earn some sympathy but is maintained against all reason and in the face of an utterly hopeless situation. The mechanism in the psyche which can lead to such a position whilst preventing the person from moving to a more rational and more merciful position suggests an underlying primitive superego at work.

Therapeutic work

James Strachey's paper on the therapeutic action of psychoanalysis (1934) laid the groundwork for understanding the kind of primitive superego that terrifies the individual to such an extent that he is unable to allow for the ambivalence which enables him to think that there might be other ways of seeing the present. Strachey looked at the formation of a harsh superego and its impact on the behaviour not only in a person's external life but also in the consulting room. He considered the cannibalistic nature of the object that the child internalises during the oral stage and points out that it is an orally aggressive object which is then, in Kleinian terms, reintrojected and projected until the process forms the basis of a hostile and aggressive environment. In Kleinian terms that could be helped by a move towards functioning in the depressive position where destructive impulses are recognised and grieved but no longer enacted. Aggressive impulses will manifest themselves through tension in the consulting room. Strachey writes about the first stage of understanding what is happening in the patient's mind and in the relationship when the analyst notices a tension in the patient who is suppressing some kind of id impulse, not necessarily aggressive, towards him. The analyst's job is to make conscious the process by a number of small steps leading to what he calls 'a mutative interpretation'. Strachey emphasises that change comes about by constant attention to the smallest indicators of anxiety caused by the superego. Since the role of the analyst is to take on some element of what Strachey calls the auxiliary superego, he becomes available for the projection of all sorts of cruelty and harshness from the past in revenge for the id impulse whatever it was and even though it was not carried out. This is where great skill is required to enable the patient to distinguish between his cruel phantasy object and the '*real*' one, the therapist who is not condemning or punishing him. The temptation for the analyst is to try to reassure the patient that one is a good object and thus become '*good*' but not 'real'.

If the analyst can convey a stream of immediate and specific interpretations recognising the impulse, followed by allowing the patient to arrive at his own understanding of the way in which his phantasy object is only a phantasy, change may be facilitated. This might serve as a definition of the thinking process which is so robustly refused in a fundamentalist mind-set. Strachey goes on to consider the reasons why analysts find it difficult to make these interpretations. One reason is that the analyst is required to acknowledge an impulse of considerable energy directed their way. This will of course arouse all the difficulties that we know accompany countertransference. In other words, a fundamentalist mind-set may evoke the same in the analyst. At the very least it will make demands for acceptance, tolerance and above all thinking in the analyst. Here the definition of thinking is again critical. The analyst too needs to be able to distinguish the present object from her primitive projections.

> *A male patient, Simon, speaks about his fear and disappointment when he participated in a conference organised by his generation of graduates but none of the older generation of graduates came to it. He reflected that his colleagues were well able to give interesting and valuable papers in their own right but that something felt dangerous to him about people talking about theory without any of the former authorities there to make judgments about whether what was said was valid.*

Simon was expressing his need for a powerful authority that can make the present and the future safe. Only through thinking can the patient tell the difference between the analyst and the cruel primitive superego in his mind. This brings us back to the point that in order for the fundamentalist to maintain his position there must be no thinking. If the therapist is able to point out the ways in which the patient is creating a new intransigent parent in the analyst, she may enable him to begin to risk some thinking. The patient needs to become aware of the fear and guilt which threaten him with punishment emanating from the harsh internal agency that he has developed in order to protect himself from guilt over the primal crime. There is a high level of magical thinking in connection with mental states located in an early stage of development. If he punishes himself he will not need to be punished from outside.

Michael's superego

Most therapists encounter the effects of a persecutory superego. Michael, a gay man, came to therapy because he was frightened by his own tendency to risk dangerous sexual encounters where he had no idea what would happen. Michael had become a gay pride activist and had been on Gay Pride marches. His friends had told him to find a gay therapist. He had chosen instead to see a woman who refused to tell him anything about her sexuality even though he asked directly. From this difficult beginning, there was a conflictual dynamic which put both into a fundamentalist position. Michael took every opportunity to say how important it was for him that everyone he knew should support gay rights. The therapist was well able to support gay rights but was concerned about Michael's risky and dangerous behaviour. His mother had told him that she was glad he was gay because he would always belong to her. His father disowned him and left the home when Michael came out as gay at the age of eighteen. In this part of his history there was a problematic relationship with his mother and guilt about what he might have done to his father. Michael was able to say that he did not think that his sexuality was the sole or maybe even the main reason why his father had left as he did not get on well at all with his wife but he was not entirely sure of the reason and his older brother Rob said that it was Michael's fault for his selfish satisfaction of his own needs. The therapist suggested that he might even have wished to be powerful enough to cause this trouble but that wishing it was not the same as doing it.

Michael demonstrated a fundamentalist position in his hatred and anger directed outwardly at his older brother and inwardly at himself. Rob was described in the most lurid terms: he had seduced a series of young women in London and always left them just when they were vulnerable, in some cases pregnant. He was so bad that undoubtedly he would come to a bad end and already some of his business success was failing. It was at this point that Michael demonstrated the power of the projected superego. He said several times, 'I hope you can see that I am different from my brother. Otherwise you would throw me out of this room right now'. The therapist was then able to move on to the second phase of the mutative process by pointing out to Michael the moments when he was experiencing his persecutory sadistic superego projected onto the therapist in order to establish herself as morally superior and free of guilt.

In Michael's case, the tendency to take up a fundamentalist position was first manifested internally in his hatred of his own gay nature, although this was not conscious at first. He said that he hated gay men who flaunted their camp inclinations or wanted to cross-dress. He went on gay pride marches and hung around public toilets but despised all the other gay men that he met. He even once said that some gay men deserved to be attacked by thugs along canal banks. Then he was ashamed and said that he didn't mean that. His defensive structure involved a rejection of thinking until after he had spoken or acted. His initial guilt over the part that he thought he had played in the breakup of his parents' marriage was enough to contribute to the formation of a very harsh superego. The first task for the therapist was to investigate his hatred of others who were like himself in order to see whether he could acknowledge that he was expressing hatred of himself. This was not far from consciousness and he was able to see that he could easily replace 'other gay men' with 'this gay man'.

Traditional thinking about transference would require that the therapist should ask the questions: 'who is speaking?' and 'to whom is he speaking?' There is value in arriving at the conclusion that, in his homophobia, Michael had taken up the place of his father in hating and despising gay men and this identification had led to an easing of the pain of his anger with his father. He had experienced an intransigent hatred of gay men in his father that could not be shifted by seeing his own son as a gay man. The seeds of rigidity and violent anger were sown.

Could transference interpretation help to solve or resolve this fundamentalist mind-set? Strachey's second phase of interpretation seems to show that the person addressed is seen as the cruel and intransigent parent. He is quite explicit that he thinks that the whole efficacy of psychoanalysis arises from the urgency and immediacy that is possible only through transference. In other words, the therapist must catch the moment when the cruel aspect of the superego is projected onto the therapist so that it can be seen in the present. In the case of Michael, the first hint of this was seen when he ascribed to the therapist the wish to punish him for being like his brother. Pointing out that this is a projection is of course difficult. The most obvious risk is that the therapist reassures the patient that of course she would not do this. In Michael's case, the therapist merely asked whether he had seen any indication that she might do that. He then had to think about what he had said and the repeated requirement to think began to make a difference to the nature of his superego.

Even if we can see how to begin to address this kind of rigid position there is often some difficulty for therapists in knowing how to prioritise vague hints of transference and how or whether to use what Strachey calls 'extra-transference interpretations' talking about third parties and leaving the focus outside the room. Contemporary analytic thinking is questioning the role of transference in the therapeutic action of analysis. Christopher Bollas (2007) brought together some of this thinking when he designated transference interpretation as a way of avoiding or closing down free association and obeying the therapist's own superego:

> In the British School 'What about the transference?' became a speech act: 'stop thinking about anything else'. It sought to resolve an anxiety; 'How can I feel effective in a place like this?' It did so by not thinking. A mantra – 'what about the transference?' – occupied these analysts' minds and rid them of any meaningful contact with the density of the analysand's unconscious life.
>
> (p. 99)

While accepting that a rigid 'me too' approach is often useless and may even be dangerously seductive, we do not need to go as far as blindly throwing it out. We can use an understanding of what is transferred from the past unconsciously and what is projected while maintaining flexibility in what we say and thus take precautions not to become a part of the patient's rigid fundamentalist defence.

The fundamentalist mind-set that Michael exhibited had included all the qualities described at the beginning of this chapter. He was frightened and guilty about the crime that he believed he had committed against his father. He then sought a more powerful authority in the shape of the therapist who would be able to prevent him from committing further crimes. The social context was also important in forming and maintaining his mind-set. He wanted to belong to the group of brothers, as Freud described them in his myth, who had all committed the same crime. Opposing this wish stood his father who had found all these gay brothers to be unacceptable. We can then see that he would need a powerful authority to make it possible to belong to the group of gay men, accepting their nature and refusing to denigrate them. Jonathon Haidt (2012) in his examination of contemporary morality points out the power of what he calls 'groupishness' (p. 221). We are tribal animals and we like to know our tribe. We can display remarkable loyalty and co-operation to the group that we have chosen to join but being shut out is too close to losing the mother in the early days of need and so can lead to a form of sadistic fundamentalism.

Michael's predicament demonstrates how difficult he found it until he was able to join the group of gay men to which he naturally belonged. To do this he had to deal with the primitive superego which at an unconscious level was telling him that he could not be allowed the pleasure of belonging. In order to move beyond this position he had also to face the danger of his mother's close embrace. She had said that she was glad that he was gay because she could keep him forever. This was not only frightening because it meant that he was usurping his father's place, it was also stiflingly incestuous or threatened to keep him forever a child.

The paranoid schizoid position in Melanie Klein's terminology (1946 [1975]) is a developmental lay-by. Modifying the superego to accept appropriate conscious guilt is the task. Before we are able to move between paranoid schizoid and depressive positions as an adult, we might spend most of our time in the position of hating and fearing the Other. Michael had found little respite from this position in his youth. As an adult he was with a female therapist in order, perhaps, to face the harm that he feared that he had done to his father and that any move into adult independence would do to his mother. The anxiety that was aroused led to a long period in which he denied any kind of thinking. The therapist had to consider his expectation that she would want to get rid of him in terms of this relationship with his mother. This led her to try to convey to him that she understood that he might wish that she would want to get rid of him. If she wished it then he could feel that he was not destroying her by moving into adulthood but was actually doing what was good for her too. If he could achieve this, a more benign superego would be able to allow a move out of the paranoid schizoid prison. The therapist could see that her task was to enable him to accept that his mother loved him and did not want to get rid of him but could survive his growth into a mature man.

The case of Michael demonstrates something of the difficulty of the emotional prison holding the fundamentalist and also shows how the therapist had to begin to think before the patient could. Most therapists have their own rigidities and areas in which they no longer think but simply refer to the library of existing beliefs. Whether or not the therapist thinks that transference interpretation is the only valid way to work tends to solidify into a kind of fundamentalist rigidity. Other areas of theory may form a religious text which must be preserved and honoured. A trainee describing a visit to the Freud Museum in London said 'It was very moving. I felt awed that Freud had actually been there'. His language sounded as though he felt that he was in a temple.

Effects on the therapist

The value of psychotherapy derives partly from the human exchange between the two participants and relies on the therapist to know something of what the patient is suffering. Unfortunately this also implies that the therapist will be adopting some of the same positions as the patient and as Warren Coleman points out (in Chapter 11) no amount of analysis will iron out all the unconscious areas of pathology in the therapist although it may strengthen 'capacity to withstand group processes'. We can therefore expect that there will be areas of rigidity and defences against thinking, not only in the areas of content that may be addressed but also in the use of a theoretical model. The reasons for this are various and individual:

> Nonetheless, the history of psychoanalysis is frighteningly similar to fundamentalist movements. (1) The organization of subgroups tend to be built around the ideas of the founder without any acknowledgement of the fallibility of the originator of the school. (2) Each theory justifies itself on the basis of the founder's ideas, which are treated as unquestionable. (3) Schools of psychoanalytic thought tend to act as though the historical movement of the field has ended at their founders' ideas. (4) Adherents of each point of view bond in a collective identity, and others tend to be identified only by their lack of belief in the system.
>
> (Summers, 2006: p. 351)

The therapist's superego supports parental authority, often with some verbal aggression. Britton (1998) developed the concept of unconscious belief. Most forms of stereotyping fall into this category where a belief is not consciously identified as a belief but is held to be a fact of the 'I have always known that' variety. The task of analytic work is partly to articulate and explore these unconscious beliefs. Just as the patient needs to do this exploration, so also the therapist needs to explore her unconscious beliefs in her supervision or self-supervision/analysis. Dr Patricia Tate, in a lecture to the Balint Society (April 2017) about some informal research about reactions to the word *rules*, found that three-quarters of the people she asked, most of whom were therapists, had negative associations. If therapists feel this way, we can expect some breaking of rules to ensue and that might be in relation to some unconscious beliefs, along the lines of breaking boundaries.

Freud's superego set him fewer boundaries than the practising clinician in the twenty-first century must have. He did, however, set out the 'fundamental rule' of psychoanalysis which states simply that the patient must say whatever comes into his head without censorship. The therapist who consciously believes that this will set him free from his prison, is showing the paradox in seeking to escape from a fundamentalist carapace. Only strict adherence to an injunction from the father of psychoanalysis will enable him to set himself free. But only assessing his actions through his own superego will free him from guilt and the need to inflict terror. The superego is both the source of the fundamentalist mind-set and the means of escape from its power.

References

Alderdice, J.L. (2005) Understanding terrorism: the inner world and the wider world. *British Journal of Psychotherapy*. 21(4), 577–587.
Benjamin, J. (2002) Terror and guilt. *Psychoanalytic Dialogues*. 12(3), 473–484.
Black, D.B. (1993) What sort of a thing is a religion? A view from object-relations theory. *International Journal of Psycho-Analysis*. 74, 613–625.
Bollas, C. (2007) *The Freudian Moment*. London, Karnac Books.
Bray, C. (2015) *A Song for Issey Bradley*. London, Penguin Books.
Britton, R. (1998) *Belief and Imagination Explorations in Psychoanalysis*. London, Routledge.
Britton, R., Chused, J., Ellman, S. & Likierman, M. (2006) Panel II: The Oedipus complex, the primal scene, and the superego. *Journal of Infant Child and Adolescent Psychotherapy*. 5(3), 282–307.
Freud, S. (1913) *Totem and Taboo*. London, Routledge, 1934.
Haidt, J. (2012) *The Righteous Mind*. London, Penguin Books.
Hamid, M. (2007) *The Reluctant Fundamentalist*. London, Penguin Books.
Hammon, A. (2017) *Jack*. Arizona, Berry Publishing.
Klein, M. (1946) Notes on some schizoid mechanisms. In: *Envy and Gratitude and Other Works*. London, Hogarth Press, 1975.
Stein, R. (2006) Fundamentalism, father and son, and vertical desire. *Psychoanalytic Review*. 93(2), 201–229.
Strachey, J. (1934) The nature of the therapeutic action of psychoanalysis. *International Journal of Psychoanalysis*. 50, 275–292, 1969.
Summers, F. (2006) Fundamentalism, psychoanalysis, and psychoanalytic theories. *Psychoanalytic Review*. 93(2), 329–352.
Tate, P. (2017) *Rules*. Paper delivered to the Balint Society, April 2017.

Part III

The superego in clinical contexts

Chapter 10

The superego as a significant factor in clinical training

Christine Driver

Unlike an academic training, a clinical training involves the totality of the self and confronts the trainee with extensive personal challenges. It requires a helpful, aspirational, protective superego to ensure that theory is learnt and integrated, course work is completed, and clinical work is carried out in a professional manner but the superego also has the potential to be persecutory and in this form can impede and disrupt the learning process. Exploring the way in which the superego affects clinical training is the focus of this chapter.

The trainee and the clinical training context

The demands of a clinical training are complex. It involves the integration of a dynamic understanding of theory, ideas, skills and clinical practice alongside the challenges of personal therapy and the development of self-awareness in relation to self and other. It requires an ego capacity that can oscillate between dependence and independence so as to achieve an integration of knowledge, awareness and skills and a learning position of openness and reflection. In addition it requires sufficient ego-strength to use the self as a tool in understanding the conscious and unconscious communications and problems which patients bring. Such a learning process requires both assimilative learning, the accumulation of new knowledge and information, and accommodative learning (Piaget, 1958), the modification of existing cognitive (and emotional) schema (Szecsödy, 1997: p. 109) and the development of the ego in relation to the self. Clinical training is therefore not just a cognitive activity, it is about psychological learning and development and presents the trainee with psychological challenges.

This is especially true in relation to clinical work and clinical understanding. This necessitates the development of an observing ego (Greenson, 1981), mentalisation and the reflective function (Fonagy, 2001: p. 165) so as to understand the mind of another and unconscious communications from the patient. It requires an ego-based perspective to help make conscious the unconscious issues and complexes that affect the patient's life and relationships and help the patient understand themselves more fully and move forward in their lives. However, the functioning of the ego, especially in a training setting, can be impeded by the superego. The superego, in its rigid and extreme form, will determine what can or cannot be thought. It entangles the ego in oughts, shoulds and should nots and limits what can be made conscious and brought into mind and, as Britton (2003) comments, '*self observation is an ego function and not a superego function*. The ego observes itself in a realistic light, the superego in a moral light' (p. 72).

The internal world, regression and the superego

A clinical training is a psychological and emotional melting pot, has a developmental trajectory (Stoltenberg & Delworth, 1987; Frawley O'Dea & Sarnat, 2001; Hawkins & Shohet, 2002) and activates the re-experiencing and reworking of the trainee's 'internal working models' (Bowlby, 1969) and the demands of their ego ideal and superego. The developmental processes of training arise through the requirement to learn and integrate new skills and information and process feelings in relation to self and others and at one level the ego ideal and superego provide the inspiration and motivation to aspire to, and achieve, internal and external goals. However, as adults we bring into every new situation 'anxieties that have their roots in our childhood and infancy . . . a memory in feeling' (Salzberger-Wittenberg et al., 1999: p. 7) and in addition 'the learning process itself can also set in motion a regressive reaction' (Frawley-O'Dea & Sarnat, 2001: p. 116) to more primitive forms of relating to self and others as the individual steps into new and unknown surroundings. This regression to more primitive forms of relating activates the amalgam of the primary 'protective superego', which organises 'experience into patterns and schemas' (Reddish, 2014: p. 39), and the developmentally formed superego. The latter emerges from the internalised 'relational patterns, parental values, parental criticisms, *and* cultural influences' developed from infancy and a 'preoccupation with what is the right or wrong thing to do' (Bateman & Holmes, 2002: p. 35). However, although 'the superego takes shape around the original parental imagos, both positive and negative . . . these imagos are later linked to the influence of teachers and other authority figures who carry ego ideals . . . or to . . . a fear of punishment for the individual' (Kalsched, 1996: p. 82). A perspective reflected in feedback from trainees and two commented: "I have quite a punishing superego which I recognise comes from internalising parental criticism and envious attack" (DS.[1] Driver, 2016) and "I am sure that feeling criticized is very much to do with my own personal history" (CP. Driver, 2016).

The superego has a powerful impact because 'a person who grew up being criticised all the time will tend to "hear" criticism in the comments of others, even when no criticism occurs' (Pally, 2007: p. 865). As a result, it can be punishing, prevent the trainee from feeling good-enough and generate anxiety, regression and persecutory states in which the trainee can feel, or fears, attack from without or within. In addition the ego ideal exerts a powerful influence. Emerging from a longing for the 'narcissistic perfection of childhood' (Freud, 1914: p. 94) the ego ideal can lead to states of either grandiosity, in which the trainee values their own perspective above others and are intolerant of criticism, or vulnerable to narcissistic injury in relation to the longed for state of perfection. Any wound to the ego ideal, as a result of perceived negative criticism or negative feedback, can lead to defensive reactions, anxiety, a longing to retain an idealised view of the self and a trainee who is not open to ego-based reflective learning. This leaves the trainee prone to either persecutory internal objects or projecting criticism onto the trainers and supervisors, seeing them as not good enough so as to protect their own ego ideal. As another trainee commented:

> Being self-critical fed my own unresolved complexes and anxieties which I projected in abundance on every aspect of the training at every stage. It was limiting and destructive of my experience and opportunity to learn.
> (SC. Driver, 2016)

The emotional exposure of training, and the inevitable regression, therefore leaves the trainee vulnerable and especially so if they have turned towards becoming a therapist because the wounded part of themselves seeks a healing relationship from the training. The unconscious hope may be that the training 'parent' will be the perfectly attuned, holding and empathic parent who values and praises them, heals the psychological wound and meets the longed for needs of the ego ideal. Such transference longings and projections can leave the trainee prone to shame when they are not 'able to evoke an empathic response in the other' (Mollon, 2002: p. 26) or to a tendency to idealise trainers, theory and theoreticians leading to disillusionment, anger and loss when the idealised 'other' does not live up to the expectations of the ego ideal or superego. In either case engagement with learning is inhibited until the disillusionment and loss of the ideal can be mourned and the limitations of the therapeutic 'parents' and the therapeutic relationship integrated. This requires trainers to be containing and non-retaliatory so that the trainee can work through their feelings of loss and disillusionment because clinicians who are ruled by ego ideals and superego imperatives will find it difficult to learn from their mistakes or be open to the complex conscious and unconscious issues that patients bring. This is not to say that trainers and supervisors should take on the role of therapist but that they use their therapeutic capacities to hold and contain the trainee's projections and not get caught into acting into them in a persecutory or retaliatory way. Such holding provides the trainee with the opportunity, e.g., in therapy, to digest and work through their disillusionment, accept limitations within themselves and others, reappraise their patterns of relating and their superego and ego ideal perspectives and move to a more ego-based position in relation to others and themselves.

Anxiety, shame and learning

The challenges of a clinical training inevitably stir up feelings and emotions, and research by Stoltenberg and Delworth (1987) identifies that beginner trainees, although highly motivated, are insecure, anxious, 'lack self-awareness and other-awareness', tend to see supervisors and trainers as 'all knowing experts' (p. 52) and are focused on 'the "right" way to do things' (p. 54). In my own survey with recently qualified trainees (Driver, 2016), findings indicated that when starting a training hopes and expectations were mixed with excitement (100%), anxiety (80%), feeling de-skilled and feeling judged (52%).[2] In terms of anxiety the survey revealed that although 47% felt criticised by supervisors and 27% by seminar leaders, the majority, 67%,[3] indicated that the most powerful factor which generated anxiety and feelings of criticism was from within themselves. Such anxiety focused on fears about not being deemed competent, not knowing enough, not grasping theory, not getting things right in the consulting room with patients, not being as good as they had hoped or not living up to their ego ideal. As one recent graduate wrote:

> I am, by nature, extremely self-critical and lacking in confidence when embarking on something new. I am conscientious and work hard and expect that I will do well by hard graft. Yet, when I heard others speak, I could not accept that my contributions were as good or clever or thoughtful. I found it very difficult to trust myself and my learning. I did not allow myself any time to feel at sea – I expected that I would get on top of it all at once.
> Starting to see real clients in Year 1 I felt the burden to do well as a therapist (for them, me and supervisor) but certain other trainees seemed more experienced and/or more able to grasp the theoretical aspects of the readings and/or more articulate and confident in seminars or client work. I felt a gulf between understanding the concepts theoretically and putting these into practice; feeling out of my depth and unable to see how to catch up; feeling I was not good enough and fearing I might not have an aptitude for the work; fearing I had made a wrong decision in embarking on the training.
> (HC. Driver, 2016)

A clinical training therefore disturbs a trainees' ego and defences, generates anxiety, stirs up dynamics linked to the ego ideal and superego and activates powerful superego activity in relation to peers, supervisors, seminar leaders, assessment committees and the requirement to demonstrate skills and competences. Anxiety can trigger regression and often a retreat to the paranoid-schizoid position in which relationships become 'split into . . . persecutory and idealised' ones (Fonagy, 2001: p. 83) and the ego ideal and superego become powerful transference phenomena and internal persecutors. As one trainee commented:

> I felt people were judging me and I retreated, as I am basically shy. I compared myself to others. I felt inferior to my peers and unable to express myself. I knew I had something to offer, but could never compete or feel comfortable enough to relax and be myself.
> (XX. Driver, 2016)

Such dynamics, if not held, contained and understood by training staff will cloud the trainer–trainee relationship and damage the trainee's capacity to learn and develop.

A beginner trainee, as well as being anxious, is also highly motivated, enthusiastic and 'wants to do a good job' (Stoltenberg & Delworth, 1987: p. 52). They are aspirational and this aspect of the superego plays an important role in motivating trainees to achieve the goals and competences of the training. They hope that the trainers will respond positively to their input in seminars or their presentations of clinical work but this is not always the case. Critical feedback from trainers, leading to a mis-match between what is hoped for and the fantasy of what the trainee feels they have achieved, leads to unsettling states of exposure, anxiety, emotional arousal and shame. Within the infant–caregiver dyad shame emerges as a means to manage intolerable states of arousal (Schore, 1991: p. 196) and is induced when the infant's mastery of skills does not measure up to the infant's ego ideals or the infant does not receive 'matched attunement' or a positive response in relation to the 'practicing sub-phase of the separation-individuation stage of development' (Mahler et al., 1975; Schore, 1991: p. 192). Such dynamics are paralleled in a training context. In training, learning and development occur through practicing within role plays, seminar discussions and actual clinical work but the way this is managed emotionally will also rest on the capacity of the trainer–trainee dyad to tolerate emotional arousal and anxiety. Evaluation anxiety is a key factor and shame is easily triggered when the trainee feels they have not measured up to their own ego ideal, not received positive attunement and feedback from the training staff or guilt when the superego reflects a sense of failure at not achieving the fantasy of how they should be (Piers & Singer, 1953). As one trainee commented:

> I think my superego made it difficult for me to accept criticism, particularly if I perceived it to be unfair or delivered harshly. However I do feel that my training helped me to recognise my internal punishing voice and enabled me to stop listening to it so much.
>
> (DS. Driver, 2016)

In a clinical training therefore the trainee is frequently exposed and vulnerable to emotional arousal, shame and guilt. In seminars trainees are exposed to internal pressures in relation to the way theory is understood, or not, and in experiential groups, or similar, the trainee is exposed through interpersonal interactions and the surfacing of personal issues. However, exposure is especially powerful in supervision because the internal world of the trainee is exposed through the presentation of clinical work and their capacity to make sense of the patient material and the supervisor's input. Supervisors can easily activate anxiety and shame when trainees take their first steps in working with patients because the supervisor holds evaluative power and for a trainee, 'to be *found empty* or to have nothing to give or suggest is a dread that haunts many' (Martin, 2005: p. 176). Here, shame at being found wanting through not living up to an internal ego ideal (Nathanson, 1987) is activated when 'there is a discrepancy between a person's ideals, their introjects and their actual behaviour' (Martin, 2005: p. 169). The potential for shame and guilt in relation to the expectations of the ego ideal and the superego, and the consequent persecutory dynamics, makes the relationship to the learning environment and learning difficult. As one trainee commented:

> I found it almost impossible to speak in seminars, because I was sure that everyone would think that what I had said was disappointingly stupid. This didn't have anything to do with the actuality of the seminars though – if I did manage to speak, no one ever made me feel criticized.
> (AC. Driver, 2016)

And went on to say:

> I think criticising myself first makes me feel safe – I've pre-empted the attack by attacking myself before anyone else can. There is also something in it about having a very critical parent, who often made me feel stupid. I've always been much harder on myself than the training has ever been on me – what I think now is that supervision over the past four years hasn't been so much about helping me to become a perfect therapist but about helping me to let go of the idea that that is what I needed to become. I hung onto the idea of right and wrong, and needing to get things right, for a long time, when all the way through my supervisors have done everything that they could to encourage me to see it all as part of a process, without any judgement attached.
> (AC. Driver, 2016)

Here the reactivation of the developmentally formed critical and persecutory superego impacted on the learning process but the containing, non-judgemental and process-oriented approach of the supervisors, together with personal therapy, enabled this trainee to move from a persecutory superego to a more benign one in which they could consider the clinical work as a process to be understood rather than conforming to a supposed 'right way' of doing things. As Caper comments, 'a victory of ego over superego' (Caper, 1999: p. 44) in which the ego is now free(er) to process and reflect on the clinical work and the conscious and unconscious dynamics that patients' bring. The role of training staff in managing and containing these dynamics is vital.

Transference however cannot be overlooked because training staff hold the power and this can generate conscious and unconscious 'family dynamics'. In childhood 'attachment bonds are appropriately normally profoundly asymmetrical' (Fonagy, 2001: p. 10) but in training asymmetry conflates with the authority and power held by the trainers and the training organisation. As a result superego and transference anxiety about being judged, criticised and deemed stupid or unworthy of being on the training will powerfully affect how the trainee relates to seminar leaders and supervisors and engage with the training processes. Linked to this is the way training staff relate to the trainee and the danger that they too get caught up in their own transference issues.

Stimmel (1995) writes of the transference risk for supervisors of having favourites who can do no wrong and of unconsciously falling into the trap of seeing a trainee in terms of their own internal objects: good or bad, loved or hated, or the recipient of the trainer's critical superego or ego ideal. It is important, therefore, that the danger of trainers acting into the power balance is mitigated by ensuring that training processes, especially assessments, are carried out by a team so that any anomalous and extreme issues that emerge between a particular trainer and trainee can be considered from all angles. This needs to include the possibility that the trainer has been caught up in an unconscious transferential link with the trainee or caught up in a countertransference enactment of a critical other.

Superego dynamics mobilised by clinical work

The patient is the most important and vulnerable person within the training context and here the superego holds an important function in terms of boundaries and professional capacities. The protective aspect of the superego promotes and holds an ethical attitude to clinical work, which is vital for trainees and qualified practitioners alike. Most trainees are aware of this and two of those surveyed commented: "The main anxiety was getting things right in the consulting room with patients" (CP. Driver, 2016) and "Starting to see real clients and feeling the burden to do well as a therapist – for them, me and the supervisor" (HC. Driver, 2016). The containing function of the protective superego therefore keeps the work safe and on task but the ego and superego also need to navigate the challenges of personal abstinence in the face of the needs of the patient. Supervision generates a triangular, oedipal dynamic and a tension between the needs of the supervisor, supervisee and patient. The focus of supervision is on the patient and their internal world and this means that the internal world of the supervisee has to struggle with feeling excluded but present enough to engage with, and reflect on, the patient material with their supervisor. The triangle of supervision 'contains three triangulation points of Ego, Id and Superego as these aspects of the psyche are present in all three participants' (Martin, 2002: p. 15). When judgemental superego dynamics between supervisor and supervisee conflate it clouds their perception of the patient, the supervisee or possibly even the supervisor and inhibits the processing and understanding of the dynamics emerging from the work with the patient and their capacity to 'learn from the patient' (Casement, 1985).

One of the most difficult areas where anxiety and the superego create a challenge is with the first patient. Beginner trainees have 'an intense focus on the self . . . resulting from anxiety which will not in itself lead to productive self-awareness' (Stoltenberg & Delworth, 1987: p. 53) and tend to be self-centred with a preoccupation about 'can I make it in this work?' (Hawkins & Shohet, 2002: p. 64).

If these anxieties dominate the trainee the needs of the patient can be lost. One trainee commented that:

> In supervision I was terrified of the supervisor and felt I had to make 'clever' interpretations and links to theory so as to avoid the supervisor's criticism. When I was with the patient I was so anxious that I ended up not saying very much. In retrospect I can see that the patient felt un-held and unheard. It must have felt as if there was no-one there and that they were on their own with a zombie. It's no wonder the patient did not come back again.
> (CR. Driver, 2016)

An equally serious impact of the superego occurs in supervision when anxiety generates unconscious links and dynamics between patient and trainee clinician. Such parallel processes (Searles, 1955), when carried into the supervision arena, requires careful discernment by the supervisor so as to ascertain what belongs to the patient and what to the supervisee. For example:

> Mary, a first-year trainee, was presenting her first two sessions with a patient named Sue. Sue lived with her parents and was embarking on a career in teaching. In supervision Mary spoke quietly when she presented and found it hard to remember what the patient had said but was able to report that Sue was beset by anxieties in relation to what her parents wanted her to achieve and the expectations of her new teaching role. The supervisor felt somewhat frustrated by the difficulty Mary had in presenting and remembering and of how young and inexperienced she seemed. The supervisor thought about this as possible parallel process and explored with Mary the anxiety-filled quality of the patient's presentation and wondered if this might be linked to the way the patient was ruled by fears of criticism by others, especially her parents, and was unable, and possibly not allowed, to access her own feelings.

Awareness of parallel process in supervision by the supervisor is not easy, but vital, so that the trainee does not become the scapegoat of superego projections and identifications or oughts and shoulds. 'Regressive experiences in the supervisory encounter are frequent rather than unusual events' (Frawley-O'Dea & Sarnat, 2001: p. 135) and for Mary they stirred up anxiety and defensive reactions and activated internal process which paralleled the patient's anxiety. To have focused on Mary in supervision would have collapsed the supervisory triangle, excluded the patient and prevented learning and self-awareness in the trainee about Sue's internal world. Subsequently Mary admitted to how scared she had been in supervision, fearing that the supervisor expected her to "have it all worked out" and to have made "clear and clever interpretations." Clearly Mary's anxiety triggered links to superego issues within herself and the patient but if the supervisor had not been aware of the power of parallel process they too would have got caught up in their own superego enactments with the trainee and inhibited exploration and learning.

The superego is one of the most challenging problems for a supervisor because of its inhibitory effect on the capacity of the trainee to explore issues relating to their patients and expose their feelings or 'mistakes' in supervision. Trainees frequently feel that they should present tidy and theoretically and clinically correct presentations to show that they are 'doing it right' but such superego perspectives prevent curiosity and exploration of unconscious dynamics, transference and countertransference. Supervisees frequently report "I was afraid to talk in supervision about how I felt because I feared the supervisor would think I couldn't cope or that I wasn't doing it right". When such perspectives dominate it is hard to connect to an ego-based reflection and exploration with the trainee about their thoughts and feelings and consider them as a resource and potential information about the patient's internal world and complexes. As Stockwell (2005) comments if supervisees 'are too anxious and are trying too hard to meet the demands of the superego' they 'are not in a sufficient state of reverie for other unconscious processes to be accessible' (p. 92). This leads to attacks on linking (Bion, 1967) and an ego-destructive superego which prevents the trainee being able to consider, in an ego-based way, the unconscious issues being brought by the patient or to use their thoughts and feelings as a means of understanding the internal world of the patient. The supervisor is probably one of the most significant relationships in a clinical training. Supervisors hold responsibility in relation to the learning and development of the work with the patient and evaluative power in relation to the learning and development of the trainee. Within the supervisory relationship supervisors have 'to overcome powerful cultural pressures to feel like competent objective experts' (Frawley-O'Dea & Sarnat, 2001: p. 122) and avoid falling prey to their own ego ideal and superego by becoming either over-critical and persecutory or overly self-effacing. Supervisors need to be aware of the dangers of a critical and persecutory superego in supervision and consider the recommendation by Hughes and Pengelly (1997) that they should model dialogic processes between thinking and feeling for the supervisee, operate from a benign authority, enable exploration and create an environment in which both trainee and supervisor are open to learning about the patient. Supervisors therefore hold a complex role in relation to the developmental level and learning needs of the trainee and require a range of skills so as to engage the trainee in a productive relationship which enables their development as a clinician.

The superego and the training context

The impact of the superego in training is clearly complex and inescapable for trainees and as one respondent to my research commented:

> Training is a self-exploratory venture. We necessarily go places where we feel vulnerable. If seminar leaders and especially supervisors are very critical and in some way reinforce one's superego, things may get pretty difficult.
> (MF. Driver, 2016)

The attitude of the training context is therefore important because superego dynamics emerging from trainees' internal complexes can be exacerbated by the training organisation and the approaches of the trainers. Kernberg (1996) lists thirty factors within a clinical training which generate anxiety, persecutory fears, persecutory superego dynamics and destroys creativity. These include the idealisation of theorists and theory, the authoritarian maintenance of hierarchy, the perpetuation of ideals, secrecy regarding decisions and, as he later comments, the 'unanalyzable idealization of the training analyst as a combination of excellent clinician, ideal supervisor and seminar leader' (Kernberg, 2010: p. 998). Kernberg identifies the impact of trainers who adopt a rigid, hierarchical approach to training thereby exacerbating superego dynamics and embodying a rigid, persecutory superego for the trainee and for themselves. Kernberg (2006, 2007) also examines the conservatism within some training institutes regarding changes to the educational methodology and content. He considers how approaches to training should reflect a more equal partnership between trainee and trainers and that supervision should be a collegial experience as well as one which 'monitors the trainees' work (Kernberg, 2006: p. 1667) and that 'deep learning, in the sense of accentuating critical thinking and confrontation with what is known and still unknown, demands an openness to new ideas, and confidence in the student's capacity to evaluate freely and independently' (Kernberg, 2007: p. 189). However, this requires a strong ego-based capacity within the trainee but for many trainees, especially those beginning training, this is the learning challenge that they are engaged in. He goes on to suggest that when trainers relate in an ego-based way with trainees they facilitate an environment in which the trainee can explore, discover, critique and challenge ideas and theory and develop their own ego-based perspective.

The presence of 'dogmatic indoctrination' (Kernberg, 2007: p. 189) within training organisations is always a danger and Kernberg's papers alert clinical training organisations and trainers to the danger of succumbing to the sway of their own superego dynamics in relation to the founding 'Mothers' and 'Fathers' and preserving the 'right way to do things'. Such dynamics create a persecutory closed system secured against change or challenge and perpetuate and exacerbate anxiety within both staff and trainees. Such a system is not containing, holding and exploratory; it is rule bound, generates a persecutory superego and a dynamic in which 'the parents' cannot be challenged (see Colman, Chapter 11). Training organisations and trainers therefore need to consider whether they are operating from a benign superego or ruled by a persecutory one which is not open to critique and stuck in an idealised relationship to 'the founders' that brooks no challenge. Maybe in this day and age such a perspective is increasingly rare but it is important for trainers, training organisations and management structures to be aware of the dangers of being ruled by persecutory superegos, especially when challenging and anxiety provoking issues come to the fore from trainees, patients or external professional bodies. In states of anxiety all of us, trained and untrained, are vulnerable to the internal bombardment of a persecutory superego and defensive rules and regulations that eliminate anxiety. A persecutory and critical superego will inhibit exploratory processes, creative dialogue and the creativity of the trainee whereas a flexible, benign superego enables a place for exploration.

The superego as a necessary factor in training

It is perhaps all too easy to be critical of the superego because we often encounter it in its defensive and persecutory form but the superego is also a necessary factor in clinical training. It spurs and inspires the trainee to meet the demands of the training and the profession and just as a benign protective superego in infancy is there to hold, contain and keep us safe (Reddish, 2014: p. 40) it holds an equivalent function for the trainee in relation to clinical work. The superego also links us to moral attitudes and provides the underpinning of a principled and ethical attitude to clinical work and learning. Within the psychodynamic and psychoanalytic profession the Codes of Ethics and competences are based on the standards required to make and maintain a safe and professional container for the patient and for trainees and trainers. They provide clear principles regarding professional standards and specify the personal and moral qualities required of a practitioner and good practice which, in order to fulfil, requires the development and nuanced operation of a benign yet critical superego and a moral and ethical attitude in relation to clinical work and learning.

A benign and discriminatory superego is also vital within the training context in the area of assessments. Assessments can create validation but also entail critique. For assessments to be creative and provide insight an ego-to-ego relationship is required between assessor and trainee in which the inevitable asymmetry of the relationship is accepted but does not overwhelm. This requires sensitivity on the part of the assessor and a sense of self-worth and ego-strength on the part of the trainee so that they can make their own reflective self-assessments. In an optimal setting, and where there is a sense of shared goals between trainers and trainee in terms of the competences to be achieved, there is the possibility of personal validation and self-development for the trainee. But, when a persecutory superego overtakes the process it dominates and prevents learning and insight developing. Assessment therefore requires sensitivity by all assessors in terms of how it affects the trainee and containment by ensuring that the trainee has a safe forum with a tutor or personal therapy to find a place to explore the issues that emerge. However, assessment inevitably involves decisions based on the trainers' authority so it is important for trainers to consider whether they are acting from a persecutory superego and a paranoid-schizoid authoritarian position or from an authoritative perspective based in the depressive position (Obholzer, 2006) and a benign superego which can tolerate and accept the 'good enough'.

Training processes and assessments need to ensure that the trainee is fit to practise and has developed appropriately in relation to the competences of the psychodynamic/psychoanalytic profession and the needs of the patient. The superego is central in identifying when the trainee's work is not fit for task and when there is a fitness to practise issue.

> Assessment, in the final analysis, is about fitness to practise in terms of clinical and ethical criteria, and to confront, if necessary, the difficult but important task of bringing someone's training or clinical work to an end in order to protect the patient
>
> (Driver, 2008: p. 340)

and equally, although it may not feel like it at the time, to protect the trainee. In this role the superego has a crucial function: 'mature superego functioning is distinguished by the way in which "moral evaluations" about both individuals and society, are made by an ego' (Reddish, 2014: p. 91) and, in a training context, ego-based decisions are made about the trainee and their development as clinicians.

Conclusion

What is being aimed for in a clinical training is a creative process of exploration, self-exploration, self-awareness and the generation of ideas and hypotheses about theory, concepts and clinical work. But, as Salzberger-Wittenberg (1999) comments:

> if we are too frightened to allow ourselves to be open enough to have an emotional experience of newness we also shut ourselves off from the perception of something different, from discovering anything new, producing anything fresh.
>
> (p. 9)

Interactive processes are required that can circumnavigate the persecutory power of the superego and enable exploration, dialogue and personal growth. Chetty comments that 'the qualities of dialogic relations are an appropriate index of creative productivity in higher education' (Chetty, 2010: p. 143) and Raiker adds that 'reflection enables creative processes' which 'expand knowledge and understanding' (Raiker, 2010: 137). To achieve this requires 'the capability to make, do or become something fresh and valuable with respect to others as well as ourselves', and emerge 'from the complexities and contradictions we have internalised' (Pope, 2005: p. xvi, 11).

In ideas resonant of Piaget's (1958) concepts of assimilative and accommodative learning, Mezirow, examining transformative dimensions of adult learning, considers the interrelationship between content reflection, process reflection and premise reflection and suggests that it is the latter which changes the learner's perspective (Mezirow, 1991: p. 104). Insight, imagination and creative thinking are ego-based activities and are vital to the development of the capacity to link theory to practise and hypothesise and conceptualise ideas about a patient's internal world and the problems they are facing. Within a clinical training it is therefore important to utilise learning styles which mirror and reflect a dialogic structure and which do not fall into the trap of replicating authoritarian, rigid and persecutory superegos. Adriansen points out that 'every theory, model or method should be related to (its) own practice' and that 'the learning design must include giving the participants first-hand experience, followed by reflection' (Adriansen, 2010: p. 78). These two points are vital because to train clinicians to be reflective practitioners and develop creative dialogues within themselves and with others, such as seminar leaders and supervisors, training methods need to mirror practice. As one trainee commented,

> I felt, with the support given to me, able and safe to begin to relinquish my rigid way of thinking as a defense against not knowing, and to develop and increase my capacity to hold uncertainty and the unknown.
> (SC. Driver, 2016)

Training is a container, educator, facilitator and gatekeeper in relation to the personal and professional development of the trainee and their clinical work. For the trainee who has navigated the demands and hoops of the training it is important that they emerge with a sense of the training as a good internalised object and a benign superego which enables them to continue to develop and work to professional standards. Salzberger-Wittenberg (1999) comments, that 'a good end helps both students and staff to retain a memory of a past they can be proud of' (p. 154) and Stockwell (2005) comments that it is hoped that as practitioners 'emerge from training and develop in their work, their egos and superegos become closer, and their superegos act in quieter and more benign ways as motivators, elements in reflection and boundary keepers' (p. 91). The dynamics of the superego within training are powerful and can inhibit learning and development when they take a persecutory form. However, in its benign form it is a vital aspirational and motivating factor and a key element in the development of a professional and ethical clinician.

Acknowledgements

I wish to thank the 2013, 2014, 2015 and 2016 Psychotherapy graduates of WPF Therapy for taking part in the research project and sharing their views.

Notes

1 The initials given before the reference Driver, 2016 refer to individual graduates who made comments in the research questionnaire. All graduates gave permission for their comments to be used.
2 The percentages add up to more than 100% because some respondents indicated more than one factor.
3 The percentages add up to more than 100% because some respondents indicated feeling criticised by more than one factor.

References

Adriansen, H.K. (2010) How criticality affects student creativity. In: C. Nygaard, N. Courtney, C. Holtham (eds.) *Teaching Creativity – Creativity in Teaching.* Oxfordshire, Libri Publishing.
Bateman, A. & Holmes, J. (2002) *Introduction to Psychoanalysis.* Hove and New York, Brunner-Routledge.
Bion, W.R. (1967) Attacks on linking. In: *Second Thoughts.* London, Maresfield Library.
Bowlby, J. (1969) *Attachment and Loss: Volume 1 Attachment.* London, Hogarth Press.
Britton, R. (2003) *Sex, Death and the Superego.* London, Karnac Books.
Caper, R. (1999) On the difficulty of making a mutative interpretation. In: *A Mind of One's Own.* London, Routledge.
Casement, P. (1985) *On Learning from the Patient.* London, Tavistock Publications Ltd.
Chetty, R. (2010) Connecting creative capital and pedagogy in postgraduate programmes. In: C. Nygaard, N. Courtney & C. Holtham (eds.) *Teaching Creativity – Creativity in Teaching.* Oxfordshire, Libri Publishing.
Driver, C. (2008) Assessment in supervision – an analytic perspective. *British Journal of Psychotherapy.* 24, 328–342.
Driver, C. (2016) *Results of Questionnaire to 2013/14/15/16 Graduates of the WPF Therapy Psychodynamic Psychotherapy Training.* Unpublished.
Fonagy, P. (2001) *Attachment Theory and Psychoanalysis.* New York, Other Press.
Frawley-O'Dea, M.G. & Sarnat, J.E. (2001) *The Supervisory Relationship.* New York, Guilford Press.
Freud, S. (1914) On narcissism: an introduction. In: *The Standard Edition.* Volume XIV. London, Hogarth Press, pp. 67–102.
Greenson, R.R. (1981) *The Technique and Practice of Psychoanalysis.* London, Hogarth Press.
Hawkins, P., & Shohet, R. (2002) *Supervision in the Helping Professions.* 2nd edition. Maidenhead, Open University Press.
Hughes, L. & Pengelly, P. (1997) *Staff Supervision in a Turbulent Environment.* Bristol, PA, Jessica Kingsley.
Kalsched, D. (1996) *The Inner World of Trauma.* London, Routledge.
Kernberg, O.F. (1996) Thirty methods to destroy the creativity of psychoanalytic candidates. *International Journal of Psychoanalysis.* 77, 1031–1040.
Kernberg, O.F. (2006) The coming changes in psychoanalytic education: part 1. *International Journal of Psychoanalysis.* 87, 1649–1673.
Kernberg, O.F. (2007) The coming changes in psychoanalytic education: part 11. *International Journal of Psychoanalysis.* 88, 183–202.
Kernberg, O.F. (2010) A new organization of psychoanalytic education. *Psychoanalytic Review.* 97, 997–1020.
Mahler, M.S., Pine, F. & Bergman, A. (1975) *The Psychological Birth of the Human Infant.* New York, Basic Books.
Martin, E. (2002) Listening to the absent patient. In: C. Driver & E. Martin (eds.) *Supervising Psychotherapy.* London, Sage.
Martin, E. (2005) Shame in supervision. In: C. Driver & E. Martin (eds.) *Supervision and the Analytic Attitude.* London, Whurr Publishers.
Mezirow, J. (1991) *Transformative Dimensions of Adult Learning.* San Francisco, Jossey-Bass.

Mollon, P. (2002) *Shame and Jealousy: The Hidden Turmoils.* London, Karnac Books.
Nathanson, D.L. (ed.) (1987) *The Many Face of Shame.* New York, Guilford Press.
Obholzer, A. (2006) Authority, power and leadership: contributions from group relations training. In: A. Obholzer & V. Zagier Roberts (eds.) *The Unconscious at Work; Individual and Organisational Stress in Human Services.* Hove, Routledge, pp. 39–47.
Pally, R. (2007) The predicting brain. *International Journal of Psychoanalysis.* 88, 861–881.
Piaget, J. (1958) *The Development of Thought: Equilibration of Cognitive Structures.* New York, Viking Press.
Piers, G., & Singer, M.B. (1953) *Shame and Guilt: A Psychoanalytic and a Cultural Study.* Springfield, Charles C Thomas.
Pope, R. (2005) *Creativity: Theory, History, Practice.* London, Routledge.
Raiker, A. (2010) Creativity and reflection: some theoretical perspectives arising from practice. In: C. Nygaard, N. Courtney & C. Holtham (eds.) *Teaching Creativity – Creativity in Teaching.* Oxfordshire, Libri Publishing.
Reddish, E. (2014) *The Petrified Ego: A New Theory of Conscience.* London, Karnac Books.
Salzberger-Wittenberg, I., Williams, G. & Osborne, E. (1999) *The Emotional Experience of Learning and Teaching.* London, Karnac Books.
Schore, A. (1991) Early superego development: the emergence of shame and narcissistic affect regulation in the practicing period. *Psychoanalysis and Contemporary Thought.* 14(2), 187–250.
Searles, H.F. (1955) The informational value of the supervisor's emotional experiences. In: H. F. Searles (ed.) (1986) *Collected Papers on Schizophrenia and Related Subjects.* London, Maresfield Library.
Stimmel, B. (1995) Resistance to awareness of the supervisor's transference with special reference to the parallel process. *International Journal of Psychoanalysis.* 76(6), 609–618.
Stockwell, R. (2005) The ego and superego in supervision. In: C. Driver & E. Martin (eds.) *Supervision and the Analytic Attitude.* London, Whurr Publishers.
Stoltenberg, C.D. & Delworth, U. (1987) *Supervising Counselors and Therapists.* San Francisco and London, Jossey-Bass.
Szecsödy, I. (1997) How is learning possible in supervision? In: B. Martindale et al. (eds.) *Supervision and Its Vicissitudes.* London, Karnac Books.

Chapter 11

The analytic superego[1]

Warren Colman

Introduction

It is unfortunate that training as a psychoanalytic psychotherapist can often contribute to the development of a strict, unforgiving analytic superego that continues to operate as a critical, threatening persecutor long after formal training has ended. Analytic goals and methods are set up as an ideal standard against which the practitioner continually measures themselves (and/or others) with moral injunction and admonishment towards deviations and shortcomings. This is often expressed in terms of anxieties about whether one is 'doing it right' and fears of what colleagues would say 'if they knew what I was really doing or saying with my patient'. Sins of omission often become focused around 'getting hold of the transference' and interpretations of the patient's destructiveness. Sins of commission usually focus on boundary issues: things one is 'not supposed' to do.

I do not think the prevalence of this analytic superego derives from the failures or limitations of therapists' personal analyses. Personal analysis may serve to strengthen the individual's capacity to withstand group pressure, but no member can be impervious to the groups to which they belong; even those who leave the group retain relatedness to it by defining themselves, and being defined, as 'outsiders'. Furthermore, the association between the authority of the organisation and the personal superego is likely to be greater in analytic organisations because personal analysis is also part of the social institution. Inevitably, there is some cross-over between transference to the personal analyst and to the wider training organisation. Even if this is not actively reinforced by the analyst reporting on the candidate's readiness for training and/or qualification, it is likely to extend the transference beyond what can be worked through in the analytical relationship (Balint, 1948; Arlow, 1972; Klauber, 1983; Kernberg, 1986, 1996; Glover, 1991; Eissold, 1994; Johns, 2000). Balint and Arlow both point to similarities between analytic training and initiation rites and the consequent tendency for candidates to 'remodel' themselves in the image of their community's ideal (Arlow, 1972: p. 562). The candidate's ego ideal is thus transformed into an analytic ego ideal to be monitored by an analytic superego identified with the wider analytic community.

Eissold (1994) points out that since being 'well analysed' is an important criterion of professional acceptance and respect, analysts always feel vulnerable in the eyes of their colleagues to the most intimate *ad hominem* arguments. A vicious circle may develop whereby feelings of anxiety, guilt and inadequacy, inevitable concomitants of psychoanalytic work, are experienced as personal failings that colleagues may identify and hold against them, thus generating further feelings of anxiety, guilt and inadequacy. The same is true, *mutatis mutandis*, for those who may actually make such attributions. Apparently objective criticism or intellectual debate may become contaminated by judgemental intolerance and condemnation, a hallmark of unmodified superego functioning. In short, there is an oscillation within the analytic community between persecution by and identification with the superego with the one frequently being used as a defence against the other. Projective identification operates both ways: analytic weakness and failure is projected into those who are seen as 'not proper analysts' while arrogant superiority is projected by those fearing receipt of such criticism. The supposedly persecuted group may then institute equally ferocious criticism against 'analytic arrogance' in a cycle of defensive retaliation. The 'pointing finger' hallmark of superego inspired blame can be seen in both positions.

An example of this process occurred in the early 1990s during the contentious debates surrounding the formation of a breakaway organisation for psychoanalytic psychotherapy (now the British Psychoanalytic Council) separate from the larger and more diverse UK Council for Psychotherapy (UKCP). Discussion amongst the various psychoanalytic organisations was continually dogged by mutual judgemental prejudices, with each group becoming pushed into defensive positions. The BPC organisations and their supporters insisted on the superiority of their 'standards' whilst the UKCP supporters became equally insistent on attacking the judgemental criticism they felt these standards implied. This is a typical example of the process of splitting in a fight/flight basic assumption group (Bion, 1961). As Kernberg (1998) describes it, 'Because the members cannot tolerate opposition to their shared ideology, they easily split into sub-groups, which fight with one another' (p. 4). Similar mutual defensiveness and projections still go between Jungian and Freudian groups, a century after the original split between their founding fathers.

These large group processes reflect the difficulties individual practitioners face as they attempt to mediate between their psychoanalytic ego ideal and the reality of their clinical practice. Since the reality of psychoanalytic work is slow, arduous and painful and its results are often meagre by comparison with the hopes and expectations of both patient and therapist, therapists will frequently be exposed to feelings of inadequacy and failure. Such feelings are most likely to arise in persecutory and destructive clinical situations, which therefore imbue the resulting superego criticisms with a correspondingly persecutory and destructive character. In this sense, the analytic superego may be regarded as a counter-transference problem. However, it is also an institutional problem, derived from the initiatory processes of induction into the analytic community. This creates a two-way reinforcement of superego anxieties: the counter-transference conflicts of the clinical situation are projected into the institutional dynamics of the analytic community which then reflect back the practitioner's own doubts, fears and uncertainties.

I approach this problem from both points of view. In the first part of this chapter I describe some of the anxieties of the clinical situation that give rise to persecutory superego anxieties, while in the second I focus on how these anxieties become institutionalised and exacerbated through the process of training and induction into psychoanalytic culture. I suggest that the leading anxiety in psychoanalytic work is a fear of helplessness and powerlessness, especially being powerless to heal the patient's distress. The analytic superego is both a legacy of these anxieties as they are continually re-evoked in the clinical situation and an attempt to defend against them through the fantasy of an analytic ego ideal believed to be immune from them. I refer to three ways of relating to the analytic superego: anxious compliance, rebellious splitting and denial and pseudo-omnipotent identification. In practice, all three may oscillate within the same practitioner although individuals may 'prefer' one or another according to their personal proclivities. None of these are stable and all compromise the therapist's capacity to function in a truly analytic manner, acting as rigid injunctions not subject to thought and evaluation, and interfering with the therapist's free-floating availability to the actual clinical situation.

In this way the analytic superego inhibits the capacity to choose the appropriate response to the patient's need, and leads to an anxious, rigid clinical style that closes down the possibility of technical diversity. Rebellion against the analytic superego may also lead to a false 'freedom', splitting-off the need for restraint and blinding the practitioner to collusions with the patient which avoid the arduous pain of analytic work (Caper, 1992). I conclude by outlining how a more positive relation to the psychoanalytic community may enhance and support the therapist in their lonely, anxiety-provoking work.

Persecutory anxieties in the countertransference

During my analytic training, I mentioned to a colleague that I had offered to reduce a patient's fee but the patient had found this very difficult to accept. My colleague smiled knowingly and said that the patient was obviously feeling guilty about her envious triumph over me in getting me to reduce her fee. I replied that I did not think this was it at all. I felt the fee reduction was well justified by the patient's difficult circumstances but it was difficult for her to accept being cared for by me.

Nevertheless, I was left feeling awkward and uncomfortable as if I had been 'found out' as a bit of a dupe. I felt somehow small, obscurely guilty, and ashamed. My explanation seemed so soft-centred while my colleague's alternative interpretation seemed tougher and more 'rigorous'. Perhaps in my attempt to be kind, I had been drawn into an unwitting collusion? Perhaps I had been 'weak' and failed to grasp the negative and destructive aspects of the transference?

It is notable that this comment came from a peer, a fellow trainee rather than a supervisor or teacher for it shows that socialisation into the analytic community takes place in a broader context than the formal elements of training. This comment came to epitomise, for me, the official 'orthodox' view that I could neither emulate nor reject. Unwittingly, my colleague had stepped into the position of a persecutory superego that closely reflected the dynamics of the relationship with my patient. I knew (as my colleague did not) that my patient suffered from a highly persecutory superego that insisted on her inadequacy and worthlessness. This was the source of her guilt about accepting a reduced fee but interpreting it was extremely difficult since such interpretations were immediately taken over by her internal persecutor and used as confirmation that she was worthless and 'stupid'.

This interaction was reflected with my colleague where I was the one who felt worthless and inadequate, squirming under the fantasised critical lash of her off-the-cuff remark. It may also be that my fellow trainee felt as insecure as me and there was an envious triumph for her in aping her own critical superego and making me the one to squirm. We may both have had exaggerated fantasies about what being a psychoanalyst was supposed to be, but the interaction served to delude us both into believing that these were realities. It served to reinforce a projection of a persecutory superego out of the clinical situation and into the 'organization in the mind' of psychoanalysis. This did evoke envy, albeit not an envious triumph but a feeling of weakness, inadequacy and helplessness in relation to psychoanalysis that echoed similar feelings in my patient, indicating a state of unconscious identity between us (Jung, 1946: para 364).

The rabbit and the stick

In this kind of persecutory climate it can be painfully difficult to find a position that is neither persecutor nor victim. The difficulty is highlighted in Rosenfeld's (1962) distinction between an early persecutory superego and a later, more Oedipal one. Rosenfeld suggests that the early superego is characterised by feelings of reproachful accusation associated with damaged internal objects. He illustrates this by a dream in which a patient was instructed by a man to kill a tame and docile rabbit by hitting it with a stick. No matter how much she hit and mutilated the rabbit, no matter how mangled its body became, it would not die, but kept looking at her in a reproachful and accusing way. Rosenfeld suggests that the injured rabbit represents the patient's anxiety about injured early objects which, being damaged beyond repair, turn into accusing persecutors. The patient attempts to defend against this by identifying with an idealised punishing father represented by the man with the stick. The identification with the later Oedipal superego (the idealised father), operates as a defence against the early persecutory superego. Rosenfeld says:

> The greater the inner persecutory anxieties [deriving from the early persecutory superego], the greater is the need to make . . . absolutely uncritical identifications with the real parents or parent substitutes as later superego figures.
> (Rosenfeld, 1962: pp. 145, 154)

I think this shows how identification with psychoanalysis as a powerful idealised father serves as a defence against the reproachful accusations evoked by the patient's damaged state. The therapist, often in projective identification with the patient, feels powerless to help and may feel that the patient is damaged beyond repair, as indeed is sometimes the case. All this evokes intense guilt that may become unbearably persecuting. In the example I described, my colleague took on the role in my mind of the powerful Oedipal superego advising me to hit the patient with the stick of interpretations about her envy. I felt as if my colleague was saying that my patient was a bad rabbit who should be hit with a stick when I felt that she was a helpless frightened rabbit who needed me to help her. In situations like this, the therapist is torn between their desperation to help the 'injured rabbit' and feelings of punitive violence toward a patient/rabbit whose injuries arouse unbearable feelings of guilt, inadequacy and failure. They become caught between a Scylla and Charybdis of persecutory superego injunctions – fearing the consequences of failing to help on the one hand, and the consequences of being too 'soft' and insufficiently analytic on the other. This creates a false dichotomy between being a good object and a good analyst whereas what is really at issue is the distinction between a good object and an idealised object (Colman, 2006).

Robert Caper refers to situations in which the therapist avoids the reproach of the archaic superego by colluding with the patient's conscious or unconscious demand for an idealised good object (Caper, 1992, 1995). The therapist identifies with the patient's *fear* of the archaic superego and cannot withstand the guilt-laden pressure to give in to its accusatory demands. However, the fusion between the archaic superego of patient and therapist that Caper describes can also result in the therapist *identifying* with the superego, enacting this by 'punishing' the 'bad' patient. Then, like Rosenfeld's patient, the therapist may turn to the idealised potency of psychoanalytic interpretation – the 'big stick' – resulting in a punitive and persecutory response that disguises the therapist's sadism as 'interpreting the patient's destructiveness'. For example, a therapist presenting to a clinical seminar of colleagues spoke of 'getting out the big guns' in his interpretation to his patient. Here, the therapist identifies with the imagined potency of the idealised father as a defence against the more primitive superego associated with the reproach of damaged objects. Such interpretations of a patient's destructiveness can become disguised sadistic attacks, driven by fear and hatred of the patient who reminds the therapist of their own damaged objects. An alternative strategy is to become a helpless rabbit oneself, complying with the dictates of analytic superego injunctions out of fear of being punished by the big stick. Here, the letter of the law is obeyed, not because it benefits the patient but because it avoids persecution by the analytic superego. In neither case is the therapist actually in touch with the patient.

Idealisation in psychoanalytic training

Although these pressures are inherent in psychoanalytic work, they may be compounded by the induction of trainees into the psychoanalytic community during the process of training. It is inevitable, and in some ways even desirable, that there should be a certain amount of idealisation of psychoanalysis by those devoting the enormous resources required to become a qualified practitioner. Similarly, trainees inevitably identify with senior figures in the profession. Nevertheless, idealisation and identification create considerable difficulties if they remain unmodified. Since it is the job of the superego to monitor and even police the ego in relation to the standards of the ego ideal, the more idealised and therefore unattainable the ego ideal becomes, the more persecutory the functioning of the superego will be (Newton, 1961). Furthermore, it is often difficult to know whether one is functioning in the desired way. For example, I have still not managed to work out whether I am capable of working 'without memory and desire' (Bion, 1970: p. 31) because I have never been sure what working without memory and desire really means. Nor, in working with the unconscious, is it ever possible to 'know' sufficiently what is going on to be in command of the situation. These pressures contribute to a tendency to compensate for feelings of helplessness and powerlessness by elevating the psychoanalytic 'parents' into super-powerful, magically effective beings. We project into them the omnipotent power we believe we need which we then hope to ingest from their words of wisdom. In short, psychoanalytic training is likely to function as a Dependency Basic Assumption Group (Bion, 1961) in which 'members perceive the leader as omnipotent and omniscient and themselves as inadequate, immature and incompetent' (Kernberg, 1998: p. 4). Hopper (2003) elaborates:

> The basic assumption of Dependency protects people from the experience of helplessness and fear that they will be unable to fulfil the requirements the completion of which is essential to life. . . . Feelings of unsafety, uncertainty, being lost, of not knowing what to expect and what is expected are also involved.
>
> (pp. 32–33)

While such feelings must be present in any training situation, they are compounded in analytic training by the trainee's own analysis where such feelings are aroused through regression to infantile states of mind. The trainee has to cope with the most acute activation of their needs for dependence while simultaneously trying to function in a work group related way. This can lead to a difficult oscillation between idealisation and denigration since, as Hopper (2003) continues:

> When Dependency fails as a defence against feelings of helplessness, envy is likely to occur and, in turn, either denigration develops and leads to Flight/Flight or further idealisation develops and leads to an amplification of Dependency.
>
> (p. 34)

In the latter situation, trainees function uncritically, looking to their analysts and supervisors to convey the magically effective power to heal. Such feelings can lead to rote imitation, taking what is said and done by analyst or supervisor and repeating it to the patient in undigested form, thus eliminating the trainee's own thinking mind, the very thing of most benefit to the patient. The tendency towards fight/flight in psychoanalytic group relations is most clearly apparent in the denigration associated with splitting and projection of 'bad' theories and practices into other groups and a defensive insistence on the superiority of one's own school.

Rigour and 'the rules'

One result is the persecutory idealisation of analytic 'rigour'. Although being 'rigorous' is often valorised in psychoanalytic discourse, its dictionary definition is surprisingly similar to the activity of a punitive superego: 'severity in dealing with persons, extreme strictness, harshness, the strict application or enforcement of a law, rule etc., exactness without allowance, deviation or indulgence' (Oxford English Dictionary). When analytic rigour becomes idealised, authority degenerates into authoritarian rigidity and the maintenance of boundaries becomes slavish adherence to orthodox technical procedures. As a result, trainees can form the erroneous impression that psychoanalytic practice is full of 'rules' that must be obeyed, fostering an over-zealous aspiration to a style of practice hide-bound by the injunctions, prescriptions and proscriptions that make up the analytic superego. The idea grows up that one must always and only interpret the 'here and now' transference, maintain a neutral demeanour at all times, never make a personal disclosure, never acknowledge mistakes, never apologise, never answer questions and preferably never ask them either, never say 'we', never accept presents, never look at photographs of the patient's family or read anything they bring to the room. Such strictures produce an essentially defensive approach to the therapeutic relationship in which the therapist is continually 'watching their back' for fear that the 'supervisor on their shoulder' will put the knife in. Instead of *thinking* about boundaries and containment, instead of recognising that it is the maintenance of an analytic attitude of thoughtful reflection in the therapist's *mind* that constitutes the real boundaries, these matters are rigidified into 'rules'. Once this kind of persecutory atmosphere takes hold, presentation of clinical material can become a fraught and inhibited experience in which the therapist fears being shown-up and criticised for all the 'enactments' he has missed and the transference dynamics he has failed to spot and/or interpret. Although it is recognised that 'errors' inevitably occur due to counter-transference pressures, these are regarded as regrettable 'failures' that the therapist should strive to avoid. This generates further competitive pressure to become a knowing and clever therapist who can not only spot the patient's attempts to 'trick' the therapist but point out where other therapists have been insufficiently rigorous and thus caught out by the tricky, devious manipulations of the patient. While this may be a caricature, it is certainly a recognisable one. I frequently find that supervisees, including qualified and experienced therapists, are maintaining rigid boundaries as 'rules' without really having thought through the reasons for them. Consequently they are hamstrung when patients question their actions and unable to consider when there might be reason to act differently. Instead of boundaries serving as a set of guidelines enabling the therapist to know where they are in relation to the yardstick they provide, they become a fetishised shibboleth measuring little more than analytic rectitude. They provide an easy target for insecure colleagues or supervisors, thus turning the screw of persecutory anxiety about presentation of clinical work.

What counts here is not what one does but why one does it: is it merely conformity to or rebellion against 'the rules' or does it have a properly thought out analytic motivation behind it? I fully accept that some practitioners take a very different view of the frame from my own, for example the view held by Langs (1976) that the frame must be kept absolutely stable. Langs' approach is a carefully thought out and closely argued clinical strategy. As such it is only likely to be effective when used by those who understand it and are able to make it their own. So, while the nature of the frame may vary, the important thing is that the frame itself should be subject to analytic discourse, not merely a given beyond discussion. Considering the frame as the expression of the analytic attitude itself frees it from superego 'shoulds', making it available for the exercise of personal judgement which, as Britton (2003) points out, is actually a function of the ego, not the superego (p. 101).

The analytic frame and the analytic attitude

External boundaries may thus be regarded as the outward sign of the analyst's inward commitment to the analytic process. In the disorienting situation of 'not knowing' that is inevitable when working with the unconscious, boundaries may sometimes provide a virtual life-raft of stability. This certainly has a positive aspect. I treasure the story of a psychotic patient who had great difficulty attending his sessions at the right time. The analyst patiently reminded him of the correct time of the session and kept to the time boundaries regardless of when the patient arrived. Several years later, when the patient had recovered from his psychotic state, he reflected: 'That was a terrible time for me. There was only one thing in the world I could be sure of – that you knew what time it was'.

Yet if this moving story were to become an unbreakable law, we would be unable to recognise circumstances in which the opposite considerations apply. An example of this occurred while I was writing this chapter. One Sunday afternoon, as I was reading over the paragraph above describing 'the rules', a patient phoned to ask if I would see him as he was in 'a desperate situation'. I could hear from his quivering voice that he was in a dreadful state such as I had never heard in several years of therapy. It dawned on me that he wanted to see me *immediately* and, as it did so, I made up my mind. I told him I would meet him at my consulting room in half an hour where I saw him for an otherwise normal 50-minute session. This swift, unhesitating decision was based on the unlikelihood of him making such a request without serious cause and that, in all the years of therapy, we had been unable to make direct contact with the raw, emotionally dependent infantile part of himself that was now so apparent. The session that day seized an opportunity that would almost certainly have been lost had I insisted on waiting until his normal session time two days later. As a result the therapy was moved forward in an undoubtedly helpful way by his increased emotional availability and my increased understanding of the part of himself he had found so difficult to bring directly into the room.

Some might argue that such action is all very well for experienced therapists but inadvisable as a model for trainees. They would argue that you have to learn the rules before you can break them. Yet it seems to me that if therapists are going to learn to relate to boundaries and the frame as an expression of their analytic attitude, they need to be taught how to do so. This is only possible if the frame is subject to analytic scrutiny and debate in the course of training. So I would argue that you have to understand the meaning and purpose of the frame before you can learn how to use it. This keeps 'the rules' in the context of exercising ego judgement as opposed to becoming superego injunctions that can be utilised defensively.

Perpetuation of the superego in psychoanalytic organisations

Unless such injunctions are actively countered in training they may become installed into the analytic superego and difficult to shake off once qualified. Worse, they may be perpetuated as therapists become supervisors and trainers themselves. Even those who have developed a more personal way of working may feel required to pass on 'the rules' to the next generation. Freud (1933) describes this process in his account of the role of the superego in passing down traditional values and ideology:

> As a rule, parents and authorities analogous to them follow the precepts of their own super-egos in educating children. Whatever understanding their ego may have come to with their super-ego, they are severe and exacting in educating children. They have forgotten the difficulties of their own childhood and they are glad to be able now to identify themselves fully with their own parents who in the past laid such severe restrictions upon them. Thus a child's super-ego is in fact constructed on the model not of its parents but of its parents' super-ego.
>
> (p. 67)

As analysts take up senior professional roles, 'identifying with the parents' may be a positive and gratifying experience, especially if they have experienced their own analysts as loved and admired parental figures. Yet, by the same token, they may feel themselves to be responsible for ensuring that the beloved, precious knowledge and traditions of psychoanalysis are preserved and protected. Consequently, a defensive conservatism sets in that unconsciously regards the new generation as the repositories of repressed rebellious impulses that must now be subjected to 'rigorous' training to ensure their continued suppression. For example, Martin describes the response of trainees on a supervision course to a teaching example of an inexperienced male supervisee who had given a female patient a lift home in the rain. The course staff were shocked by the members' suggestions that the supervisee should be reported to their professional body as an 'offender' and struck off rather than exploring with him how and why this had happened (Martin, 2005: p. 177). The course members, supervisors themselves, seem to have been so anxious about the possibility of sexual acting out that that they felt the need to ruthlessly police sexual impulses in their supervisees. Ironically, this was the supervisee's difficulty too: unable to acknowledge his own sexual response to his patient's seductive behaviour, he had become drawn into an (unconscious) enactment with her.

Infantilisation

The unconscious phantasy of psychoanalytic organisations as families where senior members are parents and trainees are children frequently results in trainees being infantilised through institutional practices that embody and perpetuate this unconscious belief (Hill, 1993; Kernberg, 1996; Johns, 2000). It is often forgotten that candidates for analytic training are usually capable and experienced adults in their own right. Johns (2000) quotes an egregious example of this from the obituary of a member of 'The Year of the Colonels', a group of psychoanalytic candidates, including Bion, who had had successful careers in the military psychiatric services during the Second World War. The obituary describes them:

> sitting on a dilapidated sofa and swallowing their indignation at being infantilized by their then teachers, and treated as if they knew nothing of life – senior officers who had been through the Desert and European campaigns and had organized the psychiatric and psychological services for the war effort.
> (p. 66)

While it is true that training promotes regression, especially given the concurrence of personal analysis, this is compounded if the organisation responds in kind. There may be powerful unconscious processes of projective identification underlying such organisational dynamics, whereby residual fantasies amongst trainers are projected into the new generation of trainees.

Anonymity and 'that distant ideal land'

These processes are also enacted and promoted in the structural relations *between* analytic organisations. The entire analytic community, at least in Britain, constitutes an organisation in the mind that is conceived as a hierarchical ladder with the Institute of Psychoanalysis at the top, the other BPC organisations on the next rung down, the rest of the psychoanalytic psychotherapy trainings below and the psychodynamic counselling trainings somewhere at the bottom. In my view, this construction cannot be avoided, since those who protest most vociferously against it thereby confirm its existence as a collective reality. The effect is to institutionalise a system that promotes the fantasy of a highly idealised and therefore persecutory analytic superego. For if, as I have suggested, the superego becomes more persecutory the greater the distance between the ideal and the achievable reality, the reduction of superego anxieties is dependent on a reduction of idealisation. Therefore it becomes imperative that therapists have opportunities to test out their fantasised idealisations of psychoanalysis against the reality.

However, the organisation of psychoanalysis fosters the opposite. The hierarchical structure is such that the 'lower echelons' rarely have direct contact with those remote idealised figures against whom their superego continually measures their competence or lack of it. As Kernberg (1996) ironically remarks in his satirical paper 'Thirty methods to destroy the creativity of psychoanalytic candidates', 'Anonymity fosters unanalysable idealisation and healthy insecurity'. Many of the methods he outlines promote such anonymity by maintaining a strict demarcation between senior and junior colleagues and the institution of powerful barriers to advancement within analysts' own societies. He also considers the discouraging effect of geographical distance:

> It may be very helpful to point out that psychoanalysis is understood and carried out properly only in places far away from your own institution.... If the demands of the training are such that the students would not be able to spend an extended part of the time in that distant ideal land, they may become convinced that it is useless to attempt to develop psychoanalytic science in a place so far from where the true and only theory and technique are taught. And that conviction will last.
>
> (p. 1034)

Nor is geography the only way of maintaining distance. The same effect is 'achieved' by a hierarchy of analytic organisations within the same city, as is the case in London where the role of 'that distant ideal land' is amply fulfilled by senior bodies such as the Institute of Psychoanalysis and the Society of Analytical Psychology. From this view, much of what Kernberg says about the barriers *within* analytic societies is even more true of the relations *between* the analytic societies and their 'descendants' – mainly the psychoanalytic psychotherapy organisations. Put briefly, the analysts train the psychoanalytic psychotherapists and the psychoanalytic psychotherapists train the psychodynamic counsellors. It is therefore no surprise to find among the latter group the greatest persecutory anxiety and the most rigid beliefs about analytic rules and boundaries for it is here that the greatest distance between analytic ideal and clinical reality is to be found. Fed on undiluted wodges of psychoanalytic theory derived from patients seen five times weekly, they are expected to apply these ideas in once weekly counselling on the basis of what is usually once weekly personal therapy. They are taught mainly by psychoanalytic psychotherapists who are often intent on impressing upon them the difficulty of achieving their own status, a reflection of the envy and sense of inferiority they feel towards the even higher status analysts. For most of these trainees, a real McCoy 'analyst' is a semi-mythical being whose papers they read but whom they rarely if ever see and then only at lectures where they are wheeled out as distant celebrities. Small wonder if they feel persecuted by an analytic superego that impresses on them their pathetic inferiority in relation to the analytic ideal. While this may be extreme, it highlights the same processes that pertain in less exaggerated form throughout the profession. Hence the anxiety or hostility with which many psychoanalytic psychotherapists measure themselves against the analysts, seeking either to impress or denigrate them – a further example of the oscillation between an exaggerated Dependency Group and the flip into a Fight/Flight Group (Hopper, op. cit).

All this clearly implies that the more contact and communication there is between different psychoanalytic bodies, the more healthy and creative the atmosphere will be and the less opportunity for persecutory analytic superego fantasies. It is also important that such contacts encourage an atmosphere of openness and sharing. It is not helpful to recreate analytic anonymity in the guise of impenetrable organisations since, unlike the analytic relationship, there is no opportunity to analyse the transference fantasies that such anonymity fosters. It is all too easy to hide behind the need for confidentiality and boundaries as a way of defending against anxieties and uncertainties, lest we be revealed as emperors without clothes (Casement, 2005).

This suggests that the barriers and inscrutable anonymity maintained by analytic organisations serve only to disguise the truth that the fantasised omnipotent analytic father (or mother) is nowhere to be found. As analysts gradually progress up the hierarchy, they become slowly acclimatised to the fact that these ordinary people who are now their colleagues are no more powerful or threatening than themselves. At the same time, though, a further insidious form of socialisation may be taking place as they are inducted into the view that it is their responsibility to maintain the illusion. For this reason, psychoanalytic organisations may display a rigid defensiveness that exceeds the personal defensiveness of its members. So the analytic superego continues in a new guise, policing senior analysts into maintaining group relations that encourage their junior colleagues to go on dressing them up in the clothes of the analytic ideal. That is, group relations in the analytic world tend to foster transference fantasies rather than acting to dissolve them.

Conclusion

When I began thinking about this chapter I was still under the sway of transference fantasies of this kind. I believed that many analysts and psychotherapists maintained attitudes of arrogant persecutory superiority towards colleagues and negative judgemental attitudes towards their patients. I saw this as a kind of tyranny from which the profession as a whole needed to be liberated (by me, presumably). It took me a long time to recognise that what I was actually criticising was my own analytic superego: an internal supervisor built on the model of my training but imbued with my own self-critical anxieties. I now see my former view as an attempt to split-off and project these self-criticisms and take up a position of rebellious denial towards them. My view changed as I became increasingly aware of the defensive and critical tone with which I sought to 'nail' the attitudes by which I felt so criticised. I discovered that in hating 'nothing at all except hatred' (Dylan, 1965) the virulent strength of the persecutory superego reveals itself in a new guise: it takes the easy option of exporting the superego by projecting it onto others and carrying on a superego-driven vendetta against them.

Although there is certainly evidence for the attitude of rigid superiority that I was so keen to 'nail' (e.g. Hill, 1993) I now see these as examples of therapists and analysts identifying with the same persecutory analytic superego that others comply with, rebel against and/or project onto the remote (and envied) psychoanalysts 'above' them. I believe that all psychoanalytic psychotherapists struggle with the same anxieties, doubts and confusions that I do. Investigating my own analytic superego has taught me the real therapeutic value of staying with such feelings and struggling to think about them with an analytic attitude. In my own development, my inability to shrug off views of the analytic process running counter to my own turned out to be an asset. I would see this as an illustration of the internal process that Jung described on the mythological level through his exegesis of the story of Job (Jung, 1952). Rather than turning against God or capitulating under the weight of his blows, Job confronts God with his own blindness and cruelty and, Jung argues, thereby brings about a change in God's nature, evinced by the shift from the Old Testament morality of 'an eye for an eye' to the New Testament morality of 'Love thy neighbour'. Britton (2003) puts forward the same view in terms of the conflict between ego and superego. It is through confronting the superego that its qualities become modified: critical persecution gives way to strong, loving support.

This confrontation represents a shift from an idealising and identifying relationship with psychoanalysis to one of love (Caper, 1999: p. 118). Giving up wishes for idealised certainties brings freedom from inner persecution. Such an internal relation to psychoanalysis has to be distinguished from a narcissistic relation where the therapist's relation to their theory, technique or fantasised view of their professional colleagues stands in the way of relating to the patient. I think of this as more like an adult couple relationship than one of parent and child. In a successful (i.e. non-narcissistic) couple relationship there are always difficult issues to be struggled with but the relationship provides a background of support on which the partners comes to rely, recognising that each of them contributes to the overall value of the relationship just as in a creative relation to psychoanalysis we are contributors as well as recipients. An alternative model is to see a more benign, transformed analytic superego as akin to a council of elders consulted by a ruler. As Britton (2003) puts it, 'the example of intrepid ancestors and the trust of respected colleagues is a source of inner strength' (p. 128). In the end, the decision is ours and ours alone. That is the joy but also the terror of our impossible profession.

Note

1 This paper was originally published in *Journal of the British Association of Psychotherapists* 44(2), 99–114, 2006, Copyright © 2006 BAP. Published by John Wiley & Sons, Ltd. It has been re-edited and shortened for this publication.

References

Arlow, J.A. (1972) Some dilemmas in psychoanalytic education. *Journal of American Psychoanalytic Association*. 20, 556–566.
Balint, M. (1948) On the psycho-analytic training system. *International Journal of Psychonalysis*. 29, 163–173.
Bion, W.R. (1961) *Experiences in Groups*. London, Tavistock Publications Ltd.
Bion, W.R. (1970) *Attention and Interpretation: A Scientific Approach to Insight in Psycho-Analysis and Groups*. London, Tavistock Publications Ltd.
Britton, R. (2003) *Sex Death and* the *Superego. Experiences in Psychoanalysis*. London, Karnac Books.
Caper, R. (1992) Does psychoanalysis heal? A contribution to the theory of psychoanalytic technique. *International Journal of Psychoanalysis*. 73, 283–292. Reprinted in: *A Mind of One's Own. A Kleinian View of Self and Object*. London, Routledge, 1999.
Caper, R. (1995) On the difficulty of making a mutative interpretation. *International Journal of Psychoanalysis*. 76, 91–101. Reprinted in: *A Mind of One's Own. A Kleinian View of Self and Object*. London, Routledge, 1999.
Caper, R. (1999). *A Mind of One's Own. A Kleinian View of Self and Object*. London and New York, Routledge.
Casement, P. (2005) The emperor's clothes: some serious problems in psychoanalytic training. *International Journal of Psychoanalysis*. 86(4), 1143–1160.
Colman, W. (2006) Is the analyst a good object? *British Journal of Psychotherapy*. 22(3), 295–310.
Dylan, B. (1965) *It's Alright Ma (I'm only Bleeding)*. Special Rider Music.
Eissold, K. (1994) The intolerance of diversity in psychoanalytic institutes. *International Journal of Psychoanalysis*. 75, 785–800.
Freud, S. (1933) New introductory lectures in psychoanalysis. In: *The Standard Edition*. Volume XXII, London, Hogarth Press, pp. 3–182.
Glover, E. (1991) Response to memorandum by James Strachey. In: P. King & R. Steiner (eds.) *The Freud-Klein Controversies 1941–45*. London, Routledge, pp. 611–616.
Hill, J. (1993) Am I a Kleinian? Is anyone? *British Journal of Psychotherapy*. 9(4), 463–475.
Hopper, E. (2003) *Traumatic Experience* in *the Unconscious Life of Groups*. London, Jessica Kingsley.
Johns, J. (2000) Future choices for psychoanalytic psychotherapy. *British Journal of Psychotherapy*. 17(1), 62–70.
Jung, C.G. (1946) The psychology of the transference. In: *The Collected Works*. Volume 16. London, Routledge & Kegan Paul.

Jung, C.G. (1952) *Answer to Job: The Collected Works*. 11, London, Routledge & Kegan Paul.

Kernberg, O.F. (1986) Institutional problems of psychoanalytic education. *Journal of American Psychoanalytic Association*. 34, 799–834.

Kernberg, O.F. (1996) Thirty methods to destroy the creativity of psychoanalytic candidates. *International Journal of Psychoanalysis*. 77, 1031–1040.

Kernberg, O.F. (1998) *Ideology Conflict and Leadership in Groups and Organizations*. New Haven, CT, Yale University Press.

Klauber, J. (1983) The identity of the psychoanalyst. In: E.D. Joseph & D. Widlocher (eds.) *The Identity of the Psychoanalyst*. New York, International Universities Press, Inc., pp. 41–50.

Langs, R. (1976) *The Bipersonal Field*. New York, Jason Aronson.

Martin, E. (2005) Shame in supervision. In: C. Driver & E. Martin (eds.) *Supervision and the Analytic Attitude*. London, Whurr Publishers.

Newton, K. (1961) Personal reflections on training. *Journal of Analytical Psychology*. 6(2), 103–106.

Rosenfeld, H. (1962) The super-ego and the ego-ideal. *International Journal of Psychoanalysis*. 43, 258–263. Reprinted in: *Psychotic States – A Psychoanalytical Approach*. London, Hogarth, pp. 144–154.

Chapter 12

The superego's role in ethical practice

Hindrance and help

Celia Harding

Introduction

In this chapter I explore the ethical standards which structure and safeguard psychoanalytic relationships, and the values which underpin the therapist's commitment to the psychoanalytic endeavour. I go on to consider the role of the therapist's superego in regulating her ethical conduct of, and engagement in, therapeutic relationships. This is vital because the therapist's narcissistic gratifications from her work are based on substantial abstinence of her personal needs, wishes and interests. I outline a model of healthy and pathological superego functioning to assess the helpful and hindering contributions of the therapist's superego in maintaining, and restoring, ethical relationships. Professional Codes of Ethics and Practice are necessarily generalised, allowing space for the therapist's clinical judgement as she applies her profession's guidelines to the ethical dilemmas arising in particular clinical contexts and individual circumstances. I propose a triangular model to assist therapists to think through ethical dilemmas and contain their uncertainties as they navigate the conflicting issues involved.

The ethical foundation of psychoanalytic relationships[1]

In daily life we exercise our moral sense to regulate our relationships with ourselves and one another. Our ethical values provide yardsticks by which to gauge the 'rightness' and 'wrongness' of actions, underlying intentions and consequences. People relate with each other on the basis of common interests as well as different, competing interests. Sometimes resolutions to differing interests can be negotiated in mutually satisfying and ethical ways. At other times one person attempts to resolve differences by forcefully exerting power over the other. Relationships between therapists and patients are no exception.

Professional ethics are necessary to regulate relationships based on unequal power. Just as mothers may abuse their powerful position in relationships with their children (Welldon, 1988) so therapists may abuse their position of trust by misusing their patients to serve their own needs. The importance of safeguarding asymmetric professional and familial relationships is reinforced by the necessarily private and confidential nature of relationships conducted 'behind closed doors'. Professionals caring for dependent and vulnerable people are accountable to professional bodies, which are in turn accountable to public institutions, just as families are accountable to state agencies.

Codes of Ethics, shared and agreed by members of the profession as standard practice, regulate the proper conduct of psychoanalytic therapy. The 'rights and wrongs' of ethical practice are internalised as an 'analytic superego', processed and executed by the therapist's superego functions. A cornerstone of ethical practice is the clinician's commitment to setting aside her needs in order to attend to her patient's interests and developmental needs. This principle can be qualified with Brenman's wise counsel:

> no love is meaningful without the donor having some self-interest. The love a mother gives *can* only be measured against giving up some self-interest. The interaction between self-interest and concern needs to be balanced lest there be adverse consequences either way.
>
> (Brenman, 2006: p. 3)

Moral values inform a psychotherapist's professional practice in different ways.[2] A practitioner's values are part of her personal belief system, often shared with other colleagues. In her conduct of therapeutic relationships, the therapist's commitment to an analytic attitude is stabilised and anchored by the values enshrined in her ego ideal. Therapists' values also underpin their adherence to their professional ethical standards and guidelines, the application of which are matters of thoughtful judgement having considered their meaning and purposes, and whether and how they may be appropriately applied in particular clinical circumstances. Within the clinical process, however, the therapist endeavours to protect her patient's thinking space from intrusions of her own values. As the patient struggles to explore and understand his own moral inclinations, the therapist utilises her values to assist her to understand what underlies the patient's perceptions and decisions, rather than to guide him to decide what he *should* do.

The role of the therapist's superego in regulating the analytic relationship

Agreement to embark on a psychotherapeutic relationship confers upon the therapist ethical responsibilities towards her patient, including prioritising her patient's interests. The therapist needs her superego to regulate her narcissism so that satisfactions she derives from the work are not at her patient's expense. The clinical process requires patients to communicate their thoughts and feelings without undue concern for the therapist's sensibilities. Primitive impulses and wishes, necessarily mobilised during psychotherapy, may threaten the therapist's self-esteem, thereby challenging her capacities to contain, think about and understand, rather than react to, her patient's communications. Gratifications of the therapist's self-esteem from such processes constitute an unintended consequence, rather than a primary outcome. 'Doing their job' ethically requires therapists to value the intrinsic rewards of developing and exercising their skills, whether or not patients consciously acknowledge and appreciate their efforts. Therapeutic changes are necessarily incremental (Strachey, 1934), often difficult for patients (and their significant others) to appreciate. A therapist needs to tolerate and accommodate assaults on her narcissism: treated as if she's non-existent, is bad and hateful or a 'toilet' into which to evacuate intolerable feelings (Saretsky, 1980). It follows that therapists are ethically obliged to ensure sufficient sources of narcissistic gratification in their lives to nourish their self-esteem beyond the treatment of their patients.

Therapists also need their superego's help to work within the parameters of the professional relationship. The profession's agreed standards of practice constitute benchmarks within which therapists utilise their clinical acumen to make ethical judgements whenever conflicts of interests arise in the relationship. The complexities of thinking through ethical dilemmas are explored later in this chapter.

Internalising ethical standards and practice is an essential ingredient of a psychotherapist's training (see Driver, Chapter 10) underpinned by the trainee's values informing their ego ideals. The trainee's superego regulates her relationships with her patients in accordance with professional analytic standards and her ego ideals. Arguably, training analysis is the most effective training component for aligning personal values with analytic practices: just as our capacities to relate to others are founded neurologically as well as emotionally in our primary relationships (Narvaez, Chapter 4) so also living an ethical therapeutic relationship as a patient, establishes, unconsciously and consciously, ethical therapeutic relating (Schore, 2012).

The therapist's superego in sickness and in health

The therapist's openness to her patients and her own process, vital for her clinical work, depends on maintaining a relatively harmonious and balanced relationship between her ego, superego and id (Freud, 1923). Her presence of mind and mental space to think can be crucially compromised by interference from her superego (Driver, Chapter 11; Colman, Chapter 12): when, for example, her self-esteem is threatened by superego recrimination, punishment and withdrawal of love (Freud, 1923; Schafer, 1960), her capacity to think is liable to become impaired or temporarily lost. Freud's aim for analyses may be seen as especially crucial for training analyses: to 'strengthen the ego, to make it independent of the super-ego' (Freud, 1933: p. 80).

Novick and Novick (2004) offer a model of healthy and pathological superego functioning which we may apply to the superego's engagement in analytic practice. In health, the superego functions as an 'open system'. In this mode the superego is characterised by its protective and guiding relationship towards the ego based on realistic ego ideals, values, standards and expectations.

The 'open system superego' is attuned and adaptive to inner and outer realities, oriented to problem-solving and conflict resolution. Its style is thoughtful rather than reactive, enlisting ego capacities to create space to think in nuanced, complex, balanced, terms, in the light of benefits and consequences, based on learning from experience. The therapist's ego is free to process and contain whatever the patient presents for understanding, neither resorting to 'easy certainties' about 'right or wrong', nor to 'anything goes' indulgences of id impulses and wishes. 'Open system superego' functioning rests on recognising the other's individuality and separateness (Novick & Novick, 2004: p. 248).

In contrast, a 'closed system superego' adopts a harsh and punitive, authoritarian position in relation to an intimidated ego. The 'closed system superego' operates in sweeping, global terms from assumed omnipotence, arrogance and narrow-mindedness (Brenman, 2006: p. 48), reacting to conflicts on the basis of false simplicities and clarities, self-evident rights or wrongs, goods or bads. Complexity is avoided and denied, without allowances for changed or extenuating circumstances. In 'closed system' mode, superego functions and processes are unadaptive and fixed, characterised by repetitive and circular logic beyond resolution, closed to other possible perspectives, contingencies and meanings. Its style is perfectionist, absolutist, tyrannical, issuing relentless punishment on the assumption that id impulses and wishes are omnipotently powerful and therefore require, in like measure, to be checked by omnipotent controls. In addition, sameness and equation are assumed: minor irritation is equated with violent rage; mistakes with heinous crimes. Clearly, in this sado-masochistic mode of functioning the therapist's ego, superego and id will be in unbalanced, conflictual relationship, pervading and pre-occupying the therapist's mind, impeding her capacity to maintain her presence of mind and openness to her patient.

A therapist's susceptibility to 'closed system superego' functioning is not only affected by the particular dynamics arising between herself and the patient, but also from a hazard of her humanity: what becomes of the aggression that accrues as she frustrates her own needs in order to prioritise her patients' needs? Freud suggests that the superego's moral zeal is driven by the aggression that the ego has diverted from its objects and represses in the unconscious (Freud, 1923: p. 54; see also Harding, Introduction, p. 4-5). This implies that a 'closed system superego' mode might provide an outlet for the therapist's unconscious hostility towards her patients disguised as morally justified judgements, presented as legitimate interpretations.

Realistically, the therapist's superego functioning moves between healthier and more pathological modes, from moment to moment, session to session, as her patient's communications challenge her emotional balance. When the therapist recognises that her superego and ego have shifted into sado-masochistic relating, it is vital that she extricate herself into 'a third position' (Britton, 1998) to create space to think through what shunted her into this internal dynamic. This enables her to utilise her lapsed 'ethical analytic attitude', to better understand her own and her patient's inner worlds, in order to further the analytic work. Successful extrication from, and resolution of, sado-masochistic relating will re-establish her presence of mind and open availability to her patient and restore the state of well-being she acquires from 'doing her job'.

We now consider the task of navigating the complexities of ethical dilemmas in psychoanalytic psychotherapy assisted by a triangulating model. With respect to the particular focus of this chapter, I illustrate my points with contributions from the superego of therapist and patient.

Creating a space for ethical thinking

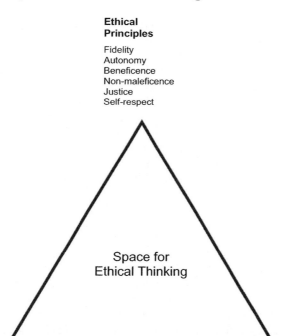

Psychoanalytic Framework
1. Benchmarks provide an early warning signal alerting us that something is surfacing
2. Provide a safe container for unconscious processes to unfold
3. A catalyst for meanings
4. The framework as a 'third' containing the therapeutic relationship

Defining features of the Psychoanalytic Model
1. The centrality of the unconscious
2. The formative influence of childhood experience on development
3. The centrality of the transference relationship
4. Therapist as container through open-minded, thoughtful presence

Figure 12.1 Triangulating modal orienting ethical thinking.

Ethical principles

The first reference point of this triangular model are principles, structuring the therapist's personal values, which underpin her ethical commitments towards her patients. These principles may differ according to beliefs, opinion and experience but those identified by the BACP (2013), defined here in psychoanalytic terms, offer a useful starting point.

Fidelity[3]

Trust underpins therapeutic relationships. The power disparity between patient and therapist confers on therapists an ethical obligation to respect their patient's dependence on them and refrain from exploiting their vulnerability. In turn, commitment to a therapeutic relationship requires patients to place their trust, provisionally, in their therapist: blind-trust would be as compromising to the therapeutic endeavour as no-trust. Patients begin therapy with preconceived expectations about the trustworthiness of relationships: for some, trust in relating has been lethally betrayed. Trust in the therapist and the therapeutic process has to be tested and discovered through the patient's experience of the therapist. The therapist's reliability, consistency and stability, her capacity to think rather than (re)act will be crucial as the patient establishes trust, and its limits, in the therapist and relationship.

Autonomy

Through respect for his autonomy, the therapist ethically safeguards her patient's necessary dependence on her and the therapeutic process. She expresses her respect for her patient's own capacities and limitations through her mindful regard for his defences. However, individuals can only make truly autonomous decisions, when equipped with the information needed to make sound judgements. Most patients implicitly accept, by seeking therapy, that they do not feel in charge of themselves when they feel driven to act by impulses and wishes beyond their conscious control. The patient is not equipped to evaluate reality as it is whilst their view of reality is distorted by unconsciousness motives and fantasies. Patients need their therapist's help to become conscious of, and understand, their unconscious wishes and impulses before they can exercise greater control over, and responsibility for, their decisions and actions (Holmes & Lindley, 1991: p. 52ff).

Beneficence and non-maleficence

These two ethical principles, to 'do good' and 'do no harm', are two sides of the same coin. Of all the therapist's ego ideals, these have the deepest roots in her 'moral function' (Rickman, 1951), connecting directly with her ambivalent feelings towards her patients in the consulting room and her endeavours to contain her aggression with loving concern, and with reparative guilt when she fails.

Patients bring to therapy their experiences of 'good and ill' from past and current relationships, often confused about what constitutes harm or benefit. Therapists too may share such confusions feeling, perhaps, that kindness and helpfulness are necessarily beneficent and saying 'no' is maleficent.

These principles require evaluation and judgement when considered in the context of ethical dilemmas: what does it mean to 'do good' and 'not harm' for an individual in each particular circumstance? In reality, ethical decisions can have both beneficial and negative possible consequences but in every case the unconscious meanings a patient ascribes to a therapist's actions carry the greatest weight.

Justice

In western cultures, justice and fairness are central to our proper treatment of one another and constitute an integral aspect of respect for an other's autonomy. This is reflected in the superego of both therapist and patient as they monitor the way they treat each other. Think of the speed at which a patient registers an unjust reflection of themselves implied in their therapist's interpretations. The therapist too registers their patient's unfair estimations of them, hopefully in reflective ways. Think too of the weight of grievance that many patients bring to their therapeutic relationship, feeling unfairly hard-done-by or denied credit when due. One manifestation of respect for justice in therapeutic relationships is a therapist's willingness to take responsibility for her part in whatever went wrong between them: this can be an unprecedented experience for some patients with potential reparative value beyond the immediate circumstance.

Self-respect

This is the therapist's responsibility to ensure her own personal and professional needs are met according to the values of fidelity, autonomy, beneficence, non-maleficence and justice. The therapist's attention to her own physical, mental and professional well-being, creating an appropriate balance between her professional and personal life, enables her to be present for her patients reliably and consistently whilst fulfilling her responsibilities to care for herself. The therapist's conduct of her self-respect crucially enables her to fulfil her own narcissistic needs in appropriate areas of her life and safeguard the patient's therapeutic space to prioritise their treatment needs.

The principles securing the ethical probity of therapeutic relationships are complex. Other reference points are also needed to orientate ourselves when navigating ethical dilemmas.

The psychoanalytic framework

My second reference point is the therapeutic framework embedding analytic technique, which preserves the therapeutic relationship and analytic space for 'uncovering [of] what is unconscious to the patient' (Freud, 1913: p. 118). Holding the framework steady allows unconscious meanings to emerge more clearly, protected from intrusions of external reality factors which could muddy the analytic waters.

Instilling an ethical attitude during clinical training includes learning the parameters of therapeutic relationships, agreed standards of practice accepted by the psychoanalytic profession. These include the regularity of sessions, at an agreed frequency, at the same time or times each week; the fifty-minute hour; an agreed fee; invoiced at a regular time in the month; charging the agreed fee for cancelled sessions; giving notice of changes to these arrangements including termination of therapy over an agreed period so that ending or absences may be gathered into the body of the therapeutic work; the limits of confidentiality.

Initially, these accepted parameters are received by trainees as the 'rules' of engagement. When these parameters continue to be treated as 'rules', their value to therapeutic work is limited to pleasing or defying an analytic superego, and restricts their potential to underpin an ethical attitude (see Colman, Chapter 11). However, there are occasions, when pressures to cross a line are compelling, for example, when a therapist feels tempted to act on an erotic counter-transference and turn the therapeutic relationship into an exciting sexual liaison: on such occasions responding to 'No! Wait!' from the therapist's protective superego, may grant her a moratorium within which to reflect. Coen (2007) distinguishes between 'boundary crossings' and 'boundary violations' at times when therapists feel driven to misuse the therapeutic relationship to serve their own narcissistic needs at the expense of their patient's treatment needs. 'Crossings' refer to occasions when therapists recognise that they have breached, or are about to breach, a boundary in time to retrieve it by working with the psychical meanings of their failure for their patient. In contrast 'violations' occur 'when the patient's treatment needs are infringed on or ignored and the analyst is unable to explore what has been enacted and so cannot restore the treatment frame' (Coen, 2007: p. 1171).

With time and experience of clinical work, reflective therapists may observe the sense of security that therapeutic boundaries confer to their patients as well as themselves, and how the rhythm of sessions starts to play a meaningful and containing role for the patient's psychic economy, anxieties and impulses. Therapists who thereby gain respect and appreciation for the boundaries may start to experience them as protective superego supports rather than sources of restriction and resentment. In particular therapeutic boundaries serve four functions:

- pressures to breach a boundary, coming from therapist or patient, often weighted with the moral force of superego pressures, may constitute an early warning signal to the therapist that something is trying to surface from the unconscious, seeking a way into thought. Therapists can only use boundaries

- as *benchmarks of unconscious activity* when they are accustomed to taking boundaries seriously; when they change boundaries casually they may miss cues that something unconscious is begging attention.
- therapists respectful of boundaries create *a safe container* enabling therapeutic work to unfold. As much as patients, or therapists, may kick against them, boundaries can provide a sense of safety and security to both parties. Knowing what to expect upholds the patient's autonomy and trust in the therapist's reliability and consistency. However patients may need to test the therapist's dependability by challenging the boundaries with the added weight of moral accusations: the therapist is cruel to not answer the door when her patient arrives early for a session; she rejects or castrates the patient by interrupting them when fifty minutes has passed; she exploits their dependence and takes advantage of them by charging for cancelled sessions. A patient's insecurities cannot come into focus when his therapist holds boundaries casually; his negative experiences of bad treatment cannot emerge for understanding when she reflexively gratifies his wishes.
- therapeutic boundaries constellate very personal meanings such that observances, or breaches, may become useful *catalysts for work and understanding*. When I forget to present my invoice at the regular time, patients may unconsciously communicate, in their own idioms, anxieties about my 'flakiness'; or when I have needed to make permanent changes to session times, patients have experienced me as rejecting, or side-lining them (whether or not the alternative time suits them better), or a sign that I am fed-up with them for being over-demanding: again, note the superego reproaches reinforcing these protests.
- therapists who respect the boundaries can experience the framework as *a therapeutic 'third' in the relationship* (Britton, 1998) holding the therapeutic couple. I recall one occasion, after many years of protest at my cruelty when sessions ended, finding myself saying to a patient 'we are both subject to the limits of time': this did seem to dilute the patient's sense that, by calling time, I was flaunting my power and sadistic control over him.

Therapists hold a boundary or not: either way it has meanings and repercussions which optimally therapists recognise and use in the service of the therapeutic task but the meaning behind boundary pressures is rarely obvious or straightforward. Often a third point of reference is needed to navigate the ethical dilemmas presented by pressures upon analytic values and boundaries coming from a patient's and therapist's inner worlds.

Defining features of the psychoanalytic model

My third reference point is the therapeutic model in which the therapist is trained and experienced, illustrated here by psychoanalytic psychotherapy. Therapists are bound by the standard practices of the therapeutic model in which they qualified and the professional body to which they belong: this is a matter of fidelity to patient, professional body and society. When patients embark on therapeutic treatment they implicitly trust their therapist to 'do their job' properly, even though neither they, nor the therapist, can know precisely what that will mean for them or where it will lead (Murdin, 2010). When the British Psychoanalytic Council extended their membership to a broader range of psychoanalytic and psychodynamic trainings five defining features of psychoanalytic work were outlined (British Psychoanalytic Council, 2011).

The centrality of unconscious processes

This feature of psychoanalytic therapies was enshrined by Freud in his dictum 'Where id was, there ego shall be' (Freud, 1933: p. 80). Freud's intuitive and clinically deduced theory of the unconscious, of 'the dimension of depth', of 'psychical structure' of which we are consciously oblivious (Freud, 1913: p. 126) is confirmed by neuroscientific research into the neurobiological substrate of the mind: our brains function largely on information outside conscious awareness (Eagleman, 2011; Schore, 2012).

Patients seek treatment for diverse problematic psychological conditions, implicitly and explicitly recognising that their attempts to overcome their maladies by conscious efforts have failed. Their mental distresses cannot be explained by known causes. Analytic therapists understand that their patients' sufferings are rooted in unconscious conflicts, expectations, fears and wishes, expressed in defensive compromise solutions that no longer 'work' for them. Psychoanalytic treatment focuses on discerning the unconscious mind to identify the sources of mental disturbances and difficulties that patients encounter repeatedly in their lives and relationships. Unconscious fantasies, motives and impulses are revealed in patterns emerging in freely associated feelings, thoughts, memories and dreams, and transference and counter-transference dynamics, as unconscious meanings surface in disguised and condensed forms (Murdin, 2010).

Even so patients may find it unsettling to admit that they are frequently unaware of what they think, feel, do and why, energetically resisting this unwelcome news by trying to convince themselves, and their therapists, that the reasons for their problems are outside themselves, beyond their control. Although this leaves patients feeling powerless, it satisfies an urgent need to bypass superego accusations of unconscious ulterior motives for their actions and behaviours. Even those who recognise unconscious sources of their suffering, may still feel, according to punitive and omnipotent superego judgements, that they should overcome their problems unilaterally through will-power. Patients may experience these superego expectations as coming from the therapist and accuse her of cruelty, not understanding, failing to allow for the realistic demands of their lives.

Early childhood experience contributes to difficulties in the present

Unconscious conflicts shaping the patient's approach to life, and unconscious expectations of relationships, originate in childhood experiences of self, others and the world. During early life, as minds (and brains) are forming, the child makes sense of their experience in childlike ways, conditioned by parental perceptions of the world and their child. Childhood is a time of actual dependence and helplessness when physical and psychological survival are paramount. Once formed, expectations of self and others resist revision in the light of later different experiences.

What cannot be cognitively recalled from childhood is nevertheless registered emotionally. Therapist and patient gradually confer meaning to adult experiences by piecing together freely associated psychic fragments into narratives of childhood experiences. This includes understanding possible origins of the harsh judgemental climate within the patient's mind and their unrealistic expectations of themselves and others, experienced as a barrage of superego recrimination for falling short of ego ideals. However many patients resist their therapist's understanding of present suffering in terms of past experiences and their current feelings in terms of childhood perceptions. Those who experienced their helplessness and dependency in childhood as unsafe, may be particularly resistant to the therapist's focus on childhood experience, adding moral weight to their protests by accusing the therapist of hurting, infantilising, patronising or exploiting them.

The centrality of the therapeutic relationship as a medium of understanding and change

The patient's difficulties with relating to others inevitably surface in their relationship with their therapist sooner or later. Consciously patients expect therapists to be non-judgemental, to treat them differently from other people in their lives, past and present. But painful unremembered experiences are repeated (Freud, 1920: p. 35ff), reincarnated and relived in the transference relationship with the therapist. The therapist experiences, at first hand, a taste of her patient's experience in his formative relationships, when he misperceives her 'as if' someone from his past.

In transference/counter-transference enactments the therapist may find herself in the emotional position that the patient occupied as a child; alternatively, the patient unconsciously manoeuvres the therapist into re-enacting the failures of an other from his past. Often these re-experiences of past relationships are painful and provoke moral reproach whether the patient criticises the therapist or feels criticised by her. Typically superego reproaches arise when a patient feels let down, abandoned, exploited, misunderstood, intruded on or controlled, this time by someone whom they consciously, reinforced with moral justification and financial payment, trusted to treat them 'right' this time.

The internal world as the location of difficulty and change

Analytic psychotherapists regard their patients' inner worlds as the source of their psychic conflicts and distresses. Patients can feel frustrated by this focus on their inner worlds, especially when they urgently need to attribute their pain to bad treatment inflicted on them; they can feel criticised when their therapist understands their experience as an externalisation of an internal dynamic; or feel harshly judged for failing to be the person they believe they should be. The therapist's focus on the patient's inner world can painfully expose his responsibility for, and part in, what has gone wrong. Therapists may unconsciously prefer to understand their patients as victims of their objects and circumstances than to identify their patients' agency in their experiences, to avoid becoming the target of superego-driven outrage (Novick & Novick, 2004). This could constitute a therapist's ethical failure since patients need her help to take responsibility for themselves before they can develop more autonomy and benefit from the expanded opportunities and satisfactions that such developments can enable.

The therapist's commitment to sustaining an open-minded, emotionally available and self-reflective attitude

This feature of the psychoanalytic method is the essence of the analytic attitude, underpinned by the ethical attitude, as defined and explored by McFarland Solomon and Twyman (2003). Achieving an open-minded, receptive, emotionally available stance towards patients, coupled with the therapist's self-reflective monitoring of her internal responses, expresses her capacity to set aside her interests during the session and prioritise the patient's interests. Her success in this endeavour is reflected by her use of any narcissistic deprivations, injuries – or indeed satisfactions – in the service of understanding her patient.

The therapist's open-minded attention to her patient's inner world is difficult to sustain in the face of powerful emotions, impulses, anxieties and wishes, pressurising her to act and react rather than think and understand (see for example Nathan, chapter 7, p. 110–11). To maintain an open receptiveness, the therapist must occupy an ego position of thoughtful understanding rather than succumb to the 'anything goes' of id impulses or the 'easy moral certainties' of the superego (Lloyd-Owen, 2007: p. 113). When the therapist's ego position shifts into id or superego modes, she needs her self-reflective capacities to recognise her failure, take responsibility for her part in the consequences and, with renewed understanding, repair the rupture in her analytic attitude and its impact on her patient. This beneficent outcome depends on the therapist's capacity to find a 'mind of her own' (Caper, 1999) in relation to her self-criticisms and restore her space for thought (see Harding, Introduction; Chapter 5).

The patient's superego enforcement of their ego ideal expectations of themselves can generate anxiety and persecution. Patients expect their therapists to criticise and judge them as they do themselves. When therapists react in kind to their patient's id demands or superego attacks, they reinforce the punitive superego in their patients' minds. Conversely when the therapist survives attacks from her patient's superego and sustains her thoughtful ego position, she offers the patient an experience of a more moderate and protective superego (Schafer, 1960; Harding, Chapter 5). These are potentially mutative experiences (Strachey, 1934). When a patient internalises cumulative experiences of a benign superego from their therapist, the internal relationships between their ego, id and superego rebalance (Barnett, 2007) and their inner world becomes more harmonious.

Using the triangulated space for ethical thought

Payment for cancelled sessions in psychoanalytic practice

I select this psychoanalytic practice to illustrate the model outlined above because it is an element of the framework, 'leasing a definite hour' (Freud, 1913: p. 126), which often generates acute conflicts, not least between ego, id and superego pressures, in the minds of all concerned. Payment for missed sessions 'preserves the analytic space and the analytic connexion despite the physical separation' thereby holding the analytic framework in the face of 'conflicting and ambiguous' pressures upon it (Furlong, 1992: p. 714). This requires the therapeutic couple to confront, rather than bypass, the conflicts arising between them around the frame, in the interests of further understanding (Brenman, 2006: p. 10).

Payment for cancelled sessions may seem to violate the therapist's values underpinning her commitment to ethical relationships by apparently: penalising patients for exercising their autonomous rights to decide whether, or not, to attend a session; taking advantage of the patient's dependence on therapist and therapy; treating patients unfairly, even cheating them, by charging for something they did not have, thereby doing harm not good. The only therapeutic principle this practice apparently upholds is 'self-respect': the therapist's legitimate need to stabilise her income, thereby providing the material security necessary to prioritise her patient's treatment needs.

Unconscious processes and meanings, embedded in the analytic frame and psychoanalytic model, confer sense to this counter-intuitive practice (Furlong, 1992). These include:

- the experience of analytic treatment as a continuous process over the entire therapy, a space preserved to optimise the uncovering and understanding of unconscious meanings;
- an experience of the analytic relationship as 'a bond between two parties which transcends their physical presence together' (Furlong, 1992: p. 705);
- experiences of working with absences and separations, which are as necessary to developing autonomy and independence as experiences of the therapist's actual presence;
- by maintaining her neutral position of thoughtful availability and understanding towards the missed session, the therapist conveys her choice to decline an omnipotent position of 'knowing best', of exerting the power of her asymmetrical position to judge the worthiness of reasons for absences;
- a communication that the therapist is separate and different from the patient, offering him an opportunity to experience and emotionally respond to this painful reality. To imply that they are in the same boat, by not charging for

the cancelled session, could constitute a seductive encouragement of his unhealthy dependence on her;
- the therapist's willingness to accept the patient's experiences of her as an unkind, exploitative object offers him an opportunity to express and explore these negative experiences of her;
- an intrusion of the therapist's need, for regular and stable payment offers the patient an opportunity to re-experience in the transference how he felt treated by his mother as her narcissistic object, there to meet her needs, rather than she to meet his;
- an opportunity for the therapist to provide the patient with an experience of 'a mother [who] is there to be left' and the developmental possibilities on which this availability depends (Furman, 1982);
- by not incurring financial cost from the patient's absence, the therapist allows him an experience of separateness and independence without giving grounds for guilt whilst accepting and exploring the patient's resentment about being charged for the session;
- experiences through which the patient may discover new ways to relate to his commitments: less as inviolable moral obligations, and more as obligations containing freedom to prioritise other things as he thinks fit.

Containing 'moral uncertainty' as integral to an ethical attitude

Having offered this triangulating model to assist ethical thought it would be misleading to imply that following it may guarantee ethically 'right' conclusions, even when supported by thorough consideration and debate of the issues with colleagues.

Therapists are human, not omniscient: they cannot know all the relevant details of their own and their patient's inner worlds or foresee with certainty the consequences of their judgements. What might seem to be the most optimal decision in the circumstances for one patient might be different for another. 'Each case, each decision, is different and requires an absolutely unique interpretation that no existing coded rule can or ought to guarantee completely' (Goldberg, 2007: p. 19). These realities make outcomes of ethical enquiry necessarily uncertain. As it happens containing uncertainty is an essential feature of the psychoanalytic method which seeks to subject any and all assumptions to exploration with an open mind (Goldberg, 2007). By contrast, moral certainties are closed to exploration contributing to their imperative force: as said of preachers in pulpits, the (internal and external) deliverers of morally infused pronouncements claim to be 'six feet above contradiction'. Goldberg argues that an approach to ethical conundrums, consistent with psychoanalytic methods, is one of open-minded uncertainty as dilemmas are considered from every conceivable angle and conclusions reached are regarded as provisional. A therapist's understandable longings for certain resolutions are based in her need for refuge in the 'false comfort' of having 'done the right thing' (Goldberg, 2007: p. 41). But when we are prepared to dig deep into our assumptions in debate with others, it is unlikely that we can reach a clearly 'right ethical decision'.

Cultivating an open-minded acceptance and tolerance of uncertainty when morally infused 'rights and wrongs', 'goods or harms' are at stake, is challenging. A frustrated quest for 'right' decisions and the necessity to manage the anxieties attendant on uncertainty, are liable to generate the therapist's aggression and challenge her maintenance of an 'open superego'. Urgent resort to a ready outlet for her aggression, disguised as moral rectitude from a 'closed superego' position, may unconsciously present a defensive solution. This may prompt a therapist to follow an 'ethic of conviction' considering only the imperative to uphold the 'rightness' and purity of a moral ideal, an ethical standard or a technical principle, without considering the possible psychological consequences (Weber, 1919). By contrast, when a therapist is able to contain her aggression which has been generated by uncertainty, she may find herself able to exercise an 'ethic of responsibility' (Weber, 1919): a decision which modifies or compromises a moral ideal in order to facilitate a 'greater purpose' having anticipated the possible destructive consequences in reality if the ideal is insisted upon. An 'ethic of responsibility' includes the therapist's preparedness to take responsibility for the consequences of her decisions, including unintended ones.[4]

An example of these two approaches applied to an ethical dilemma, from conviction and/or responsibility, was illustrated in the television drama, 'The Sopranos'. Tony Soprano, head of a mafia organisation, approaches Dr Melfi for psychoanalysis when he experiences unfamiliar feelings of loss and sadness. Despite her awareness of his psychopathic defences, which were likely to undermine and pervert the effectiveness of psychoanalytic treatment, she agrees to treat him; in effect she gives him the opportunity to discover whether he is capable of psychical change. To what extent is Dr Melfi adopting an 'ethic of responsibility', mindful of the risks (see Taylor, Chapter 8), responding to Soprano's developmental need, knowing that her judgement might be distorted and that she will take responsibility for whatever consequences unfold? Or to what extent might she be gratifying some unconscious self-destructive motives of her own? In contrast when Soprano's wife, Carmela, approaches a psychoanalyst for treatment he is categorical that unless she is prepared to give up her relationship with her mafia husband and life-style, he cannot treat her. To what extent might his decision be seen as 'an ethic of responsibility' coupled with 'conviction' based on his clinical judgement and experience that offering to work with a patient unlikely to benefit from psychoanalytic treatment would be unethical? Or to what extent is his decision based on an 'ethic of conviction': his moral certainty disguising his self-interested concern to protect his professional rectitude from becoming sullied by his attempts to help Carmela to extricate herself from her corrupt state of mind and life-style? As Twyman (2007) suggests:

> An ethicist begins with questions, and from the very beginning of the exploration of the field proceeds by . . . questioning, and continues finding that questions lead to further questions.
>
> (Twyman, 2003: p. 15)

Conclusion

The therapist's capacity to engage with the ethical dilemmas arising during analytic work depends on her availability to think openly and freely. The proposed triangular model offers three reference points to assist the therapist to navigate her ethical dilemmas towards understanding and provisional resolutions. Utilising this space for thought depends on the relationship in the therapist's mind between her id, ego and superego functions. When the therapist's superego rears up to dominate and intimidate her ego with punishing shame and guilt, zealously requiring adherence to absolutist values and standards, this unhelpful 'closed' superego fills the space needed for thought. Under siege from superego judgements and condemnations she becomes liable to comply with or defy superego injunctions undermining her capacity for ethical practice. It is then essential that she call on the help of understanding and compassionate supportive colleagues and consultants to help her restore an 'open' superego in her mind. When the therapist's ego is in an independent and respectful relationship to her superego, she is in a position to think realistically and objectively (Caper, 1999) whilst observing the analytic necessity to contain her narcissistic needs and impulses. She is then able to use her protective and forgiving superego functions to help her to face her responsibilities, support her capacity to think and restore her ethical footing.

When she has reached provisional resolutions to her ethical dilemma, the therapist cannot know in advance what the outcome will be and whether the balance will tip towards more good than harm or vice versa. In the last analysis the therapist has to hold her uncertainty and discover what, or even whether, transformative potential can evolve from her ethical thinking and the path she chooses, fully prepared to review her resolutions as the consequences of her decisions unfold.

Acknowledgements: my thanks to Gill Bannister, Sybil del Strother and David Riley for the ethical discussions we have shared and their generous contributions to this chapter.

Notes

1 For clarity of distinction I use a female referent generically to denote the therapist and a male referent to denote the patient.

2 I am indebted to David Riley for pointing out the distinctions I draw here between ethics, values and clinical process.
3 The principle of Fidelity was revised to 'Being Trustworthy' in the 2016 and 2018 editions of the BACP Ethical Framework accessible on www.bacp.co.uk/events-and-resources/ethics-and-standards/ethical-framework-for-the-counselling-professions/ from April 2018. (BACP, 2018 Ethical Framework for the Counselling Professions. Ethics: Principles, Point 5. Lutterworth, BACP).
4 The sociologist Max Weber drew this distinction in the context of the moral tension between idealism and pragmatism that runs through political decisions (The Economist, 2016: p. 40) but I suggest it has wider application in the context of any exercise of power by an authority when moral issues are at stake, including psychotherapy. This distinction also seems to me to approximate the biblical distinction between 'the letter and the spirit of the law'.

References

Barnett, B. (2007) *"You Ought To!": A Psychoanalytic Study of the Superego and Conscience*. London, Karnac Books.
Brenman, E. (2006) *The Recovery of the Lost Good Object*. London, Routledge.
British Association for Counselling and Psychotherapy (BACP) (2013) *Ethical Framework for Counselling and Psychotherapy*. Lutterworth, BACP. Revised edition: BACP *2018 Ethical Framework for the Counselling Professions*. Lutterworth, BACP).
British Psychoanalytic Council (2011) *New Associations*, Issue 7, Autumn 2011. London, British Psychoanalytic Council.
Britton, R. (1998) *Belief and Imagination*. London, Routledge.
Caper, R. (1999) *A Mind of One's Own*. London and New York: Routledge.
Coen, S.J. (2007) Narcissistic temptations to cross boundaries and how to manage them. *Journal of the American Psychoanalytic Association*. 55(4), 1169–1190.
Eagleman, D. (2011) *Incognito: The Secret Lives of the Brain*. London, Canongate, 2016.
The Economist, 1 October 2016, p. 40.
Freud, S. (1913) On beginning the treatment. In: *The Standard Edition*. Volume XII. London, Hogarth Press.
Freud, S. (1920) *Beyond the Pleasure Principle*. Volume XVIII. London, Hogarth Press.
Freud, S. (1923) The ego and the id. In: *The Standard Edition*. Volume XIX. London, Hogarth Press.
Freud, S. (1933) New introductory lectures on psychoanalysis. In: *The Standard Edition*. Volume XXII. London, Hogarth Press.
Furlong, A. (1992) Some technical considerations regarding the missed session. *International Journal of Psychoanalysis*. 73, 701–718.
Furman, E. (1982) Mothers have to be there to be left. *The Psychoanalytic Study of the Child*. 37, 15–28.
Goldberg, A. (2007) *Moral Stealth: How Correct Behaviour Insinuates Itself into Psychotherapeutic Practice*. London, The University of Chicago Press.
Holmes, J. & Lindley, R. (1991) *The Values of Psychotherapy*. Oxford, Oxford University Press.
Lloyd-Owen, D. (2007) Perverse females: their unique psychopathology. In: D. Morgan & S. Ruszczynski (eds.) *Lectures on Violence, Perversion and Delinquency*. London, Karnac Books.

McFarland Solomon, H. & Twyman, M. (2003) The ethical attitude: a bridge between psychoanalysis and analytical psychology. In: H. McFarland Solomon & M. Twyman (eds.) *The Ethical Attitude in Analytic Practice*. London, Free Association Books.

Murdin, L. (2010) *Understanding Transference: The Power of Patterns in the Therapeutic Relationship*. Hampshire, Palgrave Macmillan.

Novick, J. & Novick, K.K. (2004) The Superego and the two-system model. *Psychoanalytic Inquiry*. 24, 232–256.

Rickman, J. (1951) The development of the moral function. In: King, P. (ed.) *No Ordinary Psychoanalyst: The Exceptional Contributions of John Rickman*. London, Karnac Books.

Saretsky, T. (1980) The analyst's narcissistic vulnerability. *Contemporary Psychoanalysis*. 16, 82–89.

Schafer, R. (1960) The loving and beloved superego in Freud's structural theory. *The Psychoanalytic Study of the Child*. 15, 163–188.

Schore, A.N. (2012) *The Science of the Art of Psychotherapy*. London, W.W. Norton & Company, Inc.

Strachey, J. (1934) The nature of the therapeutic action of psychoanalysis. *International Journal of Psychoanalysis*. 15, 127–159. Reprinted in: *International Journal of Psychoanalysis*. 1969, 50, 275–291.

Twyman, M. (2003) Ethical themes in analytic practice. In: H. McFarland Solomon & M. Twyman (eds.) *The Ethical Attitude in Analytic Practice*. London, Free Association Books, pp. 15–20.

Weber, M. (1919) Politics as vocation. In: H. Gerth & C. Wright Mills (eds.) *From Max Weber: Essays in Sociology*. London, Routledge, 2009.

Welldon, E.V. (1988) *Mother, Madonna, Whore: The Idealisation and Denigration of Motherhood*. London, Guildford Press.

Index

Abraham, K. 81, 83, 85, 87
abuse 106, 130, 135; sexual 54; sexualised behaviours 51–52
action language 88
Adriansen, H.K. 169
Adshead, G. 131, 135, 136
agency 88, 90
aggression 56, 83, 89; anal 81; (un)bound by love 5, 81, 84, 89, 193; death instinct 24–25; defences against 120; from developmental deficit 4–5, 62, 66, 81, 130; driving superego functions 3, 4, 5, 6, 12, 22–23, 82–83, 145; in fundamentalist mind-set 143, 146; healthy development of 83, 89, 119; in psychopathy 127, 130–136; re-cycled 5, 7, 12, 84, 90; response to loss 84; self-preservative 4, 89, 131, 108n1; sexualization of 96, 99, 108n2; in species-typical childrearing 61, 62, 65; therapist's in clinical practice 153, 190, 193, 201; unconscious 11, 82, 96; *see also* ambivalence
Aichhorn, A. 47, 57n1
Alderdice, J.L. 146
Alexander, F. 32, 39, 40
altruism 129, 131
ambivalence 148; parental 52, 55; therapists 193; toward lost object 84, 85
anality 81; structuring obsessional defences 10, 13, 23, 37, 39, 86; *see also* aggression
analytic attitude 14, 106, 178, 179–180, 184, 188, 198; lapsed 190; underpinned by ethical attitude 198; *see also* thinking
analytic boundaries/framework 178–180, 194–195, 199–200; defensive use of 183 (*see also* clinical practice; psychoanalytic model); internalised in training 167, 189
analytic ego ideal(s): in the profession 174, 183, 189, 192; re training 57, 161, 172, 189, 173
analytic function 118; compromised 120–121, 189, 194; restore ethical footing 202; restore third position 122, 190–191; *see also* analytic attitude
analytic rigour/rules 163, 178–179, 194; *see also* authority
analytic superego 14, 172, 184; analytic ego ideal 172, 182–183; boundary issues 163, 172, 178–179; compliance with 176, 178, 180, 194; persecutory anxieties 173, 174–176, 182–183, 184; personal analysis 172; post-training 172, 173, 180, 188; rebellion against 174, 194; relating to 153, 174, 183–184, 188, 194; re psychoanalytic organisations 180–183
Andrade, V.M. 110, 111–112, 117
anti-social impulses *see* aggression; psychopathy
anxiety 49, 55; alleviation of 44; between professional colleagues 173, 183; capacity for 137; in clinical training 159–161; defences against 131, 144; driven defences 92, 146, 152, 158, 159–164; fundamental anxieties 92n6; Nameless dread 111; Oedipal 33, (primal mistaken for 34); part of personhood 66; persecutory 118, 198; presenting problem 34, 36; in psychoanalytic work 148, 151, 173–174, 174, 179, 182; re intimacy 52,

Index

105, 108n1; superego 12, 23; survival 34; in training organisations 165–167; unconscious 115
archaic superego 8, 15n3, 32–34, 110, 176; elemental superego 13, 111–116, 117–118, 119, 120, 121–124; incarcerating ego 34; origin & function 38–39; persecutory 42; as protective 33, 40; in politics and society 34–35; as primitive functioning 29, 39, 42, 146, 148; regulator of affect 39; therapists identification with 176; *see also* superego development
Arlow, J.A. 172
attachment 2, 13, 48, 66, 67; lacking 84, 85; fear of 53; in psychopathy 130, 131, 133, 137, 162
authority: of analytic organisations 172; analytic rules 178; benign119–124, 165; of clinical trainers 158, 162, 165, 167; exercise of 203n4; idealisation in fundamentalism144–49, 151, 153; limit setting 120; in psychopathy 129, 130; of superego 12
autonomy 21; development of 5, 34, 39, 65, 69, 198, 199; fallacious understanding of 9; key therapeutic value 191, 192, 193, 195
auxiliary superego 8, 87, 89–90, 148

Balint, M. 172; Society 153
Barnett, B. 9, 10, 15n1, 199
basic assumption group 173, 177
Bateman, A. 131, 158
Beebe, B. 63
beneficence 192–193
benign authority *see* authority
benign pluralism 1
Benjamin, J. 63, 143
Bereczkei, T. 131
Beres, D. 39
Berry, T. 72
Bion, W. 29, 181; attacks on linking 165; basic assumption group 173, 177; containment 112, 116, 120; ego destructive 111, 123–124; nameless dread 111; without memory & desire 177, 181
Black, D. 142
body 81; body/brain 62, 65; body-gaze 56, 96; based defences 49, 54, 55, 56, 66; female perversion 54; image 54; language 43; parental control of 81; personalisation 53, 54, 56, 62; purging 26, 86; sexualization of 99; split from mind 49, 67, 69, 70
Bollas, C. 151
borderline states 13, 110–125; contrast with normal development 111; as interpersonality disorder 116, 119; superego in 110, 113, 114, 123–124; therapist's vulnerabilities in treatment of 110–111, 115, 116, 117, 119, 120, 123
Bouchard, M-A. 8, 43, 82, 90
Bowlby, J. 130, 158
brain 5, 12, 196; development 2, 61, 62, 72; fight/flight 33; moral sense 7, 15n4; plasticity 66; in psychopathy 126, 129, 130, 132, 133, 136; right-brain 3, 66
Bray, Carys (novelist) 15n8, 144
Brenman, E. 188, 190, 199
Brenman-Pick, I. 115, 117
Brenner, I. 39
Brierley, M. 29
British Association for Counselling and Psychotherapy (BACP) 192, 203n3
British Psychoanalytic Council 173, 196
Britton, R.: developmental process 29; ego/superego relations 32, 82, 88, 98, 124, 158, 179, 184; parental sexuality 147; superego 12, 98, 99, 114, 147; triangular space/third 122, 190, 195; unconscious belief 153
Bromberg, P. M. 7, 8, 13
Byung-Chul, H. 35

Caldwell, M. 137
Campbell, D. 49, 104
Caper, R. 38, 15n3, 88, 202, 162, 174, 176, 184, 198, 202
Carpy, D.V. 110, 116, 117
Casement, P. 163, 183
certainty 184, 200–202
Chasseguet-Smirgel, J. 9, 14, 48, 105
Chetty, R. 169
childhood experience: as central to analytic model 191, 196–197; companionship care 4, 62–65; consequences of under-care 66–70; depression 83; in hunter-gatherer 60–61; in industrialised 60–61; maturational environment 49, 62; as mother's narcissistic object 11, 113; non-maturational environment 12, 49–50, 112–114

Cleckley, H.M 127
clinical practice 35–38, 40–44, 104–107, 179–180, 196–199; boundary crossings 194; boundary violations 194; closed & open system superego 189–190, 201; parameters of 194–195; problems of perversion 95–96, 100, 104, 105, 107–108; *see also* analytic boundaries/framework; psychoanalytic model
clinical training 157, 177; anxieties 158, 160, 161, 166; aspirational 161, 169; assessment 161, 168; components of 157–158; developmental processes 158; ego-destructive trends 165, 166; ego ideals in 158–159, 172; ego strengths required 157–158, 168–169; hierarchy of training institutions 166, 176, 181–182; idealisations of 159, 166, 176–177; initiation rites 172; parallel processes in 161, 162, 164; regression during 158, 159, 160; shame & guilt 161–162; superego in 158–171 (necessary to 167–168, 169); supervision 163–165; trainers & supervisors 159–160, 163, 165, 166, 180; training analysis 172, 177, 189
Coen, S. J. 99, 194
Colman, W. 14, 166, 172, 194–185, 189, 194
Cooper, A. 52
compliance 43, 61; ethic of 68; with analytic superego 174; in patient group 43
conflicts: between ego and superego 90–91, 184; between ego, superego and id 199; between individual and social 4–5, 9; psychic 8, 90–91; social 9; between value systems 8–9, 199–200
conscience 1, 4, 5, 29, 32, 106; driven by re-cycled aggression 5; harsh 52; as individual's moral function 1, 14, 21, 60; neurobiological development of 60, 65; new theory of 34; in psychopathy 126, 129, 130, 131; varieties 10–11
constituents of superego 5–8, 12
core complex 13, 105, 108n1, 134
cortisol 66, 132
countertransference: with borderline pathology 110, 115, 116, 117, 121; fundamentalist mindset 144, 149; in perversion 95, 98–99, 100, 103, 104, 107; with psychopathic pathology 129;

superego enactment in 114–118, 163, 165, 174
Cox, M. 38
criminality 95, 97, 100, 102, 126–128, 130–131, 135; *see also* delinquency; psychopathy
cumulative trauma 38, 49

death instinct 24; *see also* aggression
defences 7, 13, 192; borderline 13 (*see also* borderline states); defensive analyst 120–121; against depression 85–86 (*see also* depression); distorting ego function 5, 13, 14; fundamentalist 13, 153 (*see also* fundamentalism); illusions of omnipotence 85; manic 85–86; obsessional 10, 37, 42, 86 (*see also* obsessionality); paranoid-schizoid 25–29; in perversion 13, 52, 85 (*see also* perversion); psychopathic 13, 201; psychotic 26–27; sexualisation 96, 99, 100, 105, 107; against superego attacks 7, 13, 14, 90–91; survival 52, 60, 66–70; in training 160; against uncertainty 200–201
dehumanisation 52, 146
delinquency 50, 128
De Mijolla-Mellor, S. 48
De Mause, L. 60
dependence: of child 6, 197 (*see also* independence); of ego on superego 1, 7–8, 83, 87–91, 92; of infant 26; on 'mindless' objects 42; narcissistic pain of 85; of patient 43, 192, 199, 200, 195; of trainee 157, 177
depression 13, 79–94; antecedents 67, 82–86, 132; defences against 84, 85–86; depressed states of mind 79, 84; disclaimed superego propensities 87–88; dream representing 87; of infant 56; superego behind 79, 83, 87, 89, 95, 101, 108; therapeutic remedy 80, 87–94, 105–106; *see also* aggression
depressive position: developmental 27–29, 48, 119; state of mind 25, 152; superego functioning 97, 98, 167, 148
Derber, C. 71
Dermen, S. 52
development 1; aggression 4–5, 80–83, 84–86; brain 2, 62; of child 22, 25; of ego 5, 7, 82–83, 84–85; failure 4; of individual 1, 2; of morality 60,

61–65; neurobiological 2–5, 7; pseudo development 66–70; psychic 111–114; of sociality 2–5, 61–65; of self formation 61–64; of superego 7, 22–29, 80–82, 95, 97; in therapy 80, 87–94, 105–106
disrespect 50, 132, 144, 146
dissociation 7, 8, 99, 106
Dolan, M. 131
Dreyfus, H.L, & S.E. 70
Driver, C. 14, 158–170, 189

Eagleman, D. 2, 3, 7, 196
Economist, The (current affairs magazine) 203n4
Edmundsen, M. 71
ego 9; agency 8, 13, 44, 88, 90–91; destructive 33, 111, 123, 124, 165; development 5, 7, 8, 14, 25–29, 41, 82–83, 84–85 (pseudo 66–68; in therapy 42–44, 53, 55–57, 87–91, 92n5, 106–107); disconnected from superego restraint 9; fragile 13, 85; functions devoted to moral duties 5, 82; identified with superego 11, 13, 32, 34, 36, 142, (petrified 8, 13, 34, 36, 38, 40, 42–43); immaturity 5, 8, 32, 40; independence of superego 8, 13, 14, 32, 34, 88, 91; maturity 32, 34 ; recipient of self-directed aggression 4, 79; in sado-masochistic relation with superego 34, 43, 85, 87, 100–101, 105, 107, 108n1, 116, 190; superego as specialist ego facility 1, 5, 82–83; *see also* ego ideal
ego ideal 1, 5, 7, 14, 80; body image 52–54; in clinical practice 173, 174, 177, 188, 189, 192–193, 197, 198; in clinical training 57, 158–163, 165, 189, 172; coincide with social values 9; defined 46–47; development 6, 47–48, 80, (failure of 48–57, 82, 85); forerunner 39; of gaze 47, 53, 54, 55, 56; in health 46, 48, 159 (*see also* Ideal Ego; narcissism); as prescriptive superego 6; re narcissism 6, 47–48, 48–50; re superego 47, 80
Eigen, M. 48
Eisnitz, A. J. 38
Eissold, K. 172
elemental superego *see* archaic superego
enactments 110; in perversion 96; sado-masochistic 105, 116; superego 116, 117, 119, 121, 178, 165; in the transference-countertransference 116, 163, 178, 181, 197
equilibrium 43
Esperger, Z. 131
ethical attitude 14, 163, 167, 194, 198; tolerance of uncertainty 200–201
ethical primates 12
ethics 21, 22, 26; in clinical practice 167, 187–188, 199, 200–202 (breaches 194); Community 8, 15n6; of conviction 201, 203n4; Divinity 8, 10; of engagement 64–65; in health 61, 62; individualistic 8–9; natural 22; neurobiological substrata 7; principles 192–193; professional 187–204; of responsibility 201, 203n4; safety/self-preservative/survival 4, 11, 66–68, 70; triangular model 191–203; values 188–189, 195, 199
Evertsson, H. 130
evolutionary development 2, 3, 22; phylogenic development 3, 33

facts of life 84–85
failure: of adaptation 48–49; civilisation 4; in the countertransference 95, 116, 174; in depression 83, 85, 90, 106; of maternal provision 38, 67, 68, 95; to meet ego ideals 6, 11, 49, 82; to meet superego demands 6, 41, 85, 116–117, 161; provoke remorse 11, 28; in psychopathy 128, 131, 133 (of treatment 136); re analytic superego 173, 176, 178; therapist's 194, 197, 198; of thinking 147
Fairbairn, W. R. D. 2, 54, 64, 67
false self 49, 55, 67, 70, 131; *see also* compliance
fantasy: re ego ideal 47, 49; 161, 174; re guilt 135, 182; *see also* phantasy
father 51, 53, 54, 114, 124, 130, 134; aspect of therapist 123–124; castrating 21; founding/senior 166, 173, 183; identification with 135; representing superego figure 23–24, 87, 97, 119, 166, 175–176; underlying fundamentalism 143, 144, 145, 150–152, 153–154
Feldman, M. 118
Fenichel, O. 29
Ferenczi, S. 39, 52, 132
fidelity 192, 197, 203n3, 195; *see also* Trust

Fields, L. 136
Finney, C.G. 126
fitness to Practice *see* ethics
Fonagy, P. 3, 4, 5, 131, 132, 157, 160, 162
Frawley-O'Dea, M.G. 158, 164, 165
free association 151, 153, 154, 189, 196; *see also* Unconscious
Freud, A. 81, 84, 132
Freud, S. 12, 39, 98, 152, 189; on aggression 4, 5, 81, 130, 191; on ego ideal 6, 13, 47, 48, 158; ego independence 34, 88, 189; as heir to Oedipus complex 32, 95, 96, 145, 147, 151; manic defences 85; on melancholia 79, 83, 84, 85; on narcissism 14, 47–49, 56, 189; protective shield 37–38; on psychopathy 127; on repetition 197; on superego development 1–2, 3, 5, 6, 10, 32, 98, 180 (re Klein's views 21–25, 26, 27, 28); technique 199, 153; Totem & Taboo 3, 10, 33, 144; on unconscious 9, 194, 196 (guilt 145)
frustration 27, 64, 81, 108n2, 118; capacity for tolerating 113; in countertransference 113, 114, 115
Fry, D.P. 72
fundamentalism 142–154; defences 10, 15n7, 142; definitions 142; international stage 35; mind-set 142, 143, 144, 146, 148, 149, 151, 154; in psychoanalysis 152–154; re aggression142, 143, 146, 147; re authority 144–149, 151, 153; in religion 15n8, 142, 144; superego 10–11, 142, 143, 144, 145, 147 (*see also* archaic); transference/countertransference 144, 149, 150–151
Furlong, A. 199
Furman, E. 81, 200

Garland, C. 92n6
gaze 3, 47, 53, 63, 96, 106; self emerging through 54–57
Gilligan, J. 68, 132
Glasser, M. 1, 5, 6, 80, 98, 99; core complex 13, 105, 108n1, 134; self-preservation 10, 123; sexualization 99
globalisation 9
Glover, E. 96, 172
Goldberg, A. 200, 201
Goldberg, E. 69
Gómez-Robles, A. 61

good object(s) 25, 26, 112, 118; clinical training as 169; damage of 28; therapist as 148, 176
Greenacre, P. 99, 108n2, 127, 130
Greenson, R.R. 157
Gregory, S. 129, 136
Grotstein, J. 38
group processes 172–173, 177–178
guilt: in clinical training 161, 162; defences against 13, 144; defensive 41, 101, 149, 200; in depression 82, 83, 89, 90; in depressive position 97, 106–107, 117, 119, 151, 154, 193; ego destructive 147; in fundamentalism 143, 145, 146, 150, 151; Oedipal 145, 150; as pre-oedipal 22; primal 38, 42; in psychopathy 127, 128, 129, 132, 133; re analytic superego 173, 174, 175, 176; re conscience 5, 10, 11; regulative 80; reparative 193; superego agency 30, 88; superego punishment 6, 23, 42; in transference/counter transference 150, 200; unconscious 101, 145

Haidt, J. 3, 8, 152
Hamid, Mohsin (novelist) 144
Hamlet (Shakespeare play) 12
Hammon, Ariel (novelist) 144
Harding, C. 1–17, 5, 13, 14, 79–94, 88, 187–204, 199
Hare, R.D. 127, 128, 129
Hartmann, H. 5, 84
Hawkins, P. 158, 163
Heimann, P. 117
Herman, J.L. 132
Hewlett, B.S. 60
Hill, J. 181, 184
Hinshelwood, R.D. 2, 6, 11, 13, 15n3, 21–30, 80, 120–121, 122
Holder, A. 39
Holmes, J. 158, 192
Hopper, E. 177, 183
Horne, A. 1, 3, 6, 8, 46–59, 80
Hughes, L. 165
humiliation 35, 47; ideal ego as defence against 50–52 (*see also* shame); and violence 48, 50
Hytinnen, R. 39

id: hatred of 25; re ego & superego 9, 60, 61, 88, 14, 118, 163, 199, 202; split in 24; the unconscious 5, 7, 12, 82, 148,

190, 198, 82; unfettered behaviours 60, 61, 71
ideal ego: defence against 49, 50–53; distinguished from ego ideal 48; heir to primary narcissism 47–48, 49; omnipotence 47, 50; *see also* narcissism
idealisation: of analyst 119; of analytic rigour 178–179; of authority 147, 178, 182; as defence 104, 182; in training 166, 176–178
identification: with harsh superego 34, 142
identity 26, 39, 129; collective 153; diffusion 111, 115, 119; emerging 63; firm sense of 65; integration 119; moral 7; precarious sense of 34, 69; unconscious 175
impulses 8, 9, 12, 130, 142, 192, 194; access in therapy 88–89, 148, 188, 190, 192, 196, 198 (*see also* aggression); anti social 2, 5; frustrated 51, 81; integrate into self 8, 65; 81–82, 88–91; moral failure 89; regulated by ego 2, 5, 7, 24, 86, 90, 91; sacrificed/prohibited 10, 13, 145; sexualization of 96; socialised 80–81 (*see also* superego); superego punishment for 85; superego restraint 3, 6, 14, 81–82, 83, 181, 190
independence:expected of baby 66; fear of 152; of patient 199, 200; pseudo 40; quality for in training 157; from superego 1, 7, 32, 34, 91; *see also* autonomy
industrial civilisation 60
Ingold, T. 61
instincts 2, 24; *see also* impulses
internal object: analytic 57; externalised 12, 105, 107, 116, 198; function as superego 25, 98, 99, 100, 107; relations 34, 43, 85, 87, 100–101, 105, 107, 116, (in therapist's mind 190)
internal world 23, 123, 158; as analytic focus 169, 197; in supervision 161, 163, 164, 165
interpretation(s) 164, 172, 200; of anxieties 89, 105; disguising analysts punitive superego 116, 120–121, 122, 176, 190, 193; experienced as threat 105, 175; extra transference 151–152, 174; integrative 119, 120; of life experiences 69, 72; mutative 148–149, 151; patient-centred 43, 121; unreadiness for 120

intimacy 51; anxieties aroused by 96 (*see also* core complex); defences against 105, 134
Isaacs, S. 29

Jacobson, E. 33, 38, 39
Job (biblical story of) 184
Joffe, W.G. 83, 84, 92n4
Johns, J. 172
Jones, A.P. 129
Jones, E.21, 22
Jones Jim, cult leader 148
Joseph, B. 99, 116
Jung, C. 22, 175, 184; psychoanalytic group 173
justice 3, 136, 191, 193; injustice 146; justice system 100, 136, 137

Kalsched, D. 158
Kang, H. J. 66
Kernberg, O. 111, 115, 119, 137; of clinical training 166, 172, 181, 182; of psychoanalytic organisations 173, 177, 181, 182
Kestenberg, J.S. 39
Khan, M. 38, 66
King, A. 132
King, P. 29
Kimonis, E.R. 130
Klauber, J. 172
Klein, M. 22; positions 25–28, 29, 48, 146, 148, 152; reparation 6, 28, 79, 92n1; superego 6, 22–25, 98, 99, 118, 124, 130 (primitive 15n3)
Koch, J. L.A. 126
Kochanska, G. 65
Kupperman, J. 64

Laing, R.D. 65, 69
Langs, R. 179
Lanius, R.A. 62
Leader, D. 92n1
Lecours, S. 8, 82, 90
Lindley, R. 192
Lloyd-Owen, D. 198
Loewald, H.S. 63, 124
Lomas, P. 50
loss 35, 51, 92n6, 101–102, 129, 201; of capacity for love 132; defences against 85–89; as facts of life 84–85; of ideal states of being/object 39, 83, 159; to narcissism/omnipotence 39, 84–85, 105;

of objects 83, 84, 85, 132; of protection 35, 68, 146; of reality sense 35; re mourning 92; of self 41, 108n1
Lowenstein, R. 5, 84
Lupien, S.J. 66

Mahler, M.S. 161
Martin, C.L. 60
Martin, E. 161, 162, 163, 181
maternal object 37, 96, 111–112, 124; child as narcissistic object to 11, 51–52, 54–56; deficiencies in care 60, 80, 84, 99, 112–116, 130, 131, 146; graduated failure 6, 49, 80 (gross failure 49); infantile pathology 113; maternal affective attunement 3, 4, 49, 119, 123; as protective shield 37, 49; provision 2, 4, 62–65, 131
McFarland Solomon, H. 198
McGilchrist, I. 2
Mclean, D. 119
melancholia 25, 67, 79, 86, 87, 92n1; melancholic superego music 82–83, 86; *see also* depression
Meloy, J.R. 127, 128, 129, 132, 137
Mental Health Act 1983 127
mentalisation 43, 131, 157
Mezirow, J. 168
Midgley, M. 1, 3, 12
Miller, A. 61
mirroring 6, 47, 54, 56, 57, 118, 122; *see also* gaze
Mollon, P. 159
Money-Kyrle, R.E. 6, 10, 11, 84
moral(ity) 7, 21, 135, 184; disguising aggression 5, 8, 10–11, 12, 27, 82, 84, 86, 143, 190; bogus 103; (un)certainty 34, 36, 41, 198, 200, 201; conflated with reality 5, 12, 13, 14, 34, 36, 41, 42, 82, 91, 158; development 26–29, 17, 33, 88–91 (duties of ego functions 5, 7 (*see also* ethical attitude; ethics); evolutionary/phylogenic origins 3, 22, 33; of fear 32; function 1, 7, 12, 14, 80, 193; in fundamentalism 143, 146; individual agency over 1, 7, 14, 87, 88, 90, 91; internal agency 23; neurobiological underpinnings 3, 7, 15n4, 22; oedipal 3, 6, 32–35, 95, 97; in perversion 97, 98, 100, 102, 103, 104, 106, 107; in psychopathy 11, 12, 126, 129, 131, 136; regulation of mind 2, 89, 91; regulation of narcissism 13, 89, 91; regulation of social engagements 12, 187; in species (a-)typical environments 61, 62, 66–70; *see also* archaic superego); roots in sociality 12, 60; and sociality 2, 60, 62–65; via social pressure 8–9, 10–11, 12, 13, 14, 152; of survival 32, 33
moral insanity *see* psychopathy
Muller–Isberner, R. 137
Murdin, L. 3, 6, 10, 13, 142–154, 196
Murphy, C. 130
Music, G. 2, 10, 15n2
mutative interpretation 148

narcissism: in clinical training 159, 161, 162, 174; depression 79, 89, 90; destructive 115, 127; developmental deficit 6, 13, 47, 48–49, 50, 51, 53, 56, 83, 131, 132 (*see also* ego ideal; ideal ego); infant 63, 127; merger fantasies 9; narcissistic object 11; omnipotence 47, 49, 63, 80, 81, 85 (limits to 6, 48, 84, 105); paranoid- schizoid position 25–29, 99, 106, 119, 160; primary 47, 49 (absence of 56); regulation of in therapist 144, 188, 189, 202; regulation with shame 6, 7, 13, 37, 132, 161; as self-preservation 4, 11, 13, 67, 68; superego regulation of 10, 47, 80, 82; of therapist 188–189, 190, 193
Narvaez, D. 2, 3, 4, 7, 11, 15n4, 60–75, 80, 189
Nathan, J. 13, 110–125, 198
Nathanson, D. 162
neurobiological development 2, 60, 62; foundations of relating to others 2–5, 64–70; self-regulatory functions 65, 68
Newton, K. 177
Niehoff, D. 70
non-maleficence 192–193
Novick, J. 6, 80, 81, 85, 189, 190, 198
Novick, K. 6, 80, 81, 85, 189, 190, 198
Nygaard, C. 170

Obholzer, A. 167
obsessional 13, 37–38, 39, 42; affect regulation 39; defences 10, 13, 86; symptom in child 23; thinking 37, 42; underlying fundamentalist mind-set 10–11

oedipal 21; anxiety 34; castration anxiety 21; complex 22, 23, 24 (superego as heir to 6, 32, 95, 147); dynamics in clinical training 163; morality 32–35, 97; pre-oedipal 38, 52; superego 13, 32, 33, 34, 95, 175, 176; underlying fundamentalism 145, 147, 151–152
Ogden, T. 104
Olver, M.E. 136
omnipotence *see* ideal ego; narcissism
O'Shaughnessy, E. 98, 99, 101, 106

paedophilia 104
Pally, R. 158
paranoid-schizoid 25–29, 99, 106, 119, 160
Parsons, M. 11, 52, 81, 131
paternal 119, 120, 123, 143; *see also* father
pathological organisation 111, 117, 119, 121, 122, 123
perpetrator 52, 105
personalisation 54
perversion 127; core trauma 52, 108n1; female perversion 54, 187; problems of 95–109; reversal 85; sexualization 51–52, 96, 107, 103–104; transference/countertransference 104–105, 107, 108n2; types of superego structures 95–98, 100
phantasy 23, 26, 29, 111, 147, 148, 149, 181; *see also* fantasy
Phillips, A. 89
Piaget, J. 157, 168
Pick, I.B. 115, 117; *see also* Brenman-Pick, I.
Piers, G. 82, 161
Plumwood, V. 60
Pope, R. 168
Porter, S. 130, 135, 136, 137
power: asymmetrical relationships 145, 149, 151, 176, 177, 187, (in clinical practice 192, 195, 199; in training 162, 163, 165); coincidence of individual and social 9, 152, 165, 181; 'domination orientation' 68, 148, 187; exertion over other 131, 137, 144, 146; of feelings 116; illusion of 80, 81, 85, 107, 177; of moral imperatives 1, 12, 176; between psychic agencies 33, 99, 101, 150, 158, 160, 168, 190, 196; of secrets 104; self-regulation of 126; social-regulation of 3, 122, 144, 145, 175, 198

Prichard, J.C. 126
projection 24, 26, 56, 83; between groups 173, 178; infant's 111, 113, 130; patients 116, 117, 151; of superego 147, 148, 149, 175; in training 159, 164
projective identification: containing object 112, 113, 117, 121; as countertransference 176; excessive 113; realistic 113; rejecting-object 113, 115, 116, 117, 120; underlying organisational dynamics 181; unmodified superego functioning 173
protective shield 37–38, 66, 40
pseudo-independence 41
psychoanalytic model: defining features of 194–195, 196–199 (*see also* free association); payment for cancelled sessions 199–200; tolerance of uncertainty 200–201; *see also* analytic boundaries/framework; clinical practice
psychopathy: brain abnormalities 129, 132–133, 136; central motivations 126–128; checklist 128–129; in criminal justice system 136–138; defences 10, 130–132; definitions 126–129; early development 11, 130–133; empathy 127, 128, 129, 131; nature/nurture debate 129–130; primary relationships 130–133; psychopathic traits 11, 126–130; as 'semantic dementia' 127; superego 11, 131–132, (in action 133–135; development 130–133); in treatment 136–138; as victim 132, 133, 135; victim's of 131, 133, 134, 135

Raiker, A. 168
reality principle 21, 25–27, 48
Reddish, E. 8, 13, 15n3, 32–45, 88, 95, 158, 167, 168
Reddy, V. 63
regression 9, 105, 110, 158, 159, 160, 177, 181; therapist's 110, 116, 117, 118
remorse 51
reparation 28, 29, 79–80, 92n1; *see also* guilt
reverie 111, 112, 113; *see also* thinking
Rice, M.E. 136
Rickman, J.: personal moral function 1, 7, 12, 14, 80, 193; protective superego 6; representative-of-society-in-mind 13, 14; toilet mastery 81

Riesenberg-Malcom, R. 98
Rilke, Rainer Maria (poet) 32
Rosenfeld, H. 29, 175, 176
Roth, P. 85
Rusczcynski, S. 85
Rycroft, C. 46–47

Sacks, J. 10
sadism: anal 81; in countertransference 116, 120–121, 123, 176, 195; in depression 79, 82, 83, 87; fundamentalism 143, 146, 152; in perversion 95, 97, 99, 100, 101, 105, 107, 108n1; in psychopathy 128, 129, 134; re parental intercourse 25, 147; of superego 52, 147, 150
safety ethic 4, 11, 67, 68, 131; fears for survival 12, 13, 34, 42, 66, 69, 92, 123, 134–135; self preservative 10, 11, 14, 89; survival morality 32, 33
Sagan, E. 131
Salzberger-Wittenberg, I. 158, 168, 169
Sandel, M. J. 10
Sandler, J. 6, 11–12, 38, 48, 83, 84, 92n4
Saretsky, T. 189
Schafer, R.: action language 80, 88, 90; beloved superego 14, 38, 81, 83, 87–88, 90, 198 (withdrawal of 189); externalised superego 8; fundamental anxieties 92n6, 189, 199; parents superego 6; reified superego 6
Schecter, D. E. 38
Schmidt, M.F. 129
Schore, A.N. 196; changes to brain in therapy 92n5, 189; neurological basis to sociality 2, 3, 4, 7, 65, 66; shame 6, 7, 80, 132, 161
Searles, H. 128, 164
Sedlak, V. 118
Segal, H. 96
Self 35; awareness 49, 50, 117, 157–158, 164; conception 46–47; development of 62–65, (mis-development of 66–70, 131); directed aggression 24, 25, 100, 147, 149; dissociated aspects of 8, 68; ego destructive 101, 113, 201 (see also ego ideal); emerging 48, 53, 54–57, 62–64; esteem 12, 6, 38, 39, 80, 91, (of therapist 188, 189); expressions 2, 3, 9, 160; false 49, 55, 67, 70; forgiveness 29; harm 36, 37, 41, 42, 110, 113–114, 119, 121; idealised view 159 (see also ideal self); identifications 50, 101–103, 132 (with superego 34, 35, 100); interest 131, 188, 201; judgements 5, 33, 34, 132, 162; loss of 108n1, 132; mother's infantile 111, 116; perception 5, 50; preservation 4, 10, 11, 67–68, 123; protection 50, 131; punishment 8, 11, 12, 13, 113–114; purging 26, 86; reality 26; reflective 198; regulation 11, 60, 61, 62, 64, 71; in relation to other 3, 11, 12, 13, 28, 53, 98, 101(in training 158, 159, 163); respect 192, 193, 199; righteous 10, 143; at risk from within 28, 79, 113; sacrifice 10; as separate 49, 50; stability 13; split 26, 61, 69; worth 5, 6, 10, 128
sexualisation 96, 99, 100, 105, 107; see also sadism
Shakespeare, William (playwright) 12
shame: analytic superego 174; in clinical training 159, 161, 162, 174 (see also disrespect; humiliation); defences against 49, 147, 150; depression 79, 82, 83, 89; developmental origins 13; ego strengthening 90, 92n5; ego weakening 13, 37, 51; in perversion 102; as regulator of narcissism 6, 47, 49, 80, 88, 132; in transference/ countertransference 90, 144; traumatising 7, 11, 49; under gaze 47; underlying psychopathy 131, 132
Shaver, R. 68
Shaw, D. 63, 64, 67, 68
Shengold, L. 132
Siegel, D.J. 72
Singer, M. 82, 161
Skeem, J. 130
Sodre, I. 79, 85
The Sopranos (TV series) 201
species-atypical 66–70
species-typical 60, 61–65, 71, 72
sociality: basis of moral development 2–5, 12, 13; biology shaped by 61–62; of children 2, 15n2; impaired 5, 12, 66–70 (see also psychopathy); interwoven with individuality 4, 12; ontogenic development 3; phylogenic 3; species-typical development of 62–64
soul murder 132; see also psychopathy
Spitz, R. 38, 39
Sroufe, L.A. 67
Stein, R. 143, 144
Steiner, J. 29, 43

Stephen, K. 21, 22, 24, 32
Stern, D. 63, 64, 67
Stimmel, B. 163
Stoltenberg, C.D. 158, 159, 161, 163
Strachey, J. 8, 14, 88, 89, 189, 199
stress 29, 33, 46, 60, 62–64, 66, 68, 70, 86, 118, 132
suicidal 37, 42, 53, 83, 101; threats 120
Summers, F. 142, 145, 153
superego: behind depression 79–87, 95; benign, loving & protective 6, 14, 28–29, 38, 87, 89, 92, 111–112, 118; borderline states (*see* elemental superego); bridges individual with society 34; in clinical practice (*see* analytic superego; ethics, professional); clinical usefulness 21–22, 30; conceptual development 1, 21–25, 32, 95–98; as conscience 1, 4–5, 21, 60; constituents 5–6, 12–13, 80–83; development of 2, 3, 6, 22–29, 32–33, 38–39, 95, 104, 111–114 (ontogenic 3; phylogenic 3, 33); disclaimed self-aspects 7; dynamic workings 6–8, 98, 8, 87, 90; ego defences against 7, 10, 13, 14; ego destructive 33, 113; ego structuring function 38–39 (*see also* ego ideal); fundamentalism 147–154 (*see also* fundamentalism); harsh & persecuting 6, 70, 83, 85, 87, 89, 96, 99, 113, 147 (*see also* ideal ego); individual conflicts with social 4, 10; as judge 1, 5, 6, 95; malfunctioning 8–11, 14, 69; moral function 12, 14; morality 32 (sources of 33, 95) (*see also* morality); neurobiological sub strata 7, 62–64, 66–70; overarching concept 6–7; perverse 100–108; primitive functioning 15n3, 28, 32, 89, 152 (*see also* archaic superego); in psychopathy (*see* psychopathy); recycles aggression 4, 79; regulation of affect 39, (of individuals relation with society 34; of instinctual life 39; of narcissism 6); as reified entity 6, 8, 88; representative of society in mind 2, 4, 13; rooted in sociality 12, 13, 64; sadistic 34, 43, 85, 87, 100–101, 105, 107, 108n1, 116, 190; of therapist (*see* therapist's superego); in training (*see* clinical training); types of conscience 10–11; *see also* aggression; archaic superego; auxiliary superego

supervision *see* clinical training
survival 34, 66; loss of love 12; morality 4, 32, 33; psychic 42, 92n6, 134, 135, 197; relationships as threat to 4, 11; strategies 10, 11, 13, 66, 69, 123, 131
Svetlova, M. 129
symbolisation 52, 96
Symington, N. 49, 50, 114, 128, 132, 135
symmetry of meaning 112
Szecsödy, I. 157

Target, M. 3
Tate, P. 153
Taylor, C. 10, 11, 13, 126–138, 201
Teicher, M.H. 132, 133
therapist: abuse of power 187; analytic attitude/function 116, 120–121, 124, 174, 188; benign authority function 120–121; defensive 120–121, 176, 178; enactments 116; ethical responsibilities 110, 188; narcissism 187, 188–189; role 8, 13, 43, 14, 57, 72, 87–92, 105–106, 108, 196–199, 200–202 (with fundamentalist mindset 145, 149, 150, 151, 152, 153); in therapeutic relationship 85, 95, 100, 104–107; vulnerabilities 115, 116, 117, 137, 153, 176
therapist's superego 57, 111, 116, 151, 153, 187–203; analytic 172, 173, 184; archaic/elemental 13, 118, 123–124, 176; as auxiliary superego 8, 14, 148, 151; as boundary guardian 178–180, 194–195; 'closed system' 189–190, 201, 202; with colleagues 180; in countertransference 104–105, 137, 144, 178; guilt 143; 'open system' 189–190, 201, 202; in training contexts 159, 160, 162, 180–183, 189; underpinning treatment 187–188, 189, 192–194, 203
thinking: apparatus for 111–114, 147; defences against 153, 199–201; fixed 34, 36, 147, 169; forbidden in fundamentalist mind-set 149–150, 152; magical 86 ; obsessional 37, 42; reverie 111, 165; superego obstruction of 147; therapist's capacities for 166, 168, 178, 198, 202; third position 122, 190, 192, 195, 198
Thomas, R.M 66
toilet mastery *see* anality
Tonnesmann, M. 98

topographical model 1, 97
totem & taboo 3, 33, 144
training situations *see* clinical training
trans-generational 34
transference 104–107, 198; borderline 111, 114–116; depression 85, 90; perversion 95, 104–105; reversals 85–86, 115, 116, 197 (*see also* clinical training; superego in clinical setting)
trauma: in childhood experience 7, 49, 52, 64, 67, 69, 113; on political stage 35 (*see also* cumulative trauma); regression 39, 82, 86; from superego music 7; in treatment 43, 115
Trevarthen, C. 63, 65, 66
Trollope, J. (novelist) 15n6
Tronick, E. 63
trust: abuse of 188, 192, 197; of colleagues 184; developmental significance 64, 66, 67, 70, 71, 101; of gaze 54 (*see also* fidelity); of patients 51, 121, 197; of psychopathy 130, 134; in training 160; in treatment 42–43, 89, 114, 160, 184, 192, 195, 196, 197, 203n3
Twyman, M. 198, 202

uncertainty 25, 79, 169, 177, 200–201
unconscious 97; aggression 5, 11, 82, 84, 90, 190; anxieties 96; awareness 42, 86, 90; belief 36, 153, 181; central to psychoanalysis 192, 193, 194, 196, 199; communications 157, 195; expectations 3, 85, 196; free association 196; gratifications 9, 15n7, 176; group dynamics 9, 34, 35, 181; guilt 145; id 5, 82; inhibition 91; meanings and processes 43, 80, 91, 96, 106, 147, 162, 199–200; phantasy 23, 29, 147, 181, 196; subscription to morality; superego roots in 5, 87; of therapist 110, 115, 116, 117, 151, 153, 177, 180, 198; in training 159, 162, 163, 164, 165
United Kingdom Council for Psychotherapy 173

vagus nerve 66
values: community ethic 8, 9, 15n6; divinity ethic 8, 10, 11, 15n8; of ego ideal 48, 158, 159, 189; of ideal ego 52; individualistic ethic 8, 9; personal values 1, 12, 91, 189; of superego 32, 35, 36, 41, 68, 158; therapist's 188; underpinning analytic endeavour 187, 189, 192–193, 195, 199, 202; underpinning social order 3, 5, 8, 9, 13, 80, 82, 90, 180
Van den Berg, A. 128, 131
Vaslamatzis, G. 111
victim: experiences as 100, 103, 105; in psychopathy 131, 132, 133, 134, 135, 136; in transference/countertransference 116, 120, 121, 122, 175, 198
violence 4, 50, 89, 142; domestic 49, 54; identification with violent objects 50, 52, 135; non-verbal 110, 115; reaction to humiliation 52, 132; reaction to powerlessness 146; re fundamentalism 142–143; self-harm 36, 37, 41, 42, 110, 113–114, 119, 121; self preservative 123; social/political 34, 50, 143, 146; superego 79, 176; terrorist 146; verbal 7
Volkan, V. 35

Waddington, C.H. 21, 22
Watson, J.B 61
Weber, Max (sociologist) 201, 203n4
Weber, S. 129
Weiss, G. 68
Weissman, P. 39
Welldon, E. 54, 187
Winnicott, D. 39, 48, 49, 54–57, 62–63, 67, 131
Wood, H. 13, 95–109, 96, 100
Wright, K. 2, 3, 56
Wurmser, L. 1, 6, 39

Yablonsky, L. 69, 70
Yeomans, F. E. 115
Yorke, C. 82, 83, 84